Hammer and beyond:
the British horror film

Hammer and beyond: the British horror film

Peter Hutchings

Manchester University Press

Manchester and New York

distributed exclusively in the USA and Canada by St. Martin's Press

Published by Manchester University Press
Oxford Road, Manchester M13 9PL, UK
and Room 400, 175 Fifth Avenue, New York, NY 10010, USA

Distributed exclusively in the USA and Canada
by St. Martin's Press, Inc., 175 Fifth Avenue, New York, NY 10010, USA

British Library Cataloguing-in-Publication Data
A catalogue record for this book is available from the British library

Library of Congress Cataloguing-in-Publication Data
Hutchings, Peter.
    Hammer and beyond: the British horror film / Peter Hutchings.
        p.   cm.
    Includes bibliographical references.
    ISBN 0–7190–3719–0 (cloth): £35.00 ($59.95). —
    ISBN 0–7190–3718–2 (paper): £10.95 ($19.95).
    1. Horror films—Great Britain—History and criticism.   2. Hammer
Film Productions.   I. Title.
PN1995.9.H6H835   1993
791.43 616 0941—dc20   92–46534

ISBN 0 7190 3719–0 *hardback*
ISBN 0 7190 3720–4 *paperback*

Typeset by J&L Composition Ltd, Filey, North Yorkshire
Printed in Great Britain by Bell & Bain Limited, Glasgow

Contents

Introduction

> Certain branches of the British cinema are able to weather any crisis:
> they do not so much rise above it as sink beneath it, to a subterranean
> level where the storms over quotas and television competition cannot
> affect them. This sub-cinema consists mainly of two parallel institutions,
> both under ten years old: the Hammer horror and the Carry On comedy.[1]

Francis Wyndham's remarks, written in 1964, reflect upon the way
in which through the last part of the 1950s, into the 1960s and then
on to the 1970s, British horror was one of the most commercially
successful areas of British cinema.[2] As Wyndham indicates, easily
the most prolific of horror producers was the relatively small
company called Hammer Films, from which there emerged from
1956 onwards a series of gothic horrors, most notably those featuring
Peter Cushing as Baron Frankenstein and Christopher Lee as Count
Dracula, which were to become famous throughout much of the
world.

But the story of British horror involves much more than the
activities of the filmmakers at Hammer. For one thing, well over one
half of British horror production comes from companies other than
Hammer. For another, the significance of British horror derives as
much from the critical and popular responses to the films on their
initial and subsequent releases as it does from the filmmakers
themselves. In order to ascertain the importance and the merit of
British horror, as well as the reasons for Hammer's dominance, we
also need to recognise that both creators and audiences exist within
and in relation to a particular historical context. Of course, this does
not mean that British horror reflects in any unmediated way aspects
of British post-war reality. Nevertheless, this book will demonstrate
that these horror films do draw upon, represent and are always
locatable in relation to much broader shifts and tendencies in British
social history. It is equally important, however, to think of these

films, on the most basic of levels and regardless of how one values them, as aesthetic and artful constructs which are to a certain extent separate from the everyday concerns and experiences of their intended audience. What this means when we look at the films themselves is that we need to be aware of how they fit into and sometimes diverge from the characteristic practices and concerns of British cinema at the time of their production. Only in this way can a sense be gained both of their social resonance and their cinematic specificity.

It follows from this that the aim of this book is primarily a cultural-historical one. In particular, the book will trace the changing nature of British horror from the mid 1940s to the present day as it constantly seeks to redefine itself in the face of social change. In so doing, films of some distinction will be identified and discussed. But the worth of British horror does not reside entirely, or even perhaps mainly, in these. Instead, the genre itself, or movement if you prefer, the possibilities it offers and all the films it contains, can be seen in total as offering a rich, fascinating and multifaceted response to life in Britain over the past few decades.[3]

I would like to thank Charles Barr for his invaluable comments on an earlier version of this book. I would also like to thank the students and colleagues with whom I have worked over the years who, in all sorts of ways, have supported and encouraged this project. Hammer posters are reproduced by kind permission of the Maxim Décharné Collection. Finally, I am grateful to Hammer Film Productions Ltd for giving permission to reproduce stills from various Hammer films.

This book is dedicated to my parents, John and Rosemary Hutchings.

Notes

1 Francis Wyndham, 'The Sub-Cinema', *Sunday Times Supplement*, 15 March 1964.
2 On the Carry On films – still a relatively unexplored area of British film production, see Marion Jordan, 'Carry On – Follow That Stereotype' in James Curran and Vincent Porter (eds), *British Cinema History*, London, 1983, pp. 312–27.
3 British horror can be considered both as a sub-genre, a category of international horror production, and as a nationally specific movement with a finite beginning and end. I discuss this in more detail in the first chapter of this book. Suffice it here to indicate that later in the book when I discuss the genre of British horror, I mean to refer to a distinctive area of British cinema which has affinities with and can be related to horror films produced elsewhere, but in very important ways is separate and unique.

For sadists only?
The problem of British horror

Horror is often a problem for critics. The all too visible stress in many horror films on morbid themes and acts of violence; the openly exploitative nature of much horror; the association of the genre with a predominantly adolescent audience: all these factors militate against the horror genre being viewed in anything but the most derogatory or patronising of terms. So much is this the case that even those critics who want to argue for the worth of these films sometimes find themselves negotiating what appears to be an inhospitable terrain, with their work taking on an accordingly defensive tone. Nowhere is this unease more evident than in the various critical responses provoked by British horror cinema over the years. From the outraged to the laudatory, these responses are part of the baggage which British horror inevitably brings with it to any critical discussion. If we are to move beyond some of the less helpful longstanding assumptions about horror and towards a more systematic understanding of this sector of British film production, we need to consider this legacy of criticism.

For our purposes, the press reviews and other critical articles and books that appeared between 1956 and the early 1970s – the period which saw British horror's great box-office success – are of particular interest. These critical pieces form a significant part of the cultural climate within which British horror was created and developed, and for that reason alone are relevant to a contextual understanding of the genre. The relationship between criticism and film production needs to be seen as a two-way process. It is not just a question of films being made and then being critically appraised. It is much more interactive than this, with critical attitudes being defined and redefined in relation to trends in film production and, at the same time, filmmakers responding to these attitudes, sometimes reacting against them (see my later discussion of Michael Reeves in this respect) but often, as in the case of Hammer, cheerfully accepting the place allotted them within a particular map of British cinema.

It is fair to say that the critical verdict on British horror during the time of its proliferation was overwhelmingly negative. More positive critical evaluations began to appear in the early 1970s when horror production (and indeed much of the rest of British cinema) was beginning to wind down. Most notable amongst these was David Pirie's 1973 book *A Heritage of Horror* which sought to locate horror cinema within a British gothic tradition.[1] Another approach which has since become apparent is to view British horror as part of 'the dark side' of British cinema, 'a lost continent' still waiting to be rigorously explored and mapped. The 'dark side' metaphor is especially potent in that it suggests not only a repression on the part of earlier critics who have refused to engage with the genre but also that the films themselves are dealing with the release of forces that are repressed in other, more respectable areas of British cinema.

The first part of this chapter explores the various responses to and readings of British horror. It will demonstrate that while some of these, most notably Pirie's, are more convincing than others, important issues are still not being addressed. In particular, more thought needs to be given not only to the way in which these films relate to the social and historical circumstances of their production but also to how the aesthetic and the commercial imperatives of the genre interact. The chapter will conclude by offering another way of thinking about British horror, one which seeks to take all these factors into account in an attempt to identify what it is that makes the horror film so distinctive and important a part of British cinema.

The press response

The attitudes of British film critics to British horror were to a large extent formulated in response to. a series of immensely popular horror films produced by Hammer in the last part of the 1950s. Two things are apparent from a consideration of the press notices of the Hammer horrors of this period. First, British horror, and Hammer in particular, was not as controversial as some histories of horror have suggested. In discussing the critical receptions of two non-Hammer films, Michael Powell's *Peeping Tom* (1960) and Sam Peckinpah's *Straw Dogs* (1971), Ian Christie and Charles Barr respectively stress the way in which the critics almost unanimously refused to engage with these films on any level.² A product of this was symptomatic factual errors in the actual reviews. Hammer horror did not receive such treatment. It was, quite simply, not as threatening as the two films cited above. Certainly, emotive words were used to condemn it, but significantly one finds very few factual errors in the reviews in question. One reason for this might be that the Hammer films tended to lack those formal and rhetorical devices used by both Powell and Peckinpah to implicate the spectator in the violence depicted on screen.

Second, perhaps as expected, the reviews of British horror films become shorter in length as time passes. Linked with this, they also begin to use a recognisable shorthand based on the name of 'Hammer'. For example, only two of the available reviews of *The Curse of Frankenstein* mention Hammer at all (*Sunday Express*, 5/5/57, *Evening News*, 2/5/57). The reviews for *Dracula*, released one year later, contain a few scattered references to the studio. A year after that we can find, amongst other references, 'the horror boys of Hammer films' (Nina Hibbin, *Daily Worker*, 28/3/59 on *The Hound of the Baskervilles* – 'the horror boys' recurs in other reviews by other writers, implying a certain childish, 'naughty' quality about the filmmakers) and 'Hammer Films' own baleful province' (*Evening Standard*, 3/12/59 on *The Stranglers of Bombay*). By the late 1960s one finds, typically: 'Directed by Terence Fisher, *The Devil Rides Out* is no better nor worse than any other Hammer horror and, of course, stars Christopher Lee' (Nina Hibbin, *Morning Star*, 8/6/68 – complete review) and 'There's not much to say about *The Devil Rides Out* except that it's the latest Hammer horror release' (*Guardian*, 7/6/68). Incidentally, *The Devil Rides Out* is considered by many supporters of the British horror genre as one of its most distinguished films.

Here the name of Hammer is being used as a reductive, descriptive category. Merely to utter it implies a certain type of film, and in particular a certain type of horror film. Merely to invoke it implies a critical response which no longer requires elaboration. On one level at least, this can be viewed more as a response to Hammer's self-image, its unabashed foregrounding of the formulaic nature of its product. (Another possible reason for the brevity of the later reviews might be the fact that Hammer simply stopped showing certain films to the press from the mid-1960s onwards.)

Of course, this does not mean that the press reviewers were the passive victims of the manipulations of the Hammer selling machine. Undoubtedly they were sensitive to it, often mentioning, in rather distasteful tones, the gaudy posters and tasteless promotional stunts that surrounded the films. One particularly memorable example of the Hammer approach to marketing is provided by the invitations to the press screening of *The Stranglers of Bombay* – filmed, according to the poster, in 'Strangloscope' – which were written on silk scarves similar to those used as murder weapons in the supposedly factual film. In the midst of such activity, and to a certain extent as a reaction against it, the British critics worked to identify Hammer, and British horror in general, in their own way. As we will see in a later chapter, the evaluation of Hammer that emerged was subsequently used as a yardstick against which non-Hammer horrors were judged and valued.

Perhaps the best way to understand this process of identification, as well as the array of critical attitudes that it involves, is to look at the reception of one particular film, in this case *The Curse of Frankenstein*, Hammer's first colour horror film, released in 1957.

David Pirie describes the critical reaction to *The Curse of Frankenstein* thus: 'at the time outraged critics fell over each other to condemn it'.³ While this is certainly true, it is also the case that the virulently negative reviews were far outnumbered by reviews that were, on the whole, either indifferent to or amused by the film. Of the twenty-three press notices available in the BFI archives, only five could conceivably be described as 'outraged'. These include the reviews in *The Daily Worker* (4/5/57, Robert Kennedy) and *The Daily Telegraph* (4/5/57, Campbell Dixon), in the latter of which the following appears:

> But when the screen gives us severed heads and hands, eyeballs dropped in a wine glass and magnified, and brains dished up on a plate like spaghetti, I can only suggest a new certificate – 'SO' perhaps; for Sadists Only.

Similar attitudes are expressed in *The Sunday Times* (5/5/57, Dilys Powell), *Tribune* (10/5/57, R. D. Smith) and, perhaps most notably, *The Observer* (5/5/57, C. A. Lejeune).

> Without any hesitation I should rank *The Curse of Frankenstein* among the half-dozen most repulsive films I have encountered in the course of some 10,000 miles of film reviewing.

Looked at in this statistical way, one could say that *The Curse of Frankenstein*'s critical reception was not extreme at all (as indeed it wasn't compared, say, with *Peeping Tom* – there is clearly no unanimous condemnation of the film here). Yet if the reviews are examined in detail, the positive (*The Daily Herald* and *The Sunday Express*), the negative, and the rest, one finds a shared set of assumptions about British cinema, horror and the film audience. In particular, this audience is assumed to be split into two distinctive groups, on the one hand, 'us', supporters of 'entertainment', who can really see what a shameful and exploitative thing the horror film actually is, and, on the other hand, 'them', credulous horror fans, possibly childish and/or stupid, perhaps even mentally disturbed.

This process of separating out the audience is at its clearest in the early days of Hammer horror. For instance, R. D. Smith's negative review begins with: 'For all lovers of the cinema only two words describe this film – Depressing, degrading!'

Having thus established who the film is not for, Smith goes on

> The whole business of Grand Guignol . . . needs an analyst rather than a critic . . . in the cinema there are those who find it profitable to keep alive in people – (and especially, one feels, in the case of children) – primitive fears and cruelties. (*Tribune*)[4]

Here the audience for horror is conceived as completely Other, primitive, childlike, easily exploited, possibly in need of an analyst. This is admittedly an extreme version. But this process is not by any means confined to the wholly negative reviews. The notice in *The Times* (6/5/57), for example, is, on the whole, neutral. Yet at the end one finds:

> Not a film for the nervous, nor for that matter for those without a morbid taste for the revolting and who feel that the world has supped full enough of horror without having more, in colour, thrust down their throats from a wide screen.

The tone might be different from that of R. D. Smith's invective, but the critical terms are the same.

In a mildly dismissive review, this time in *The Financial Times* (6/5/57), Derek Granger discusses the way in which people react to horror films:

> Only the saddest of simpletons, one feels, could ever get a really satisfying frisson. *For the rest of us* they have just become a rather

eccentric and specialised form of light entertainment, and possibly a useful means of escape for a housewife harrowed by the shopping. (My emphasis)

A device which features widely is apparent here, namely humour. Humour in this context works to secure a distance between 'us' and 'them'. They take the films seriously; we don't. This will be returned to below. But first it is useful to look briefly at one of the positive reviews of *The Curse of Frankenstein*.

The most consistent champion of Hammer films in this period was Paul Dehn (later to become himself a film screenwriter). An appraisal of his approach to the genre is instructive in relation to the critical terms outlined above. For example, from his review of *The Curse of Frankenstein* (*Daily Herald*, 3/5/57), which went out under the heading 'I Like It Grisly':

> When titles like *The Curse of Frankenstein* come shuddering through the scrambled smoke, blood and flame of the Warner Theatre screen, I put on my spectacles, and spell them out and smile, and say 'Very good indeed'. *I know that it's uncritical to say this sort of thing before the picture has even begun, but I can't help it.* Monsters are my addiction and my sustenance. I like my vegetables two-legged. I like people who have roots. (My emphasis)

Also relevant here are his remarks on an earlier Hammer film, *The Quatermass Experiment* (*News Chronicle*, 28/8/55): 'This is the best and nastiest horror-film that I have seen since the war. How jolly that it is also British.'

What Dehn does here is maintain a division between a good/tasteful and a bad/tasteless audience, while – and this is where he is different from other critics – identifying himself wholeheartedly with the latter. He is deliberately being, in his own words, 'uncritical', surrendering himself in a fetishistic way to the dubious delights of the horror genre. The critical terms are the same as in the other reviews – the pleasure to be gleaned from horror is still illicit – but the position within these terms has shifted.

Many of the reviews for *The Curse of Frankenstein* and later horror films make humorous remarks at their expense. Perhaps most typically (in a review of *Dracula* and *The Moonraker* in *The Daily Herald*, 23/5/58): 'My reaction to them is: gore blimey. Because of seeing these two pictures, I would probably have fainted if I had cut myself shaving this week.'

Most of the complaints against Hammer accrue from the idea that its films are in some way too 'realistic', that it is too unpleasant to be laughed at. The position of the disbelieving spectator ridiculing events on the screen is threatened, it seems, when the most overtly fantastic or stylised elements of the genre are absent. Here, a lighthearted but revealing criticism of *Dracula* (*The Star*, 22/5/58): 'probably the best acted, directed and photographed horror film yet made. But to be effective Dracula needs a certain amount of bad acting. Ham as well as blood is what he feeds on.'

On another level, Nina Hibbin writes in *The Daily Worker* (24/5/58),

> I went to see *Dracula*, a Hammer film, prepared to enjoy a nervous giggle. I was even ready to poke gentle fun at it. I came away revolted and outraged . . .
>
> Laughable nonsense? Not when it is filmed like this, with realism and with the modern conveniences of colour and the wide screen.

If, in this light, one returns to Hammer's champion, Paul Dehn, one finds: 'My readers know me to be a sucker for the sort of Draculine horror film *which is rooted harmlessly in fairytale soil*.' (review of *The Stranglers of Bombay*, *News Chronicle* 4/12/59 – my emphasis) A similar attitude is apparent in all three, a need to push the film away through distancing laughter. Some critics, like Dehn, succeed in doing this; others, like Hibbin, do not. (Significantly, Dehn did not like *Peeping Tom*, a film which works to implicate the spectator in the text.)

These critical attitudes, the division between 'them' and 'us', the bad and the good audience, and the use of humour as a support for this division, are a constant structuring element in the press reaction to British horror throughout the 1950s and 1960s (although, in later years, they do become more attenuated, subordinate to the name of Hammer). The inevitable outcome of this way of approaching the genre is that horror is held firmly at a distance and functions either as a source of humour or as a cause for concern.

This is equally the case in most of the critical histories of British cinema that appeared in the 1960s and 1970s – including those by Roy Armes, Ernest Betts, Charles Oakley, George Perry and Alexander Walker.[5] In these, horror, one of the most commercially successful areas of British film production, is usually conspicuous by its absence or its marginality. The formulaic nature of much British horror, the way in which it seems to define itself entirely in relation

to the demands of the market place, ensures that the films involved
are accorded a lesser status than those films which are seen to have
been made by 'artists' who in some way or other have transcended
commercial constraints. At the same time, the pleasures afforded by
horror films, arising as they apparently do from a fascination with
violence, pain and death, are often seen by critics as being rather
dubious, with this impression encouraged by advertising which
stresses the illicit and forbidden nature of the horror experience.

The influential British film critic Roger Manvell, writing in 1947,
provides an early example of what would quickly become a standard
model for dividing up and valuing British cinema.

> The high film is comparatively rare, sometimes successful with the public
> and always valuable for prestige: it excites the artist and technician into
> making new discoveries, gladdens the columns of the film-weary critic
> and normally enters the pages of film history. The middle film is the
> staple box-office product, the reliable success, the film which offers
> sound entertainment without demanding too much or too little of the
> greater audience's sensibilities. The low film is the quickie, the noisy,
> raptureless programme-filler, the B film in every implication of the
> letter.[6]

Manvell distinguishes not only between 'art' and 'entertainment' but
also between entertainment that is in good taste, 'sound entertainment' in his words, and entertainment that is not (and perhaps is not
even entertainment). It tends to be the bad taste elements – most
notably horror – which are marginalised or done down in the British
film histories. An example of good taste commercial filmmaking
might be the James Bond films. This is most evident in Alexander
Walker's *Hollywood England* where Hammer is hardly mentioned
and James Bond has a whole section devoted to him. Roy Armes,
on the other hand, devotes as much space in his book to Hammer
as he does to Bond. He approves of the latter, 'the most potent myth
of British cinema'[7], and dislikes the former, seeing it as 'a new
manipulation of the old clichés with a little more visual or verbal
explicitness'. He goes on to describe Hammer's exploitation of these
clichés as positively unBritish, 'more characteristic of Hollywood
than the British film industry'.[8]

The role played here by the horror filmmakers was an interesting
one. In particular, Hammer, the principal producer of British
horror, seemed to contribute wilfully and enthusiastically to its
own critical disreputability. Indeed this disreputability became an

important factor in the way in which Hammer sold itself and its
products to a mass audience. The following remarks made by
Hammer's head James Carreras clearly signal what he saw Hammer's
position to be:

> if back parlour dramas look like clicking and somebody submits a good
> basic idea for one, we can act fast and have the finished article on screen
> while demand is still there . . .
>   Showmanship – and I'll go on saying that 'til I'm blue in the face – is
> still this industry's lifeblood, a fact that is too often ignored by many.
> When I see producers who are reluctant to bang the big drum about their
> product, it makes me wonder why they bother to make films at all.[9]

A repeated stress on both the need to be sensitive to market trends
and the value of showmanship characterised many of the public
statements made by Hammer personnel. The company constantly
identified itself as a commercially minded purveyor of entertainment
for a mass audience. Other areas of British cinema can be grouped
generically – Gainsborough melodramas and Ealing comedies, for
instance – but none other than Hammer foregrounded in so extreme
a way the mass-productive elements of genre. Not only did Hammer
use a stock company of actors, but up until the late 1960s when it
moved its production base it also used and reused for the sake of
economy the same sets and props (much remarked upon and derided
by critics when the films were released). It made little or no attempt
to hide the cyclical, formulaic and serial nature of its products – a
structure which will be shown later as largely inherited from an
American conception of horror developed in the 1930s. Indeed this
aggressive exploitation became part of a consciously created product
image, something of which to be proud.

Largely as a consequence of this, Hammer, and horror production
in general, found itself on the critical margins from the 1950s
through to the early 1970s when David Pirie's *A Heritage of Horror*
initiated a slow process of reappraisal. We can now consider what
insights are offered us by more positive accounts of British horror,
most of which appeared at a time when British horror production
was itself in decline.

Positive reports

David Pirie's claim in his groundbreaking work, *A Heritage
of Horror*, that British horror was worthy of critical attention

undoubtedly ran counter to the readings of British cinema dominant in the early 1970s when the book first appeared. However, Pirie himself denied that his work was a polemic, and indeed a close examination of it reveals that the two main strategies Pirie adopts to bring horror into the fold of critical respectability are closely connected to an already established way of understanding and valuing British cinema.

The first of these involves the construction of the horror genre as an important part of a national culture, with links to other aspects of British cinema, to literary traditions and also to a distinctive British character: 'it may be that the themes relate to certain psychopathological aspects of the English temperament'.[10]

The second entails bestowing upon Terence Fisher, Hammer's main film director, the status of auteur, someone with a vision that transcends commercial constraints: 'Indeed, once one begins to look at Fisher's films closely, it becomes clear that, unlike almost any other director working in the British commercial cinema, they appear to embody a recognisable and coherent Weltanschauung.'[11]

At the same time, Pirie is more sympathetic than other critics to Hammer's market-led production philosophy which, like Armes, he associates with Hollywood.

> There is a very slight echo of Ealing in the structure that emerged, but perhaps the most obvious analogy is with one of the small Hollywood studios of the 1930s and forties like Republic or Monogram; for almost overnight Hammer became a highly efficient factory for a vast series of exploitation pictures made on tight budgets with a repertory company of actors and a small, sometimes over-exposed, series of locations surrounding their tiny Buckinghamshire estate.[12]

A Heritage of Horror is full of valuable insights, and my own account of British horror is indebted to it. However, in his attempt to endow horror with a certain cultural respectability and worth, Pirie does not engage to any great extent with the reasons why the genre was disreputable in the first place. Also, while he includes an account of the economic circumstances within which Hammer was working, the implications this might have for the aesthetic and ideological properties of the films being made by Hammer are rarely taken up in his otherwise very provocative analyses of specific films. Generally, these analyses instead seek to locate the films in question within a longstanding gothic tradition or as products of an individual director's vision.

Writing in the early 1970s, Pirie was unable to avail himself of recent developments in film theory and history, with those concerning the relation of film aesthetics to the economic structures of the film industry especially pertinent to an understanding of British horror.[13] From the vantage point of today, the commercial nature of much film production seems less of an obstacle to a consideration of any film as a cultural artefact than perhaps it did in the past. Because of this, my own discussions of the aesthetic qualities of particular films will incorporate the fact that, without exception, these films were made primarily to make money.

It is surprising given the upsurge of critical interest in British cinema that has taken place in the 1980s that so little has been written on British horror outside of a few isolated essays and remarks in essays on other related subjects since *A Heritage of Horror*. One shift in attitudes that has taken place registers, albeit ambivalently, in one of the press reviews of *Hellraiser* (1987, d. Clive Barker): 'This, in fact, is a horror fantasy: the genre it has become fashionable to view as the repressed underside of British filmmaking.'[14]

The idea that British horror constitutes one aspect of what might be termed 'the dark side' of British cinema has been developed by Julian Petley in an article entitled 'The Lost Continent'. Petley argues that British films which are realistic have been valued by critics above all others. Consequent upon this, an awareness of other areas of British film production has been repressed. These areas are characterised by non-realistic or fantastic themes and styles: they include Gainsborough melodramas, the iconoclastic work of Michael Powell and Emeric Pressburger and, of course, the British horror film. This strain of fantasy permits the expression of that which is inexpressible elsewhere in British cinema. In so doing, it reveals the limitations of, perhaps even works to deconstruct, a critically privileged realist aesthetic.[15]

The metaphor of the dark side has provided a way of thinking about films which were not afforded much attention before. However, at this point we need to identify some of the shortcomings of this approach and, at the same time, indicate other possible ways of conceptualising British horror's position within British cinema. Two principal problems are apparent.

First, while it is clear that the realism/fantasy dichotomy upon which this metaphor depends is a central one in much critical writing on British cinema, it should also be clear that in an important sense the British horror film is operating in the same way as other, more realistic areas of British film production. The fact that horror films invariably come in the form of 80–120 minute fictional narratives peopled by psychologically individuated characters means that on a basic level and regardless of any aberrant or disreputable content they are unexceptional. For example, Hammer nearly always relied on straightforwardly conventional narratives. As Andrew Higson notes, 'Clearly, different films, and particularly different genres of film mark themselves as more realistic or more "fantastic" (this is particularly evident in British film culture), but it needs to be recognised that such marking is always in relation to a particular understanding of cinema.'[16]

Second, 'the dark side' offers itself as something which arises nightmarishly from within and is subservient to a dominant realist cinema. This fails to take account of the fact that these 'subterranean' films in themselves comprise an immensely popular cinema. When dealing with critical discourses that are primarily evaluative, it is often easy to lose sight of some of the commercial realities of British cinema. By any account, Hammer was a far more profitable enterprise (especially in the long term) than, say, the 1960s 'kitchen sink' productions from the likes of Woodfall and Bryanston, simply because more people saw its product than they did the products of the latter. In this sense, it is the dark side of British cinema rather than its realistic component that can be viewed, in the 1950s and 1960s at least, as dominant.

The contradiction between British horror's popularity, its centrality in the market place, and its critical marginalisation is not satisfactorily addressed by placing British horror on 'the dark side'. Looking at horror in this way, in its relation to realist discourses, can certainly be productive. However, it needs to be recognised that the horror genre as developed within this country has its own distinctive and complex history which encompasses a literary tradition (explored by Pirie), links with other horror movements and an aesthetic identity which in many instances is quite different from as opposed to deconstructive of a realist approach. What this means is that British horror does not merely reveal what is unsaid or repressed elsewhere in British cinema but is also capable of offering different ideas and a new way of seeing.

National cinema and genre

The main aim of this book is to explore the 'Britishness' of British horror, the way in which it functions within a specifically national context. It does seem that the various approaches outlined above, despite the usefulness of some, are in the end not fully adequate to this task. What is helpful at this stage is to think about British horror films as being part of a British national cinema, where this cinema is simultaneously a cultural and an economic institution which, in Geoffrey Nowell-Smith's words 'in some way signifies itself to its audiences as the cinema through which that country speaks'.[17]

Defining such a cinema is not as straightforward as one might suppose. This is readily apparent in *The British Film Catalogue 1895– 1970: A Guide to Entertainment Films* where Denis Gifford lists a number of films which one does not usually think of as British; for example *The Haunting* (1963, d. Robert Wise) and *The Masque of the Red Death* (1964, d. Roger Corman).[18] Gifford's definition of what makes a film British depends on trade and legal designations, avoiding any consideration of theme or style and including films which might appear in their formal qualities to be more American or European. Conversely, films thought of as, say, unproblematically American can be shown to have had a significant British input in terms of the creative personnel who fashioned them. Charles Barr has shown this for the 1935 Universal horror film *The Bride of Frankenstein*.[19]

While an important component of a British national cinema must be its propensity to address specifically national issues and concerns, account also needs to be taken of films like *The Haunting* and *The Masque of the Red Death* which, while not connecting with a British context in any thematic or stylistic way, do testify to the importance of American-financed production in Britain throughout the 1960s. Similarly, that *The Bride of Frankenstein* can to a certain extent be seen as a British horror film in exile signifies rather pointedly the hostility of 1930s British film censors to the development of an indigenous horror genre.

Thinking about the similarities and differences between British and American horror films leads to another difficulty in our attempt to locate horror within a specifically national cinema: namely that the operations of the horror genre are not restricted to any one country or culture but rather are spread across much of the filmmaking world. What has to be considered here then is the role of this genre, and for that matter genre in general, within British cinema. For French critic (and later filmmaker) Jacques Rivette, this role is perfectly clear:

> British cinema is a *genre* cinema, but one where the genres have no genuine roots. On the one hand there are no self-validating genres as there are in American cinema, like the Western and the thriller . . . There are just false, in the sense of imitative, genres.[20]

Rivette's view (which in retrospect has a certain irony to it inasmuch as it was expressed in 1957, the year which saw the release of *The Curse of Frankenstein*, Hammer's first important colour horror film) can be contrasted with David Pirie's claim that the British horror film is in fact deeply rooted in British culture, 'the only staple cinematic myth which Britain can properly claim as its own, and which relates to it in the same way as the western relates to America'.[21] Is British horror 'rootless', merely a local example of a transnational cultural mode? If not, what relation does it bear to its American and European counterparts?

British horror's place in the standard accepted history of the horror genre lies in between American Cold War SF/horror and the modern American horror film (usually seen to have been initiated in 1968 with the release of *Night of the Living Dead* and *Rosemary's Baby*), with considerable overlaps at either end. In what is usually seen as a constant process of generic regeneration, Hammer and other British companies – alongside Italian filmmakers such as Mario Bava and Riccardo Freda and American filmmakers such as Roger Corman – introduce into the genre in the late 1950s colour as well as relatively graphic depictions of violence and sexuality, with all this played out in period settings. However, by the late 1960s gothic horror is superseded by a series of American films boasting modern settings and even more explicit images.

One factor that enables the construction of such a 'grand narrative' is the presence of 'horror' (regardless of how it is defined) as a distinct category within the organisation of different national film industries. But it is uncertain whether one can actually abstract from the extraordinarily wide range of horror films specific aesthetic elements or structures which can be seen to characterise the genre as a whole. Attempts that have been made, particularly in their insistence on the genre having either a fixed function or a central core of meaning ('the Ur-myth . . . a tale still hidden'),[22] have necessarily lifted films out of the national contexts within which they were produced, thereby evacuating them of much of their socio-historical significance.

Despite operating from different theoretical and methodological perspectives, many of these generalising approaches manifest a social conservatism. Horror tends to be identified as a means by which an audience comes to terms with certain unpleasant aspects of reality. For example: 'The horror film teaches an acceptance of the natural order of things and an affirmation of man's ability to cope with and even prevail over the evil of life which he can never hope to understand.'[23]

Psychiatric and psychological concepts have been especially influential in the development of the notion of horror as offering an essentially healthy and life-enhancing experience. Perhaps the baldest statement of this is found in Dr Martin Grotjahn's article 'Horror – Yes It Can Do You Good': 'There is, perhaps, a healthy function in the fascination of horror. It keeps us on the task to face our anxieties and to work on them.'[24]

A related view of the genre has been argued at some length by James B. Twitchell who in his book on the genre writes:

> horror sequences are really formulaic rituals coded with precise social information needed by the adolescent audience. Like fairy tales that prepare the child for the anxieties of separation, modern horror myths prepare the teenager for the anxieties of reproduction.[25]

Drawing on Lacanian psychoanalysis, Steve Neale has offered a different approach to the genre. He argues that horror addresses the fascinations and anxieties of sexual difference, particularly as they register for the male spectator. In discussing horror's use of chiaroscuro lighting he notes that:

> all the elements involved here are central to the problematic of castration and . . . the horror film – centrally concerned with the fact and the effects of difference – invariably involves itself in that problematic and invariably mobilises specific castration anxieties.[26]

Horror is seen as 'centrally concerned' with questions of gender, not in the sense of providing role models but rather in its seeking to produce a secure spectatorial position for the male subject situated within a patriarchal social formation.

The insistent return in all the work cited above to an essential core of human experience or meaning enables their identification of horror as a distinctive body of work operating in a number of different social and historical situations. Even in Neale's apparently more socially aware approach, social specificity is acknowledged only inasmuch as the genre is seen to relate to a patriarchal society. The ahistorical qualities of his argument are clear from the examples he uses. These are picked, apparently at random, from British and American cinema of the 1930s, 1950s, 1960s and 1970s, the implicit assumption being that when reduced to their defining and invariant function these films are more or less the same.

It is also the case that those feminist critics of horror who have argued that the genre is an irredeemably misogynist area of culture, with its female characters functioning solely as victims, fail to grasp that particular horror films might – depending on the context in which they are produced and received – challenge or problematise certain patriarchal attitudes and definitions. For instance, the position of the woman in British horror from the mid 1960s onwards can be seen as offering a degree of resistance to an attempted male objectification of her. The forms this takes, and the extent to which it can be taken as a significant disruption of a male-centred narrative, can, however, only be determined through an analysis of specific films which does not presuppose the genre having fixed, immutable qualities.

One way of initiating a more comprehensively historical approach to horror is to see it as at any one time comprising a set of aesthetic conventions or norms (with these relating both to stylistic and thematic factors and narrative structure), the actual interplay and development of which takes place within particular national contexts. Jan Mukarovsky, in a discussion of aesthetic norms, provides a way of thinking about horror in these terms when he writes:

> we can state that the specific character of the aesthetic norm consists in the fact that it tends to be violated rather than to be observed. It has less than any other norm the character of an inviolable law. It is rather a point of orientation serving to make felt the degree of deformation of the artistic tradition by new tendencies . . . If we look at a work of art from this point of view, it will appear to us as a complex tangle of norms.[27]

What this suggests in the case of Hammer (and for that matter British horror in general) is that in its construction of horror within the context of 1950s Britain, it was negotiating with pre-existing generic norms, engaging in a process of product differentiation which necessarily involved 'common sense' definitions of what a horror film actually was. The motivation for this differentiation can be found in the company's search for a new, expanded market.

This approach helps us in locating British horror as part of a specifically national cinema. The relation of British horror films to non-British horror, rather than arising from a shared generic identity, is instead constituted through a series of negotiations and differentiations, in effect through different interpretations of what horror actually is. This also has implications for our understanding of the internal development of British horror production, for, as will be shown, Hammer horror increasingly came to function in the 1960s as the 'norm' from which British horror filmmakers – including some working for Hammer itself – sought to differentiate their own work.

The norms in relation to which Hammer initiated its own distinctive horror cycle were primarily those of the American cinema, and particularly the type of horror associated with Universal Studios throughout the 1930s and 1940s and featuring stars such as Boris Karloff, Bela Lugosi and Lon Chaney Jnr (with some of these films still proving popular in British cinemas in the 1950s). This is most apparent in Hammer's producing films centred on monsters already established in film horror by Universal: Frankenstein, Dracula, the Mummy and the Wolfman.[28]

Both Dracula and Frankenstein were 'stars' on the stage before the 1930s.[29] Universal's main innovation was to place them in cycles of films, in so doing removing them even further from the novels in which they first appeared. This cyclical structure, which was reproduced in the subsequent Mummy and Wolfman cycles, helped the studio to make the most of its limited resources: sets, costumes and, in some cases, footage could be reused. But this also had implications for the type of monster that was being produced. In particular, the relationship between the monster's creation and its eventual destruction changes when it is assumed (both by filmmakers and audiences) that the monster will return in a later film. It would seem that the elements of spectacle associated with these moments on the stage become even more important in the movies. As Steve Neale has noted, the horror film is often marked by a fascination with the appearance and disappearance of the monster, turning as these do on a 'fetishistic division of belief'.[30] These moments, codified for the first time in serial Universal horror production, are usually linked with a display of cinematic techniques (make-up, special effects, set design, etc.), so that not only the monster but aspects of cinema itself are involved in the spectacle. It is within such a conception of horror that Hammer, initially at least, operates, most visibly in its Frankenstein and Dracula films but also throughout the rest of its horror production in the 1950s and the first part of the 1960s.

As has already been indicated, British horror in the late 1950s was also part of a much wider renaissance of the genre: this included films from Italy (Riccardo Freda's *I Vampiri* in 1956 and Mario Bava's *La Maschera del Demonio* in 1960), America (Roger Corman's *The Fall of the House of Usher* in 1960 and his subsequent Poe adaptations, Hitchcock's *Psycho* in the same year) and Spain (Jesus Franco's *Gritos en la Noche* in 1962). All of these exploited a general relaxation of censorship through an increased explicitness in their representations of sex and violence, while many also utilised the relatively cheap colour systems that had just become available. They also, to a limited extent, shared some creative personnel. (This was mainly the case with actors: for example, British cult actress Barbara Steele made films in Italy, America and Britain.)

However, the ways in which British, Italian and American cinema responded to these common elements were in the main determined by factors operative within their respective national contexts. Moreover, while there was undoubtedly an international market for horror at this time (an important consideration for filmmakers), with films from the countries listed above regularly distributed in other countries, it is most unlikely that the response of the various audiences was a uniform one. As will be shown in subsequent chapters, many of the issues with which British horror was working were of specific relevance to British life, and, because of this, certain aspects of the films would simply have lacked resonance for non-British audiences. This does not mean that audiences in America and Europe (where British horror, initially at least, proved very popular) were 'misreading' these films; rather that they were locating them within and making sense of them in relation to their own national cultures. The extent to which a film lends itself to this process determines its international success or failure.

When the horror genre is viewed in this way as a collection of different horror cinemas, the relations between which are mediated via numerous national institutions, it becomes much easier to think about British horror both as an important intervention into the international horror genre and as a significant part of the post-war British cultural scene.

Entertainment value

> when the National Film Theatre gave us a two-week season I was horrified. I thought if they made us respectable it would ruin our whole image. When one reads all those criticisms such as the ones that appear in the NFT programme and the little ones that appear in *Time Out* when one of our films appears on TV, one is simply amazed. (Michael Carreras, Hammer executive and filmmaker)[31]

Carreras's words are a salutary reminder of the fact that the vast majority, if not all, of British horror films were intended primarily as 'just entertainment'. However, this begs the question of what the nature and function of entertainment for profit actually is. While this book will identify some of the economic factors at work in the production of horror, these factors in themselves do not wholly explain the forms which the films take. This is because films do not arise naturally, ready-made, from the conditions of their production, but are instead imagined by groups of individuals working within particular institutions. An account of the 'entertainment value' of British horror needs to discover what was entailed in the imaginative work done by the filmmakers. It will become clear that in seeking to make horror attractive to an audience, these filmmakers necessarily had to address what they perceived to be the lived experiences, fears and anxieties of that audience, with the terms of this engagement both aesthetic and ideological. In fact the history of horror in Britain can in part be read as a number of attempted (re)identifications of an audience, the nature of which (because of demographic factors and changing definitions of youth, class and gender) was unstable.

British horror films did not merely reflect or reproduce socially specific trends and issues but instead imaginatively transformed whatever they incorporated. For example, in the case of Hammer in the 1950s, its work can be seen to have involved seizing upon aspects of a contemporaneous social reality that were not naturally connected – in particular, shifts in gender definition and changing notions of professionalism – and weaving these into an aesthetic unity in the interests of making horror relevant to a British market. While it is clear that much of this work would have been unconscious, this does not render any of these creative processes any less effective. Only through an awareness of such activities is one able to engage with both the conditions of British horror's existence and the nature of that existence.

Notes

1 David Pirie, *A Heritage of Horror: the English Gothic Cinema 1946–1972*, London, 1973.
2 Charles Barr, '*Straw Dogs*, *A Clockwork Orange* and the Critics', *Screen*, 13, no. 2, summer 1972, pp. 17–31; Ian Christie, 'The Scandal of *Peeping Tom*', in Christie (ed.), *Powell, Pressburger and Others*, London, 1978, pp. 53–9.
3 Pirie, *A Heritage of Horror*, p. 40.
4 It is interesting that the five negative reviews of *The Curse of Frankenstein*, of which Smith's is one, came from three 'highbrow' (*The Daily Telegraph*, *The Sunday Times*, *The Observer*) and two left-wing newspapers (*The Daily Worker*, *Tribune*). Their collective revulsion from the film might be related to a broader critique of various manifestations of popular culture, particularly in its association with American culture, within which the right and left were concerned in the 1950s to defend different values and hierarchies; conservative standards of cultural literacy in the case of the former, working-class identity in the face of consumerism in the latter.
5 Roy Armes, *A Critical History of the British Cinema*, London, 1978; Ernest Betts, *The Film Business: a History of British Cinema 1896–1972*, London, 1973; Charles Oakley, *Where We Came In: 70 Years of the British Film Industry*, London, 1964; George Perry, *The Great British Picture Show*, London, 1974; Alexander Walker, *Hollywood England*, London, 1974.
6 Roger Manvell, 'Critical Survey', *Penguin Film Review*, 3, August 1947, p. 10.
7 Armes, *A Critical History of British Cinema*, p. 254.
8 Ibid., p. 249.
9 A 1962 publicity handout reprinted in *Little Shoppe of Horrors*, 8, May 1984, p. 22.
10 Pirie, *A Heritage of Horror*, p. 11.
11 Ibid., p. 51.
12 Ibid., p. 42.
13 For example, David Bordwell, Janet Staiger and Kristin Thompson, *The Classical Hollywood Cinema: Film Style and Mode of Production to 1960*, London, 1985.
14 *The Guardian*, 10 September 1987.
15 Julian Petley, 'The Lost Continent' in Charles Barr (ed.), *All Our Yesterdays: 90 Years of British Cinema*, London, 1986, pp. 98–119.
16 Andrew Higson, 'Critical Theory and "British Cinema"', *Screen*, 24, no. 4–5, July–October 1983, p. 91.
17 In Pam Cook (ed.), *The Cinema Book*, London, 1985, p. 36.
18 Denis Gifford, *The British Film Catalogue 1895–1970: a Guide to Entertainment Films*, Newton Abbot, 1973.
19 Charles Barr, 'Amnesia and Schizophrenia' in Barr (ed.), *All Our Yesterdays*, pp. 9–10.
20 Quoted in Jim Hillier (ed.), *Cahiers du Cinema: Volume 1*, London, 1985, p. 32.
21 Pirie, *A Heritage of Horror*, p. 9.
22 James B. Twitchell, *Dreadful Pleasures: an Anatomy of Modern Horror*, New York, 1985, p. 99.

23 R. H. W. Dillard, 'The Pageantry of Death' in Roy Huss and T. J. Ross (eds), *Focus on the Horror Film*, New Jersey, 1972, p. 37.
24 Martin Grotjahn, 'Horror – Yes, It Can Do You Good', *Films and Filming*, November 1958, p. 9.
25 Twitchell, *Dreadful Pleasures*, p. 7.
26 Steve Neale, *Genre*, London, 1980, p. 43.
27 Jan Mukarovsky, *Structure, Sign and Function*, New Haven and London, 1978, p. 52.
28 An important connection between the British and American 'schools' of horror lies in the copyright agreement struck between Hammer and Universal permitting the former's 'remakes' of Universal horror classics. This was only one of a series of agreements between UK and US companies that signalled the importance attached by British film producers to the US market. In this respect, it makes sense that Hammer should turn to Americanised models of horror, if only to transform them.
29 For a discussion of stage adaptations of Mary Shelley's *Frankenstein*, see Radu Florescu, *In Search of Frankenstein*, London, 1977, pp. 163–71; Albert J. Lavalley, 'The Stage and Film Children of *Frankenstein*' in George Levine and U. C. Knoepflmacher (eds), *The Endurance of Frankenstein: Essays on Mary Shelley's Novel*, Berkeley and London, 1975, pp. 243–89. See Donald F. Glut, *The Dracula Book*, Metuchen NJ, 1975, and *Dracula: Universal Filmscripts Series: Classic Horror Films – Volume 13*, Absecon NJ, 1991 for details of stage adaptations of Dracula.
30 Neale, *Genre*, p. 45.
31 Quoted in John Brosnan, *The Horror People*, London, 1976, p. 118.

1945–55:
From *Dead of Night*
to *The Quatermass Experiment* 2

Universal's influential Americanised version of the horror genre was formulated in the 1930s. Throughout this period British cinema was strikingly deficient in horror production. The small number of horror films that were made were either pale imitations of the American product (a plot synopsis for *Castle Sinister* – 1932, d. Widgey Newman – reads: 'Mad doctor tries to put girl's brain into apeman's head'[1]) or isolated attempts to locate horror within a recognisable British landscape (for example, *The Clairvoyant* – 1934, d. Maurice Elvey; and *The Man Who Changed His Mind* – 1936, d. Robert Stevenson, the latter featuring Boris Karloff).

One of the reasons for there being no considerable body of British work in the horror genre throughout the 1930s was the nature of British censorship at that time. As Jeffrey Richards has shown, British cinema in the decade was carefully regulated by the censors in order that those films which were perceived by them as having the potential to disturb social, political or moral order did not reach the screen.[2] It follows from this that if there had been a demand for horror in Britain at this time or before, any attempted satisfaction of this by the industry would almost certainly have met with substantial censorship problems. As one censor wrote in 1935:

> Although a separate category has been established for these films, I am sorry to learn that they are on the increase, as I cannot believe that such films are wholesome, pandering as they do to the love of the morbid and horrible . . . Some licensing authorities are already much disturbed about them, and I hope the producers and writers will accept this word of warning, and discourage this type of subject as far as possible.[3]

Given the standard practice of submitting scripts for the censor's unofficial approval before filming actually began, the absence of horror becomes not merely comprehensible but inevitable.

However, while horror films as such were discouraged, other genres of the period were regularly incorporating the macabre and the morbid into their narratives. One can note in this respect a number of 'low-life' thrillers which often dealt in the grotesque, as well as a series of gruesome melodramas starring Tod Slaughter.[4] These included *Maria Marten, or the Murder in the Red Barn* (1935), *Sweeney Todd, the Demon Barber of Fleet Street* (1936), *The Crimes of Stephen Hawke* (1936) and *The Face at the Window* (1939). Of the last-named of these Graham Greene wrote on its initial release, 'it is one of the best English pictures I have seen and leaves the American horror films far behind'.[5] While a detailed account of the inter-war period is beyond the scope of this book, it does seem that elements which would later be mobilised within a distinctive British horror genre were already in existence in British cinema before the war.

Similarly, while throughout World War Two no horror films were produced in Britain, and, significantly, the censor declined in general to pass 'H' – that is horror – films between 1942 and 1945, potentially gothic or horrific elements were occasionally present in disguised or submerged form; for example, *Tower of Terror* (1941, d. Lawrence Huntington) which centred on the activities of an insane lighthouse keeper, and Michael Powell and Emeric Pressburger's 1944 production of *A Canterbury Tale*, in which perverse sexuality – in the form of the Glueman, an apparently deranged magistrate who pours glue into the hair of various women – was seen as an integral part of rural life.[6]

It is clear then that, while not without its precursors, Ealing Studios' *Dead of Night* (1945, d. Alberto Cavalcanti, Charles Crichton, Basil Dearden, Robert Hamer) is the first important recognisably British horror film. However, to view *Dead of Night* as marking the 'birth' of British horror cinema is rather problematic for in many respects Ealing's film is very different from the long stream of horror films that eventually followed from the mid 1950s onwards. This 1950s wave of horror was in large part initiated by the enormous commercial success of Hammer's SF/horror *The Quatermass Experiment* in 1955. In seeking to explain the transition from *Dead of Night* to *The Quatermass Experiment*, as well as the virtual absence of horror from British cinema in the intervening years, one needs to take into account both the broadly social and the specifically cinematic context of each film's production. Such an approach will reveal the way in which the identity of British horror cinema was subject to constant and substantial revision.

Dead of Night: 'Oh Doctor, why did you have to break your glasses?'

Dead of Night is arguably the most famous ghost story ever produced within British cinema. It tells of an architect by the name of Walter Craig who arrives at a house party only to find that he has dreamed in extraordinarily accurate detail of both the house and its inhabitants. The guests then take it in turn to recount their own experiences of the supernatural. As their stories proceed, and the architect begins to remember some of the more horrifying aspects of his dream, a division between fantasy and waking reality becomes increasingly difficult to sustain. In the film's celebrated conclusion, the architect wakes up and realises that he has been dreaming all along. This dream quickly fades from his memory as he leaves for the very same house party at which we saw him arriving at the film's beginning.

Previous accounts of *Dead of Night* have tended to concentrate on two of the guests' stories, 'The Haunted Mirror' and 'The Ventriloquist's Doll'.[7] However, if one considers the film as a whole, paying particular attention to the ways in which all the stories – both those told by the house guests and the architect's 'dream-story' – relate to each other, then *Dead of Night* emerges as an intense and obsessive meditation on issues arising from the transition from a wartime to a post-war society.[8]

An appraisal of the film's opening few minutes provides a useful starting point for it is here that its project is laid out in an almost schematic fashion. The first three shots of the film are exemplary in this respect. The first shows a road, with a car driving towards the camera. It pulls up and Walter Craig looks offscreen. As an audience steeped in the conventions of mainstream filmmaking might expect, the next shot is his point of view of an apparently innocuous house. The third, again as expected, returns us to Craig. However, he seems puzzled by what he sees, and the audience in turn is puzzled by his puzzlement. He shakes his head as he drives out of frame. A wipe separates off this triad of shots from the rest of the film. Immediately the act of looking, of vision as it is constructed within cinema, has been problematised. Craig's hesitation before his own point-of-view shot – which is repeated throughout *Dead of Night* – is symptomatic of the whole film's hesitation before the image, its constant refusal to confirm whether what we the audience are seeing is 'real' or an illusion. As argued by Mark Nash in an article on Dreyer's *Vampyr*, such a hesitation is a mark of the fantastic, and clearly *Dead of Night* falls into that category (whereas Hammer horror, with its altogether more solid monsters, does not).[9] However, it will be suggested below that there is another, nationally specific motivation behind this hesitation.

As Craig enters the house, it is revealed that he is an architect – a symbolically charged occupation at a time of national reconstruction – who has been asked to design, significantly, two new bedrooms for the house. In both American and British cinema, 'upstairs' often functions as a resonant image of the private, psychological aspects of life. The bedroom is, of course, also the site of dreams and is referred to repeatedly as the film progresses.

Eventually Craig finds himself in a living room where six people wait to meet him. They offer greetings or handshakes, all of which Craig, still apparently dazed and unsure of what he is seeing, ignores. Instead he begins to tell them of his dream, a recurrent dream which predicts in exact detail the group now before him. Five of the people present then tell their own 'ghost' stories, with each of these comprising a separate episode within the film. They occur in the following order.

Narrator	*Story*
1 Granger	An encounter with a sinister undertaker
2 Sally, an adolescent girl	An encounter with the ghost of a murdered boy
3 Joan	The haunted mirror: a man becomes murderous under the influence of a mirror
4 Eliot Foley	A whimsical tale in which a dead golfer haunts an old friend
5 Dr Van Straaten, psychoanalyst	A ventriloquist is apparently possessed by his dummy

Audiences of the mid 1940s would undoubtedly have been familiar with this multiple-narrative structure, for it was one that character-ised numerous wartime British films. A principal theme running through many of the more overtly propagandistic feature films of the war years was the need for the individual to put aside his or her own personal ambitions and desires and enter into a national community, with this thematic impulse having distinct consequences for the ways in which the films in question organised their narratives. Often a sense of what this wartime community/nation was like was articulated via a film's dispersing its drama across a number of only loosely connected mini-narratives. Such a structure enabled the portrayal of the activities of a group of characters from different walks of life who in the course of the film would overcome their differences and together form a cohesive unit, a unit which could then be used by the filmmakers as a symbol of national unity. As Andrew Higson notes of some of these films, 'it is difficult to identify any single line of narrative emphasis which is clearly structured in terms of a goal to be achieved, a wish to be fulfilled, a disruption to be resolved. On the contrary, these films are structured as a *series* of interweaving narrative lines, following a *multiplicity* of characters rather than a single central narrative protagonist'.[10] The representation of an individual's desires – in narratives which did have clearly identifiable central protagonists – was left to other, less reputable areas of British film production during the war. Perhaps the most notable examples of wartime fictions of desire were the extremely successful Gainsborough melodramas (the first of which, *The Man in Grey*, was released in 1943), in which sexuality tended to be placed at a safe distance in a pseudo-historical past.[11]

In its multiple-narrative structure, *Dead of Night* seems then to refer back to a wartime fiction of collectivity and national unity. But the differences between *Dead of Night* and earlier war productions are as striking, if not more so, as any similarities. For example, while wartime films frequently showed the movement of their characters away from home and family into a more community-based social structure (exemplified by a military unit), *Dead of Night* takes place almost entirely within the home of one of its characters. Even more significantly, Ealing's film seems to be playing itself out inside a particular character's head.

One way of explaining *Dead of Night*'s return to the home would be to see it as reflecting things actually happening in British society at the time, with many men returning home from overseas and many women giving up, willingly or otherwise, their wartime occupations and adopting again the nurturing roles of housewife and mother within the domestic household. As another aspect of this, one can also note the stress in government social policy of the immediate post-war period on the need to rebuild traditional family life after the disruptions of war.[12]

Certainly *Dead of Night* does show a return to the home – quite literally, as the opening sequence demonstrates. But what it does not show is a reconstituted family. Fathers, mothers and children are present, but never all together in the same story. The people who do gather in the opening sequence are a curiously unintegrated group, the interrelationships of whom (outside of a few very sketchily drawn mother–son, husband–wife relationships) are never elaborated in any detail. Neither is this a dynamic community in the manner of wartime features, a community that is coming into being. Rather it seems to function as a community in the process of disintegration, caught up as its members are in essentially private fears and memories. A sense of uncertainty pervades the film; about the respective values of domesticity and community and the roles played by men and women within each; about reality itself.

It can in fact be argued that the more one considers the tone of *Dead of Night* – the way in which, for example, its domestic settings are increasingly marked as claustrophobic and confining – as well as its convoluted narrative structure and its systematic turn to fantasy, the more necessary it becomes to start thinking about the film in terms of its cinematic specificity (as opposed to seeing it as merely mirroring a particular social trend). As the analysis below will demonstrate, *Dead of Night* is working with and seeking to resolve in imaginary terms a problem which is primarily aesthetic and cinematic but which has its root cause in the broader historical conditions of the film's production. This problem can be expressed as follows: how does one produce credible cinematic representations of human desire and sexuality within recognisably contemporary settings after a period in which desire had been either banished from or marginalised within those very same settings?

Importantly, *Dead of Night* is not alone in its seeking to trace a passage from a wartime collectivity to a more desire-centred, in-dividualistic fictional world. Writing about mid-1940s British film production, Charles Barr has noted 'a spectacular shift which occurs in British films around this time from the public sphere to the private, with a stress on vision and fantasy'.[13] Each film he cites (of which *Dead of Night* is one) is marked by the difficulty of showing desire in a contemporary domestic and familial environment. In *Brief*

Encounter, home and family are traps repressing both male and female sexuality while in *A Matter of Life and Death* the heterosexual and technicolour romance of hero and heroine is threatened by and has to justify itself before a monochrome Heaven. Significantly for our later argument, both *Dead of Night* and *A Matter of Life and Death* produce a sense of desire as something which is difficult or impossible in two connected ways: first, via a problematisation of the film image itself (in *Life and Death* the hero is never quite sure whether his 'visions' of Heaven are real or hallucinations) and second, through a questioning of male vision and sanity.

These various cinematic meditations on the problem of desire are not reducible to the various social disruptions attendant upon the end of the war. But they do connect with social changes which also impinged upon and helped mould the lived experience of the film's intended audience (as indeed they had to for the films to be meaningful). As has already been suggested, one important factor in the immediate post-war situation was the partial dislocation of conventional ways of thinking about and defining the capabilities and nature of each gender – with men and women alike to a certain extent separated from traditional social roles (and with women in particular being asked, sometimes compelled, to relinquish the limited in-dependence they had gained during the war). Such a situation was fraught with potential tensions, frustrations and anxieties for both genders. The question of desire, and the form which heterosexual relationships would take in a reconstructed post-war society, were very real issues at this time.

In order to trace the ways in which *Dead of Night* operates in this area, the following discussion of the film will be divided into two sections. The first will deal with the way in which the figures of the independent/strong woman and the weak/emasculated man are used within the film to produce a sense of there being some-thing wrong with conventional heterosexual relationships. The second part will deal with the relation of *Dead of Night* to some of the aesthetic practices that characterise British cinema at the time of production, especially as they are constructed through the look. In the end, these two elements are inseparable, and the latter part of the analysis will link them together in order to give an overall view of the complex relation of *Dead of Night* to the context of its production.

Gender crisis: 'strong' women and 'weak' men

The first of the guest's story told within the film concerns Granger, a racing driver. It begins with his crashing during a race, after which he is wounded, both physically and mentally. One can profitably equate this race with the opportunities for a conventional male heroism provided by the war. It can also be argued that no male in the film as a whole quite recovers from the crash, i.e. the end of that war. The post-war trauma often takes the form of male neurosis; in this case, Granger has a portentous vision of doom and begins to doubt his own sanity. The final image of this first episode is interesting in this respect: a close-up of Granger as he sees his vision come true, it shows him as passive, quiescent, qualities more conventionally linked with representations of femininity.

The second story features a young girl, Sally. It takes place at a children's party in a large house; significantly, aside from a briefly glimpsed aged butler, there are no adult men present. During a game of sardines, the eldest boy makes a pass at Sally and she strikes him. Immediately afterwards, she finds herself in the bedroom of a sobbing boy, Francis Kent, whom we discover later was murdered eighty years previously by his elder sister. (This is based on a famous, true-life murder.) The method of killing is important. Constance Kent cuts her brother's throat. This act, this cutting of the human body has often been read as an inscription or writing of sexual difference onto the body, particularly in the context of the horror film where the body in question is usually female, the wielder of the weapon usually male and the outcome a reassuring (for men) reimposition of traditional gender roles.[14] In *Dead of Night* this is reversed, so it is the male who is marked by what can be read in this context as a symbolic castration (which becomes a self-inflicted act in 'The Haunted Mirror' episode). Moreover, this castrating act is shown as causatively linked with Sally's violent rejection of the advances of a pubescent boy, someone who is not completely a man.

The third story in the film is perhaps the most famous and discussed – 'The Haunted Mirror'. From the very beginning of this story its main male character, Peter is signalled as being inadequate in the face of Joan, his fiancée's strength. The episode opens with him seated in his flat waiting for Joan to appear, a position usually reserved – in cinema, at least – for the female half of a relationship. There is also a suggestion in this first scene that Joan is enjoying the company of two men, Peter and their mutual friend Guy, as if one

is insufficient (an idea taken up in more detail by the next story).
Later exchanges such as Joan's 'You've been a bit broody all evening'
– 'broodiness' another conventionally feminine attribute – and
Peter's reply 'A bit limp with the heat, I expect', as well as the fact
that it is Peter rather than Joan who suffers from the again
conventionally feminine eve-of-wedding nerves, obviously connect
with this partial reversal of roles. This is further underlined by Joan's
gift of a mirror to Peter, which emasculates him in two related ways.
First, the mirror in art has frequently been used to symbolise female
vanity.[15] Second, the male gaze is here associated with a narcissism
which signals a fascination evident throughout the film with images
of male introspection. In *Dead of Night*, men seem to spend most of
their time staring anxiously into space (and, implicitly, into their
own minds). As Joan herself puts it, 'I thought you'd like to look at
yourself.'

The mirror's original, nineteenth-century owner was, we are told,
a man of 'dominating influence' who, confined to his bedroom by
an accident, murders his wife in a fit of jealousy and then cuts his
own throat before the mirror. The parallels between this and the
Joan–Peter relationship are clear. Peter's repressed jealousy over
Joan's friendship with Guy is apparent from the beginning, a
jealousy which by the end of the episode and under the influence of
the mirror has become murderous. A crisis point is reached, during
which Joan, after herself seeing for the first time what up until then
has only been visible to her fiancé, succeeds in smashing the mirror.
Peter's first words after this are 'I've cut myself.' The wounding of
the male inflicted behind the mirror is reinflicted before it. Those
traces of resistance to Joan's dominance are brought out and then
vanquished. 'I thought you'd like to look at yourself': the mirror
reinforces Peter's effeminacy, a state consequent partly on his
general insipidness and partly upon Joan's usurpation of the 'male'
role in their relationship. As with the previous two stories, this story
also gives us contemporary heterosexuality as weak and listless. The
only imaginable sexual energy here emanates from the past (the room
seen in the mirror could easily be a set for a Gainsborough
melodrama) and is viewed as dangerous and destructive.

The fourth story, a comic relief sketch in which a dead golfer
returns to haunt an old golfing acquaintance, and which features
character actors Basil Radford and Naunton Wayne, is usually
considered the weakest element in the film. But even here one can

find in operation those concerns outlined above, although not in such a complex form. For example, the idea suggested by 'The Haunted Mirror' of one woman to two men is here made literal as both Radford and Wayne leave the church with the bride for the honeymoon.

The fifth and final story, 'The Ventriloquist's Dummy', can be read as representing on a barely submerged level a homosexual love triangle, with Sylvester, an American ventriloquist, at one point, Maxwell Frere (Michael Redgrave) at the second, and the dummy, Hugo, at the third. The 'bitchiness' of the dialogue between Maxwell and Hugo, and Maxwell's neurotic fear of Hugo leaving him for Sylvester, both testify to this level of meaning, however stereotypical a representation of homosexuality this might be. Maxwell's highly pitched, nervous voice and his 'feminine' mannerisms also signal him as the passive/'female' half of the relationship.

In the previous two stories a situation is envisaged in which one woman requires two men. As a bizarre but logical development of this idea, and one which connects with and underlines the fragility of Maxwell's male identity, Hugo can be seen to function in this story as a kind of detachable phallus, a symbol of an extreme male insecurity. In support of this one can note Maxwell's neurotic possessiveness of the dummy, his terror that Sylvester will take it away from him, the way in which his very identity, his 'complete-ness' depends upon his possession of it. Indeed the psychiatrist describes it as part of Maxwell, who is unable to speak of his crime until it is restored to him.

The end of the episode is revealing, especially bearing in mind the number of wounded men present in the film. Hugo is brought to Maxwell, who, realising that he cannot keep his doll, destroys it by stamping on its head. Later, as he lies in an asylum, he is made to speak. He opens his mouth and we hear Hugo's voice, that is, an even higher-pitched voice than Maxwell's own. The destruction of the dummy/phallus – equivalent to the self-inflicted throat-cutting in 'The Haunted Mirror' – has, quite simply, left Maxwell a castrato.

The conclusion of the film as a whole, in which Craig kills Van Straaten, strikes Sally (returning the blow she earlier delivered to another male), asks Peter if he can hide in his mirror, and is finally attacked by Hugo, both summarises the stories and thoroughly implicates the architect in them.

Seen in this way, the film is a complex imagining of a gender crisis, one which focuses in particular on fears, anxieties and uncertainties about the role of the male in a post-war British society. Hence the film's insistent stress on male neurosis and the impossibility of heterosexuality. However, such a reading is necessarily incomplete for *Dead of Night* can also be seen as evincing a concern with vision as it was figured within British cinema at the time.

Seeing/looking

Walter Craig hesitates before his own point-of-view shot in *Dead of Night*'s opening sequence. This hesitation is reiterated throughout the film; Granger hesitating before his own 'vision', Peter staring disbelievingly into the mirror and Basil Radford staring, again disbelievingly, at Naunton Wayne's ghost. In the case of Granger and Peter, as with Walter Craig, this hesitation tends to be presented via point-of-view shots. In both Granger's and Peter's stories, the 'visions' are created not through the use of any special effects but simply by cutting from the person who sees to what is seen. The presentation of supernatural events as spectatorial events, things to be looked at by characters within the film, echoes the way in which spectators in the cinema respond to what they see. When the audience looks at the screen, its reaction to objects that are visibly there but are also absent is split between belief and disbelief. What it sees when it watches *Dead of Night* is this mixture of belief and disbelief reproduced within the narrative world of the film itself, reproduced and brought to a moment of crisis. Both Peter and Granger look and see things which cannot actually be there – and yet they both accept what they see as being in some sense 'real'. Significantly, both of these 'visions' refer themselves back to cinema. The curtained window in Granger's room before which he experiences his vision of the hearse parallels the covered cinema screen, another 'window onto the world' and Peter's mirror provides another particularly suggestive metaphor for the nature and function of cinema (one that has been explored by psychoanalytical film theory.)

On one level, these stories can be read as self-reflexive pieces, through certain mechanisms foregrounding their own cinematic nature. If one takes a wider perspective, however, and looks at the film as a whole, then the meaning of these mechanisms changes somewhat. It is on this new level that *Dead of Night*'s peculiar relationship with social history becomes apparent.

The whole film is of course caught up within Walter Craig's

dream. A passage from film theorist Christian Metz is helpful here. It deals with one of the ways in which cinema can dramatise notions of belief and disbelief:

> Or else, in so many films, the character of the 'dreamer' – the sleeping dreamer – who during the film believed (as we did!) that it was true, whereas it was he who saw it all in a dream and who wakes up at the end of the film (as we do again).[16]

For Metz, the dreamer waking assures the audience that the images they have been seeing were *really false* while the images they are seeing now are *really real*. No such comfort or assurance is offered by the conclusion of *Dead of Night*. Craig wakes up and the audience realise that what has gone before was a dream. But then the dream (if that is what it is) begins to reassert itself, so that now we do not know whether the images we see and have seen are 'real' or 'false'. The whole film has turned over on itself; the ending is exactly the same as the beginning, giving us Craig's hesitation of vision twice-over, a hesitation which the film takes up in a complex and disturbing way.

Granger's and Peter's visions, and the play of belief and disbelief apparent in them, are associated with a crisis of gender (and especially male) identity. This of course is an anxiety specific to the post-1945 transition from war to peace and the social and representational dislocations that this involved, an anxiety acknowledged throughout this film, in all of its stories. But the film does not merely reflect this or work it through in an unproblematic fashion. All of its images are operating within a narrative structure which problematises *every* image in the film. The ontological certainty of wartime cinema – exemplified by the use within fiction films of documentary techniques – has gone. Not only are the images in the mirror now questionable but also every character and object before the mirror and indeed even the mirror itself (and also the 'dreamer', Walter Craig). One does not even know whether this is an actual dream that one is seeing. *Dead of Night* refuses to construct a hierarchy of meaning on the level of the image – it challenges the structures of belief outlined by Metz – in what is essentially a process of fetishistic disavowal, seeing and not seeing, both acknowledging and denying that there is something 'wrong' with heterosexuality and male identity. In a sense, this is why the film does not end in any conventional way, why it cannot arrange its narrative elements into a suitably reassuring point of closure.

British cinema during the war was generally devoid of formal experiments which explored the nature of the image. Even in the more flamboyant, formally excessive genres such as Gainsborough melodrama, there was no questioning of the image on the scale of *Dead of Night*. This is particularly interesting when one notes that the film was made for Ealing Studios, which, as Charles Barr has observed, played a key part in the wartime cinematic construction of a national community. 'Ealing had been the dominant studio for war-effort production, absorbing documentary ideas and personnel . . . and making films for – to appropriate Grierson's phrase again – social use.'[17] (Wartime Ealing films included *San Demetrio London* and *The Bells Go Down*.) Whereas the contemporaneous Gainsborough melodramas were dealing with the expression of sexuality, in these more respectable films sexual desire tended to be subordinated to the interests of the group or community.

It can be argued from this that in *Dead of Night* one finds Ealing's attempted reconstruction of the male as a sexualised individual as opposed to a desexed participant in the national community. In this it can be aligned with two other Ealing films of the immediate post-war period, the prisoner-of-war drama *The Captive Heart* (1946, d. Basil Dearden) and the social problem film *Frieda* (1947, d. Dearden), both of which, although not as complexly structured as *Dead of Night*, contain equivalent representations of a troubled masculinity.[18] In the case of *Dead of Night* an attempt to solve or erase this 'trouble' is imagined in such terms as make it, in the end, an impossible task. On the one hand, there is clearly an awareness in this film of certain problems around male identity and sexuality at this time. On the other hand, and as a condition of the former, there is at work a complex strategy of denial, as if Ealing were not prepared or, given the type of filmmaking associated with Ealing, able to follow this through in any systematic fashion, which results in one of the most formally aberrant films British cinema has ever produced. It is perhaps not surprising that Ealing retreated from what in many ways was a complete dead end and took another course. *Dead of Night* was a false start for the horror genre in this country, intense and disturbing but a horror film without a recognisable monster, or rather a film where the monster turned out to be the film itself.

One small but telling point: the psychiatrist in the film wears glasses. Throughout the framing story he is constantly, obsessively taking them off and putting them on again. A tiny detail which signals yet again a process of disavowal, of seeing and not seeing. The centrality of this to the film, the way in which it blocks the film at every level, is made clear at the moment the narrative collapses, when the doctor accidentally breaks his glasses and Craig strangles him. Craig's line of dialogue here is 'Oh doctor, if only you hadn't broken your glasses.' And then Craig wakes up. The glasses are smashed, the process of disavowal is momentarily halted. But then it begins again . . .

Quatermass and 1950s SF/horror

Very few horror films were produced in Britain between *Dead of Night* in 1945 and *The Quatermass Experiment* in 1955. In accounting for this, both the changing industrial structures of British cinema and the films actually produced in the period need to be considered. Through an analysis of these two factors one becomes aware of the relationships the post-1955 British horror films bear not only to *Dead of Night* but also to the films that fall between.

The discussion of mid-1950s production that follows will centre on three science-fiction/horror films made by Hammer Films which can be seen as precursors to a 'full-blooded' colour Hammer horror, namely *The Quatermass Experiment* (1955, d. Val Guest), *Quatermass II* (1957, d. Val Guest) and *X – The Unknown* (1956, d. Leslie Norman). It was with the production in 1956 of *The Curse of Frankenstein* and later *Dracula*, *The Hound of the Baskervilles* and *The Mummy*, amongst others, that Hammer constructed a particular model of British horror that was to hold dominance for almost a decade. In these three SF/horror films, two of which were made before *Curse*, one finds this model in the process of construction, as an original aesthetic mobilisation of form and theme which draws heavily upon the contemporaneous structures and concerns of British cinema. In effect, what Hammer is doing at this moment in history is seeking its constituency, a process which involves finding both a distinctive voice and a profitable audience.

The industry

The 1950s was a period of economic crisis for the British film industry. A substantial decline in admissions (down 66 per cent between 1948 and 1960) and the closing down of many cinemas (34 per cent in the same period) were only the most visible signs of the way in which cinema's position in society was shifting. The growing popularity of television in this period (TV licence ownership, just under 764,000 in 1951, rose to almost 10.5 million by the end of the decade, with ITV beginning transmission in 1955) was also an important factor, although there is a need to place this in a wider social context, as John Hill does when he observes: 'Ironically, those very elements which in one light betokened affluence only spelt decline for the cinema. Rising incomes, increasing home-ownership and home-orientated consumption, the diversification of leisure facilities and increasing popularity of motoring all seemed to conspire to diminish the cinema's importance.'[19]

What this notion of a declining cinema does sometimes serve to obscure, however, are changes in the composition of the ever-decreasing audience, and most significantly its increasing youthful-ness. In 1951 those aged 16–24 went to the cinema nearly three times for each visit by older people, while by 1960, as Stuart Laing notes, '44 per cent of those between 16 and 24 still attended cinema at least once a week and a further 24 per cent at least once a month. Against this 68 per cent of reasonably habituated cinemagoers, the figures for other age groups were considerably lower'.[20] In *The Decline of Cinema*, an important 1962 study of the industry, John Spraos saw this as a continuing tendency as the products of the post-war population boom grew to maturity in the early 1960s.[21] Clearly, the days of the 'family' audience were more or less over, not only in terms of actual audience figures but also for the exhibition and distribution practices adopted by the major cinema circuits.

The 1950s also saw an opening up of what could be represented on the cinema screen. The impetus for this initially came from Hollywood as the studios attempted to regain an audience lost to television by offering them what their supposedly more anodyne competitor could not, namely an intensified visual experience (through Cinemascope, 3–D, etc.) and, more importantly as far as an under-standing of horror is concerned, an increased explicitness on a wide range of issues.[22]

The 'X' certificate had been introduced in Britain at the beginning of the decade partly as an acknowledgement of an increasing non-family audience. Both Rank and ABC, the two major cinema circuits, resisted it for some years; Rank, openly committed to a family audience, released only fourteen 'X' films in the decade, a more open-minded ABC fifty.[23] Significantly, most of these appeared in the late 1950s when the circuits, realising that their old audiences were dwindling, were beginning to accept 'X' films as a way of targeting a new market.[24] British film censorship at this time, while not in any way as liberal as it would become later, was far less restrictive than it had been in the 1930s and during the war. (John Trevelyan, a censor whose policies very much embodied a liberal and, to a certain extent, permissive approach, was appointed Secretary of the British Board of Film Censors in 1958.) A period of limited decensorship, commencing with the Obscene Publications Act in 1959 and the subsequent unsuccessful prosecution of *Lady Chatterley's Lover*, was about to begin.[25]

While most of these important changes occurred in the late 1950s, the situation to which they were a response was in existence from the early to mid 1950s onwards. In British cinema of this period one finds a predominantly young audience (traditionally the target audience for horror films) coupled with a growing, although still limited, permissiveness in terms of what could be shown on screen. It seems that for what was probably the first time in British cinema history there was a space – in terms of both market potential and what would be allowed by the censors – in which an indigenous horror genre could conceivably operate.[26] How it was that the Hammer company rather than any other came to fill and dominate that space, what it was about this relatively small production set-up that enabled it to exploit this situation so effectively, are questions that can now be considered.

Hammer Film Productions came into being in 1947. Between that date and the release of *The Curse of Frankenstein*, its first colour horror film, in 1957, it produced approximately fifty films, both features and shorts, only five of which were in a SF/horror mould: these were *Stolen Face* in 1952 and *Four-Sided Triangle* and *Spaceways* in 1953 – with all three directed by Terence Fisher – as well as *The Quatermass Experiment* and *X – The Unknown*. The majority of the films were 60- to 80-minute programme-fillers and often featured imported American stars, especially after 1951 when Hammer made its first American distribution deal. They were also frequently adapted from radio – and later TV – plays and serials. Examples include versions of the radio serials *Dick Barton* and *PC 49* in addition to, of course, BBC TV's *The Quatermass Experiment*.

Three elements that bear on Hammer's subsequent pre-eminence in horror are clear from its pre-horror history. First, this small company had already established itself as a producer of films, the subject matter of which was more often than not known to an audience beforehand through another medium. This meant that Hammer was already highly sensitive to what was actually in demand within the market rather than being blindly committed to any notion of 'family entertainment'. One example of this sensitivity was the questionnaire circulated to cinema managers by the company in order to ascertain whether it was the horror or SF elements in *The Quatermass Experiment* that had made it so popular.[27] Alongside this, there was a flexibility within the company that enabled it to take swift advantage of any new trend, with perhaps the best example of this being its last minute reorganisation of its production schedule in 1956 in order to accommodate and exploit its growing success with horror productions.[28]

Second, Hammer had by 1951 located itself at Bray Studios – its base for the next sixteen years – and had assembled a group of highly proficient craftsmen and technicians. This provided the basis, both in terms of personnel and physical resources, for a continuity of production, so that the company's eventual move into horror could be achieved without any substantial and time-consuming transformation of its internal structures.

Third, Hammer had already forged a link with an American distributor. In the past, and particularly since the war, Hollywood had been commonly perceived as an economic and cultural threat to a national British cinema.[29] Even at this early stage Hammer apparently did not share this view and was attempting to secure long-term American finance. In this, it anticipated the increasing reliance of the British film industry on American capital in the 1960s. Later this pro-US stance would assist Hammer in its gaining access to a worldwide distribution network and also facilitate its seeking of copyright permission to remake old horror classics.

As the composition of the British audience changed, and censorship and exhibition practices also shifted, Hammer was well prepared, perhaps more so than any other company, to move quickly into the gap thereby opened up. In so doing, however, it also helped to forge what would prove to be one of the most durable of British genres, and to understand the nature of this durability, one needs not only to look at the economic conditions that enabled horror to come into being and helped to maintain it thereafter but also to examine the particular aesthetic forms that the genre took within this new industrial context. How do Hammer's first sustained efforts in the horror genre relate both to concerns and issues in British cinema and British society of the period and to the colour horror films that were shortly to follow?

The unknown

The Quatermass Experiment and *Quatermass II* can be located within the production practices developed by Hammer through the late 1940s and first part of the 1950s. Both were adapted from pre-existing properties, in this case two enormously successful BBC TV series, the first transmitted in 1953, the second in 1955. At the same time, *The Quatermass Experiment* in particular (as well as *X – The Unknown*) marked a distinct break, the moment at which Hammer identified and began to address through a distinctive aesthetic form a set of problematics to do with gender definition that would subsequently occupy much of colour gothic horror.

At one point in *The Quatermass Experiment*, Inspector Lomax (Jack Warner) says to Quatermass (Brian Donlevy) 'No one wins a Cold War.' Certainly one way of approaching these three Hammer SF/horror films is to view them as 'Cold War' thrillers (as David Pirie does in discussing *X – The Unknown*),[30] close paranoid cousins to the American invasion fantasy. However, it does seem that the inspector's remark – an apparently defeatist statement by a figure of social authority – underlines the film's lack of commitment to and interest in a 1950s superpower conflict, and in this it suggests another, potentially more profitable reading. One can further argue that while these films are operating within the same global political and military situation as their American counterparts, there is something distinctively 'British' about the position they adopt within that situation, and this 'Britishness' is to be found in the way in which a specific social and cinematic context organises their respective narratives. In this case, the central metaphor of invasion has a meaning very different from its meaning in American SF invasion movies such as *Invaders from Mars* (1953) or *Invasion of the Bodysnatchers* (1956).[31]

One striking and distinctive element in all three British films is the vaguely specified origin of the monster. In *The Quatermass Experiment* it is a thing floating in the depths of space, in *X – The Unknown* a shapeless blob that emerges from a bottomless hole in the ground, and in *Quatermass II* an unidentified object in the upper reaches of the Earth's atmosphere. This can be contrasted with American 1950s SF where if the monsters were not assigned to a particular planet (usually Mars, the *red* planet) then they were implicitly seen as stemming from a communist society (either Russia or China). While American 1950s monsters tended to be signalled as completely Other within a context of extreme social 'normalcy', the monsters in the corresponding British films are shown as Other quite simply because the films do not seem to be able to specify exactly what they are or where they come from. Hence their amorphous, shapeless forms, with the fluid monster in *X – The Unknown* as the most extreme example of this. Hence also the tentative endings of all three films. *The Quatermass Experiment* concludes with Quatermass repeating his first disastrous experiment, while *Quatermass II* ends with his suggestion that the alien invasion might not after all have been defeated. Perhaps most notably, *X – The Unknown* concludes with the monster exploding followed by the scientist–protagonist advancing upon the hole whence it came and remarking of the explosion 'It shouldn't have happened' (which is his last line of dialogue in the film). After all, these films seem to suggest, how can one destroy a monster, the origin and substance of which remain unspecified?

The two *Quatermass* films and *X – The Unknown* concern themselves with a military and scientific mobilisation in the face of a largely unspecified threat which comes from somewhere 'out there'. Considering this 'trilogy' as British Cold War cinema, 'out there' in this context could signify outside an ever-decreasing British sphere of influence. This was the period which saw a growing public awareness of the decline of Empire and Britain's reduced status as a world leader, with Suez in 1956 functioning as a particularly visible instance of this process. Connected with these changes, a social fear of the time involved Britain being caught up in a military conflict that was not of its own making (CND was formed in 1958). On one level, the threat from 'out there' given us in these films can be seen as a representation of this fear, a condensation within narrative forms of a changing perception of national identity, of what it actually meant to be British, especially in the area of foreign relations and world status.[32]

Much writing on British cinema views the 1950s, at least until the advent of the British New Wave, as an artistically undistinguished period for British filmmaking. The decade's output has been seen as

both socially and formally conservative and repressive of emotion
and sexuality; the 'stiff upper lip' is often invoked as a derisory term.
In his study of British horror, David Pirie largely subscribes to this
model, reading the opening sequence of *The Quatermass Experiment*,
in which a rocket crashes into the peaceful English countryside, as
Hammer's phallic, sexualised intervention into this 'sexless' cinema.[33]
Other work on the period, however, has mounted a critique of this
position, noting strains and tensions within films which were previously conceived of as cinematically lifeless and repressed. Charles
Barr has traced the implications of this for a revised understanding
of the British horror film: 'The relation of such films to the later
horror cycle, and indeed to the later "New Wave" cinema, has to be
seen, in fact, as more complicated than one of straight difference,
the bland giving way to the full-blooded.'[34] It follows from this that
a contextual analysis of these SF/horror films will be concerned not
only to judge the difference and innovation they might represent but
also to identify the ways in which they interconnect with earlier and
concurrent strands of British cinema.

What Pirie does not do in his analysis of *The Quatermass Experiment* is relate the opening sequence to the rest of the film or to the
opening sequence of its companion piece, *X – The Unknown*. This
latter film commences with a crack opening up in the earth; a vaginal
image to go alongside the phallic one that opens the first *Quatermass*.
But rather than merely holding up these two sexually charged images
as examples of sexuality per se bursting into a sexually repressed
cinema, a more profitable approach might be to examine how they
function as problems for the types of narrative and representational
norms characteristic of British cinema at this time. Significantly in
this respect, there are indications that the disruptions which initiate
The Quatermass Experiment and, to a lesser extent, *X – The Unknown*
are particularly extreme, functioning not only as disruptions of a
narrative world but also as interventions into a particular way of
seeing and making sense of reality.

In *The Quatermass Experiment* the crash breaks the camera that is
on board the rocket. The camera as an image of cinema is an analogy
of which the film is insistently aware, as is demonstrated at one point
when Inspector Lomax, referring to the film salvaged from that
camera, remarks, 'This is one premiere I don't want to miss.' Just
as the various mirrors and windows in *Dead of Night* direct a viewer
back to cinema, one can argue that this remark also represents a

moment of self-reflexivity, a reference to the film itself, the 'premiere' film of its type, an awareness on whatever level of its special relationship with earlier cinematic practices. In *X – The Unknown* the advent of the 'monster' is announced by a bizarre geiger counter reading. As a soldier remarks, 'We're getting a reading on the counter where there shouldn't be one.' While there is no obvious cinematic parallel here, once again a device which symbolises a perceptual certitude is shown as being inadequate.

It is instructive at this point to see what were the most popular British films at the box-office in the mid 1950s. In 1953 *The Cruel Sea* was the top British moneymaker, in 1954 it was *Doctor in the House* and in 1955 (the year of *The Quatermass Experiment*) *The Dambusters*.[35] Two war films and the first in an enormously success- ful 'Doctor' series: in this context, *The Quatermass Experiment*, the most influential of the SF/horror films as far as the later development of British horror is concerned, produces a violent collision of these two groups of films, and in particular the opposed – although connected – definitions of masculinity that are offered by each. It follows from this that these SF/horror films need to be understood not only as inflections of the Cold War thriller but also as a constituent part of what might be termed here Welfare State cinema.

Both Elizabeth Wilson and Jeffrey Weeks have argued that the British Welfare State in the 1950s was centred on a particular conception of the nuclear family.[36] This was seen both as the site for the reproduction of the nation/workforce and as a centre for a burgeoning domestic consumerism, 'a fountainhead of consumption' as Weeks puts it. Discourses supportive of this structure – in the form of legislation, government reports, newspaper articles etc. – dealt largely in the case of the woman with definitions of femininity and motherhood and for the man, perhaps surprisingly, in debates about homosexuality.[37] Underlying this and acting as a possible contradiction and source of tension was, to quote from Weeks again, 'the generalisation across all classes of the ideal of mutual sexual pleasure, but very much within the context of a stable marital relationship'.[38] The family was seen as both the proper place for and the container of male and female sexuality, and any sexual activity outside its domestic auspices was marked as deviant.

One of the areas in which these various debates were being worked through was the cinema. As far as the aforementioned war and 'Doctor' films were concerned, what was at stake in their narratives appeared to be a definition of masculinity within a nurturing state where family and home comprised the central repository of ideological and economic value.

In the war films one finds what is in effect the negative imprint of the Welfare State in the conditions necessary for 'the hero', the male role model par excellence, to exist; namely, his separation from that State, from home and family, and only a tenuous connection with the female, women remaining marginal throughout. That is to say, he must not be contaminated by certain aspects of Welfare State ideology. Paradoxically, he must live outside the time that has fashioned him. Hence the cinematic return to and recreation of World War Two. Hence too the intense repressiveness involved in these war films; present-day reality has at all costs to be kept out.[39]

In the 'Doctor' films, however, the male is inserted into a 'present-day' world (indeed into the Welfare State in the narrowest sense of the term), no longer a hero but instead indulging in comic, romantic and sometimes childish antics under the benign gaze of one of the major castrating fathers of British cinema, Sir Lancelot Spratt. What is gained here is the ability to move within what was a loose approximation of contemporary reality, and also to relate to members of the opposite sex. What is lost is the opportunity to risk all for a mythic ideal of nation, to live up to the cultural definition of what a hero actually is. On one level at least, the war films can be read as a resistance to a new masculinity demanded by a dominant ideology organised around family and home. While the 'Doctor' films can accommodate a 1950s 'new man', they work to trivialise and diminish him through humour and ridicule.

This then is the situation into which the Quatermass rocket crashes. What *The Quatermass Experiment* works to do in such a context is to expose this uneasiness around masculinity, an uneasiness which relates both to a particular moment in British social history and to the representations being produced by British film-makers, with a series of calculated and precisely executed acts of violence.

The Quatermass Experiment commences with an astronaut falling from the sky. His Christian name is Victor, and repeatedly throughout the film he is referred to as a hero. In the 1950s war film the RAF was the most mythic of all the fighting services, the open sky the most suitable arena for a staged escape from the world 'down there'. One could say that what Hammer's film is doing, in a sense, is pulling down a hero, one of the RAF victors, from the sky and propelling him into a world which, as will become clear, is very much structured by a Welfare State ideology. What is given us in this film then is a particular construction of masculinity, a heroic role model, decaying (quite literally) before our eyes under the onslaught of a contemporary reality.

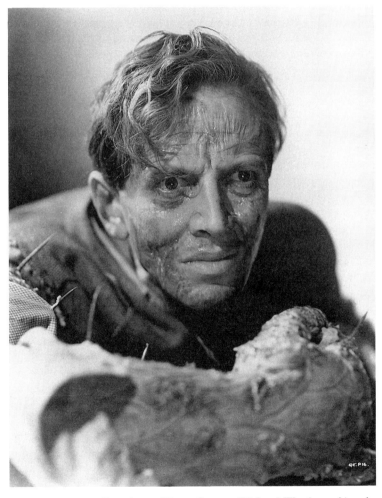

I *The Quatermass Experiment*: Victor Caroon (Richard Wordsworth) – the decaying hero

But what is the exact nature of this 'reality'? And how does it cope (or fail to cope) with the returning hero as he appears in this film? One can compare *The Quatermass Experiment* with *Reach for the Sky* (most successful British film of 1956), which also featured a pilot crashing to earth, in this case suffering the loss of both of his legs. This war film concerns itself with the attempts of the central character to negotiate between air (a war situation) and ground (peace-time society), and shows him coming to terms with the loss of 'masculinity' (his injury functioning in this respect as a symbolic castration) that being on the ground involves. *The Quatermass Experiment* is more disturbing than this. One can note here the iconography of the sexual pervert that gathers around the Victor Caroon character – his shabby raincoat, scruffy appearance and shambling walk, the inarticulate animal-like sounds that he makes, his physical decay, his preference for areas of wasteland, and so on. The famous publicity still for the film which shows Caroon holding out his deformed and decaying right hand, when seen in this light, could quite easily function as an advertisement warning against the dangers of self-abuse. All the repressive force that works to maintain the purity and virginity of the war hero has collapsed and, like Dorian Gray, he has now become a physically corrupted figure.

Immediately after the crash, Caroon is directed into the arms of his wife. She tries valiantly to reestablish a conventional marital relationship, rescuing him at one point from the significantly named Central Clinic (not even the Welfare State can hold Caroon). But upon seeing her husband's deformed hand – its position in his lap just before the moment of revelation underlining its function as a symbol of monstrous sexuality – she promptly, and somewhat improbably in terms of psychologically realistic motivation, collapses into insanity. Later a child offers Caroon a doll and, in one of the film's more disturbing moments, he knocks it aside, decapitating it in the process. In so doing, he alienates himself both from wife and child and from the possible family unit they might represent, with this alienation associated with a sexual force that cannot be contained by the family as it is portrayed in the film.

The challenge presented by Caroon to this world is further defined in a scene where he stumbles into a chemist's shop. As the chemist tries to help the pain-racked astronaut who is in the process of being transformed into an alien being one can clearly see on the right-hand side of the frame a sign which reads 'Get your National Health prescription here.' The pathetically inadequate attempts of the chemist, and by extension the National Health Service, to deal with this patient and his peculiarly sexualised 'problem' underline the fact that the nurturing state and its attendant ideologies posit and depend for their effectiveness on an altogether more compliant, conformist and socialised model of male behaviour.

In line with this, there is a general sense in *The Quatermass Experiment* that the national landscape through which Victor Caroon moves and within which he is alien is an enervating one, with its 'normal' inhabitants constantly seen as somehow anaesthetised and pliable, unaware of what is happening around them. At the beginning of the film, a crowd stands idly by at a moment of crisis: 'What do they think this is – a bank holiday?' remarks a policeman. Later in the narrative there is an apparent and curious lapse in continuity. The morning of Caroon's encounter with the little girl is signalled as being a Sunday – through the sound of church bells, the deserted docks upon which the camera lingers, the carefully constructed sense of pervading peace. And yet the day before this event has itself already been identified by a sign on the door of the chemist as a Sunday as well. Two Sundays, one directly after the other: thus is created a sense of the nation 'at rest', pacific, not to be disturbed.

As an elaboration of this, when a TV outside broadcast team stumble across a fully transformed Caroon in Westminster Abbey at the conclusion of the film the TV director's frantic shouts of 'Cut transmission' ensure that no potentially disturbing images find their way into what is implicitly the location for this peace and passivity, namely the home. It can be argued at this point that Caroon's method of killing his victims – draining away their lifeforce – is merely an extension of what is happening to them already in this increasingly conformist and domesticated world. *The Quatermass Experiment* focuses exclusively and intensively on the fate of a particular model of masculinity within such a world. In *Reach for the Sky* the clean-cut hero adapts to the demands of his new life at the cost of his legs. Victor Caroon, who returns intact, can never be assimilated into this particular concept of nation and so must be destroyed.[40]

It would make for a satisfying symmetry if one could read *X – The Unknown* as the 'female' equivalent of *The Quatermass Experiment*. Certainly a film which begins with a vaginal crack opening up in the earth and a nameless object emerging from that crack, heading directly towards a phallic tower and burning to death a boy called Willy, is operating, no matter how unconsciously, in the area of sexuality and sexual difference. Unfortunately, *X – The Unknown* never fully realises the fascinating possibilities suggested by this opening. Throughout the remainder of the film the monster tends to be identified in terms of irredeemable Otherness, with the potential relationship of complicity that it might bear to the world which it disrupts remaining undeveloped. The surprise expressed by the chief scientist at the monster's demise could be seen in this light as standing in for the filmmakers' lack of confidence in their own entirely arbitrary conclusion.

One of the important differences between *X – The Unknown* and *The Quatermass Experiment* lies in the decisive figure of Professor Bernard Quatermass. In the original BBC TV production he is a caring middle-class scientist who at the narrative's conclusion appeals to the remnants of humanity within the monster, thereby causing its death. In Hammer's version he is played as a brusque, bullying authority figure by Brian Donlevy, an American actor whose accent (for British audiences at least) renders him more cosmopolitan and 'classless'. At the film's climax, unlike his humanitarian TV predecessor, he causes the monster to be blasted out of existence. It is in the exercise of this irrefutable male authority that Hammer proposes a solution to the problem of masculinity it is at the same time working to identify and formulate. In this case the solution fails and Caroon dies. But subsequently these structuring elements will be taken up and developed in a more affirmative and commercially successful fashion in colour gothic horror.

The third film in this unofficial 'trilogy' – *Quatermass II* – is undoubtedly the most coherent and finely executed of the three. Its narrative – an alien invasion effectively conceals itself behind British bureaucracy – enables a further representation of the nation as asleep, here run by an apparently benign authority that can no longer be trusted.[41] The fact that the film is produced at about the same time as the inception of the colour horrors is significant insofar as concerns around the representation of masculinity central to *The Quatermass Experiment* are at this point being siphoned off into and remodelled by the gothic horror form. *Quatermass II* does not deal with the same issues as *The Quatermass Experiment*: it provides a more political and class-orientated account of 1950s Britain than does its predecessor. In this respect, the representation of industrial workers rising up to fight their alien bosses at the end of the film is an extraordinary event which almost certainly would have met with censorship problems if located within a more realistic narrative. *Quatermass II* also records the weakening of old class ties as workers are shifted to new housing estates, their distrust of strangers (which in the film inadvertently aids the invaders) symptomatic of their growing insularity.

While *Quatermass II* is the most formally perfect of the three films, it does seem, however, that *The Quatermass Experiment*, with its comparatively fragmented narrative structure, its ellipses and confusions, is perhaps more interesting and important as far as the development of British horror is concerned. It is in the decisive representational work done by *The Quatermass Experiment*, the partial rift in British cinema that it creates, that the aesthetic and ideological possibilities of the extensive horror production to follow are first suggested. The concern with questions of male identity becomes an important part of the subsequent Hammer horror films. The no-nonsense attitudes of Quatermass himself, as well as the entirely physical nature of the monster, are also carried over (especially in the Frankenstein cycle). Perhaps most significantly, the exploitation of a particular market signalled by the fact of the film being sold initially as *The Quatermass Xperiment* (the spelling of Xperiment referring of course to the 'X' certificate, a marketing tactic repeated with *X – The Unknown*) suggests that Hammer had finally found its place in British cinema. Clearly *The Quatermass Experiment*, rather than being another dead end like *Dead of Night*, opens the door to one of the most important interventions into British cinema since the war.

This does not mean that the colour horror films followed on naturally and unproblematically from this. On the contrary, a great deal of work – economic and aesthetic – had yet to be done. In Hammer's film Quatermass's experiment fails. As he is leaving the scene of the disaster, someone asks him what he is going to do next. 'Start again,' he replies as he walks into the distance and an unknown future. Another experiment, another attempt to deal with the 'problem' of male identity, is proposed. What lay ahead, both for Hammer and the horror genre in general, is the subject of the next chapter.

Notes

1 Synopsis taken from Denis Gifford, *The British Film Catalogue: 1895–1970*, Newton Abbot, 1973.

2 See Jeffrey Richards, *The Age of the Dream Palace: Cinema and Society in Britain 1930–1939*, London, 1984; for a slightly different perspective, see Tony Aldgate, 'Comedy, Class and Containment: the British Domestic Cinema of the 1930s' in James Curran and Vincent Porter (eds), *British Cinema History*, London, 1983, pp. 257–71.

3 Quoted in Guy Phelps, *Film Censorship*, London, 1975, p. 36.

4 For a discussion of some of these films, see Robert Murphy, 'Riff Raff: British Cinema and the Underworld' in Charles Barr (ed.), *All Our Yesterdays: 90 Years of British Cinema*, London, 1986, pp. 286–305.

5 Graham Greene, *The Pleasure-Dome: the Collected Film Criticism*, London, 1972, p. 245.

6 On the banning of 'H' films, see Phelps, p. 163; on *A Canterbury Tale*, see Jeffrey Richards and Anthony Aldgate, *The Best of British: Cinema and Society 1930–1970*, Oxford, 1983, pp. 43–59, and Ian Christie, *Arrows of Desire: the Films of Michael Powell and Emeric Pressburger*, London, 1985, pp. 67–71.

7 On 'The Haunted Mirror' see Charles Barr, *Ealing Studios*, Newton Abbot, 1977, pp. 55–8; and David Pirie, *A Heritage of Horror: the English Gothic Cinema 1946–1972*, London, 1973, pp. 23–5.

8 In a later chapter I will discuss later multiple-narrative films, mainly those associated with the Amicus company in the 1960s; films such as *Dr Terror's House of Horrors* and *Torture Garden*. Suffice it here to indicate that the motivation there for such structures is very different from that found in *Dead of Night*.

9 Mark Nash, '*Vampyr* and the Fantastic', *Screen*, 17, no. 3, autumn 1976, pp 29–67.

10 Andrew Higson, 'Five Films' in Geoff Hurd (ed.), *National Fictions: World War Two in British Films and Television*, London, 1984, p. 25. The films he discusses include *Millions Like Us*, *The Gentle Sex* and *The Bells Go Down*. To these can be added *San Demetrio London*, *The Way to the Stars*, *The Way Ahead* and *In Which We Serve*.

11 The Gainsborough melodramas were *The Man in Grey* (1943), *Fanny by Gaslight* (1944), *Madonna of the Seven Moons* (1944), *The Wicked Lady* (1945), *Caravan* (1946) and *Jassy* (1947). For a discussion of the representation of sexuality in these films, see Sue Harper, 'Historical Pleasures: Gainsborough Costume Melodrama', in Christine Gledhill (ed.), *Home Is Where the Heart Is: Studies in Melodrama and the Woman's Film*, London, 1987, pp. 167–96; and Sue Aspinall, 'Sexuality in Costume Melodrama' in Aspinall and Robert Murphy (ed.), *Gainsborough Melodrama*, London, 1983, pp. 29–39.

12 See Elizabeth Wilson, *Women and the Welfare State*, London, 1977, pp. 59–62. For a slightly different perspective on this, see Jeffrey Weeks, *Sex, Politics and Society: the Regulation of Sexuality since 1800*, London, 1981, pp. 232–3.

13 Charles Barr, 'Amnesia and Schizophrenia' in Barr (ed.), *All Our Yesterdays*, p. 16.

14 For a discussion of this, see Carol J. Clover, 'Her Body, Himself: Gender in the Slasher Film', *Representations*, 20, autumn 1987, pp. 187–228, and Linda Williams, 'When the Woman Looks' in Mary Ann Doane et al. (ed.) *Re-vision: Essays in Feminist Film Criticism*, Frederick MD, 1984, pp. 83–99.

15 John Berger, *Ways of Seeing*, Harmondsworth, 1972: 'The mirror was often used as a symbol of the vanity of woman. The moralizing, however, was mostly hypocritical . . . The real function of the mirror was otherwise. It was to make the woman connive in treating herself as, first and foremost, a sight.' (p. 51)

16 Christian Metz, *Psychoanalysis and Cinema: the Imaginary Signifier*, London, 1982, p. 73.

17 Barr, 'Amnesia and Schizophrenia', p. 18.

18 For discussions of *Frieda* see Barr, *Ealing Studios*, pp. 74–6 and Terry Lovell, 'Frieda' in Hurd (ed.), *National Fictions*, pp. 30–4.

19 John Hill, *Sex, Class and Realism: British Cinema 1956–1963*, London, 1986, p. 35.

20 Stuart Laing, *Representations of Working-Class Life 1957–1964*, London, 1986, p. 110.

21 John Spraos, *The Decline of the Cinema*, London, 1962.

22 See Phelps, *Film Censorship*, pp. 52–5; and Tino Balio, 'Retrenchment, Reappraisal, and Reorganization: 1948 – ', in Balio (ed.), *The American Film Industry*, Madison, 1976, pp. 315–31.

23 Phelps, *Film Censorship*, p. 40.

24 Ibid., p. 115 for a table that shows the rising number of 'X' films in the late 1950s and early 1960s.

25 See John Sutherland, *Offensive Literature: Decensorship in Britain 1960–1982*, London, 1982.

26 John Hill has argued that the British New Wave established itself within the confluence of the major circuits' changing business practices and a relaxation of censorship: Hill, *Sex, Class and Realism*, pp. 35–52. It can further be argued here – and Hill suggests it in passing – that British horror, rather than wholly arising in a deconstructive fashion from a set of realist discourses, represents a different form of exploitation operating within the same market conditions.

27 Mentioned in a *Daily Cinema* tribute to Anthony Hinds (available in the BFI Library's file on Hammer).

28 For details, see Pirie, *A Heritage of Horror*, p. 38.

29 See Margaret Dickinson and Sarah Street, *Cinema and State: the Film Industry and the British Government 1927–84*, London, 1985.

30 Pirie, *A Heritage of Horror*, p. 31.

31 See Peter Biskind, *Seeing is Believing*, London, 1983, pp. 101–59, which locates these American SF/horror films in their national context.

32 A similar situation was evoked in John Wyndham's enormously popular trilogy of SF invasion novels from the 1950s – *Day of the Triffids* (1951), *The Kraken Wakes* (1953) and *The Midwich Cuckoos* (1957), all published by Michael Joseph – which also depicted Britain as the virtually helpless victim of monsters and aliens, the origins of which remain shrouded in mystery. See Christopher Priest, 'British Science Fiction', in Patrick Parrinder (ed.), *Science Fiction: a Critical Guide*, London, 1979, pp. 187–202, for a discussion of Wyndham in the context of SF literature of the period.

   Also relevant here is Val Guest's film *The Day the Earth Caught Fire* – made in 1961 but planned earlier – in which the existence of the earth is threatened by superpower nuclear tests. The journalist–hero can do nothing except report the planet's rapid decline. Britain is again seen as powerless.

33 Pirie, *A Heritage of Horror*, p. 29.

34 Barr, 'Amnesia and Schizophrenia', p. 25.

35 Information from Gifford, *The British Film Catalogue*.

36 Wilson, *Women and the Welfare State*, pp. 59–68; Weeks, *Sex, Politics and Society*, pp. 232–9.

37 Weeks cites a relevant example from a 1953 publication entitled *Social Casework in Marital Problems*: 'It provided a catalogue of success stories achieved through therapeutic casework, with women "making astonishing moves towards femininity", learning to become competent mothers, and men overcoming homosexuality, achieving new status in work, and doubling their earning capacities.' Ibid. p. 236.

38 Weeks, ibid., p. 237.

39 See Christine Geraghty, 'Masculinity' in Hurd (ed.), *National Fictions*, pp. 63–7 for a helpful discussion of some of these points.

40 *The Quatermass Experiment* bears obvious comparison with Don Siegel's 1956 American production *Invasion of the Bodysnatchers* insofar as both stress the dehumanising powers of social normality. However, the fact that they are operating in different national contexts results in each identifying and adopting a position in relation to this normality in a substantially different way: for a discussion of the politics of Siegel's film, see Peter Biskind, *Seeing is Believing*, pp. 137–44 and Stuart Kaminsky, 'Invasion of the Bodysnatchers', *Cinefantastique*, 2, no. 3, winter 1973, pp. 16–19.

Another interesting comparison that can be made here is with the British film *Seven Days to Noon* (1950, d. John Boulting), in which a scientist threatens to destroy London with a nuclear bomb. As with *The Quatermass Experiment*, one is given images of a military mobilisation, as a rogue male capable of causing the absolute destruction of a post-war world is tracked down and destroyed. While in each case, the threat is ostensibly a scientific one – a nuclear bomb, a monster about to reproduce – in both films it can in fact be seen to involve shifts in gender definition attendant upon the formation of the Welfare State. However, it can further be argued that *The Quatermass Experiment*, perhaps because of its status as a horror film, provides a more intense and disturbing exploration of this situation. (A further link between the two films is that James Bernard, who wrote the music for *The Quatermass Experiment* and many other Hammer films, was involved in the screenplay for *Seven Days to Noon*, as indeed was Paul Dehn who, as we have seen in the previous chapter, was a critical champion of the Hammer horror film.)

41 Pirie, *A Heritage of Horror*, pp. 35–8.

1956–64: Hammer and other horrors

3

To a certain extent 1956–64 can be seen as the classic phase in British horror production, years during which a particular national horror movement emerged. The most famous (or infamous), influential and commercially successful sector of British horror at this time was that produced by the Hammer company, and this chapter will be devoted in the main to a discussion of Hammer horror.

It is worth noting in this respect that the 1956–64 period is 'book-ended' by two important Hammer films, *The Curse of Frankenstein* (Hammer's first colour horror, produced in 1956 and released in 1957) and *The Gorgon* (1964): these were, respectively, the first and last of the five Hammer films on which horror stars Peter Cushing and Christopher Lee and principal Hammer director Terence Fisher collaborated.[1] This fact alone marks the 1956–64 period as a distinctive stage in Hammer's development. Importantly, *The Gorgon* also represents a key point in a wider shifting of terms within the genre that occurred in the mid 1960s away from a preoccupation with aspects of masculinity towards what will be shown in later chapters to be a broader exploration of gender roles. That *The Gorgon* was a commercial failure, as well as the way in which, despite the participation of Cushing, Lee and Fisher, it has not until now attracted much critical attention, even from horror aficionados, might be seen as arising precisely from the absence within it of some of those qualities which had characterised previous Hammer horror films.

Any discussion of British horror production in this period should not lose sight of the fact that while Hammer was certainly dominant, approximately two-thirds of horror did not fall under Hammer's auspices.[2] The latter part of this chapter will show that while these films were often working with the same issues as those addressed by Hammer, on the whole (and with a few distinguished exceptions) they lack the richness and energy of Hammer's more successful approach.

Of course the years 1956 and 1964 have a much wider significance to them, representing as they do important moments in British social history. It has already been argued that the relation between this history and British horror production needs to be seen as somewhat more mediated and indirect than the notion of the latter simply reflecting the former might suggest. However, it is useful at this stage to have an awareness of some of the events and trends associated with 1956 and 1964. The historical sketch that follows is intended in this light merely to introduce some of the social issues and concerns that will subsequently be discussed in terms of the way in which they impact upon and illuminate our understanding of specific horror films.

Robert Hewison has written of 1956 as 'the first event of history after the Second World War about which there is anything like a persistent myth, and like the myths of wartime, it is a combination of historical truths and popular distortion'.[3] It was a year comprising a tightly overlapping number of momentous events and more insidious changes which were seen by many as forming a composite, multifaceted threat to a traditional British way of life. The incursion of 'Americanised' mass culture that threatened established standards of good taste, a further and substantial growth in consumerism (with independent television – which began transmission in 1955 – a key factor in this) that obscured class boundaries, an apparent weakening of the family unit that was associated with a younger generation who seemed to some to have become rebellious and disrespectful, and the ongoing dissolution of the Empire and along with it Britain's international influence as symbolised in this year by Suez; all, compressed together as they were, gave the overwhelming impression of an unstoppable wave of change.[4]

Several commentators have noted how this move from being a world power to being a somewhat less powerful, consumerist society was represented culturally via shifting notions of gender. For example, John Hill has read Suez as 'a symbolic castration – the final humiliation of a nation no longer in possession of its manhood'.[5] He has further argued that the 'kitchen sink' films of the British New Wave often identified the woman as a symbol of undesirable social change, this inasmuch as she had been constructed – by advertising and other discourses supportive of a consumerist ideology – as the figure of 'the housewife', both a symbol and the manager of an increased domestic consumption which was seen as threatening to an older system of (implicitly male) social organisation.[6] D. E. Cooper's remarks on the Angry Young Man phenomenon indicate that this also applied to many of the shifts in theatre and literature that were taking place from the mid 1950s onwards: 'What these writers really attack is effeminacy . . . the sum of those qualities which are supposed traditionally . . . to exude from the worst in women: pettiness, snobbery, flippancy, voluptuousness, superficiality, materialism.'[7]

Such a situation had a certain irony about it insofar as it was at this time that increasing numbers of women, supposed embodiments of all for which the domestic household stood, were going out to work, earning the money required to sustain the consumption boom. Hill notes one of the implications of this: 'the increasing involvement of women in the labour force and occupation of traditionally male roles deprives the male worker of his privileged status as head of the family and sole breadwinner'.[8] In fact, this was only one aspect of the contradictory relation of women to a dominant ideology of consumption and needs to be linked with an increasing stress at this time on the importance of female sexuality (although this was nearly always discussed within a marriage context). As Stuart Hall puts it, 'It was difficult to reconcile all these roles (wife/mother/worker) within the dominant representational forms and discourses of a fully fledged ideology of domesticity and motherhood.'[9]

In 1964 the first Labour government for thirteen years came to power under the leadership of Harold Wilson. It had won the election on a platform of managerial efficiency, of breaking away from what had been perceived as an amateurish management of economic and social affairs. In so doing, a different set of social values was proposed, a new definition of national identity constructed.[10] In the immediately preceding years, leading up to this transformation, one finds intensive debate on the nature of 'British-ness' and a growing sense that there was something 'wrong' with Britain. (Noteworthy random examples of this process include the Profumo scandal and the apocalyptic 1963 edition of *Encounter* magazine entitled *Suicide of a Nation?*)

This admittedly schematic rendering of a small part of post-war British history at the very least provides a sense of some of the pressing issues upon which British horror would seize in its attempt to address a particular market. What needs to be done now is to consider how this activity manifested itself in specific films. The obvious starting point is the most successful British horror producer of all.

Hammer horror

Hammer made a variety of films in the 1956–64 period. Of these, twenty-four might be considered as horror films – including fourteen colour gothic horror films, three SF/horror (*X – The Unknown*, *Quatermass II* and *The Damned*), four psychological thrillers (*Taste of Fear*, *Maniac*, *Paranoiac*, *Hysteria*), in addition to films that crossed from one generic area to another (historical drama and horror in *The Stranglers of Bombay*, comedy and horror in *The Old Dark House*).[11] However, it was the company's colour gothic horrors which proved its most distinctive and successful product, and it is to these films we can now turn. They were, in order of release:

	Year of release	*Director*
The Curse of Frankenstein	1957	Terence Fisher
Dracula	1958	Fisher
The Revenge of Frankenstein	1958	Fisher
The Hound of the Baskervilles	1959	Fisher
The Mummy	1959	Fisher
The Man Who Could Cheat Death	1959	Fisher
The Curse of the Werewolf	1960	Fisher
The Brides of Dracula	1960	Fisher
The Two Faces of Dr Jekyll	1960	Fisher
The Phantom of the Opera	1962	Fisher
Kiss of the Vampire	1964	Don Sharp
The Evil of Frankenstein	1964	Freddie Francis
The Gorgon	1964	Fisher
The Curse of the Mummy's Tomb	1964	Michael Carreras

One of the most immediately striking qualities of these films, a quality which informs them on several levels, is a robust physicality, an insistence on the solid and corporeal nature of the conflict between the forces of good and evil. Random examples of this physicality include the doors and windows that are continually being smashed open in this period, the ferocious fight scenes in *Dracula* and *The Mummy* with the assailants quite literally at each other's throats, an athletic Van Helsing leaping off a table, pulling down some drapes and letting in the fatal sunshine at the conclusion of *Dracula*, a dead body tearing through stage scenery at the beginning of *Phantom of the Opera*.

Both the settings and the style of Hammer horror function to accommodate and highlight a sense of this physicality. The castles, pubs and drawing rooms which comprise Hammer's characteristic Victorian or Edwardian milieux provide a suitably ordered backdrop against which various acts of violence are rendered even more striking than they would be otherwise. (These sets are also often characterised by a sensual, luxuriant feel which in turn connects with another important aspect of Hammer horror, its fascination with sexual matters: a discussion of this follows below.) Similarly, the camera work in Hammer horror is on the whole fairly restrained. Extravagant camera movements are few and far between at this time

2 Peter Cushing and Christopher Lee in *The Mummy*: Hammer's characteristic physicality

(and indeed afterwards). While one possible reason for this might have been the limitations of space within Bray Studios, which was a converted country house, this method of filming also accorded perfectly with Hammer's overall stylistic identity.[12] Complementing it was an undeviatingly conventional form of editing.

It is in this carefully constructed sense of physicality, and the formal restraint that usually accompanied it, that Hammer horror distinguished itself from other types of horror. In other words, Hammer chose not to indulge in the disturbing self-reflexive games played in Ealing's *Dead of Night* and Michael Powell's *Peeping Tom*. It also contained little of the evocative use of darkness and shadow that characterised, say, the 1940s American work of B-movie producer Val Lewton or the Poe adaptations directed by Roger Corman in the early 1960s.

It has been on the basis of these very distinctive and easily recognisable qualities that Hammer's colour horror films, and the work of Terence Fisher in particular – and the two are nearly synonymous at this time – have in the past been described as pedestrian, over-literal and cinematically lifeless. What can be argued here is that this negative appraisal of these films rests on a misapprehension of the relationship between the various stylistic and thematic elements deployed within Hammer horror; and that these elements, rather than lying lifelessly alongside each other, are working together, mobilised within an aesthetic that has not as yet been fully appreciated critically (although several critics, most notably David Pirie, have begun to construct such an appreciation).

One further point needs to be made in our introductory comments about Hammer, and this is to note the substantial contributions of director Terence Fisher and actors Peter Cushing and Christopher Lee to the period horror films now under discussion. Out of these fourteen films, Cushing appeared in eight, Lee in seven and a remarkably prolific Fisher directed eleven. Of course, Hammer horror, like the vast majority of cinematic enterprises, was the product of a collaborative process, with significant input from, to name but a few, producer and screenwriter Anthony Hinds, writer Jimmy Sangster, art director Bernard Robinson, directors of photography Jack Asher and Michael Reed, and composer James Bernard. In this sense, Cushing, Lee and Fisher need to be seen as mere members, albeit important ones, of the Hammer team. Nevertheless, it is the case that the five films upon which all three worked, *The*

Curse of Frankenstein, *Dracula*, *The Hound of the Baskervilles*, *The Mummy* and *The Gorgon*, embody the Hammer aesthetic in its most accomplished form. These five films can be seen as centres of gravity within Hammer horror, in the same way that Hammer horror itself provides a basic definitional model of British horror cinema in general. Consequently, much of what follows will be centred on these films, although the other nine will also be considered in some detail. (The Frankenstein and Dracula films will be dealt with at greater length in the next chapter.)

In our account in the previous chapter of *The Quatermass Experiment*, Professor Quatermass was identified as an early version of a character-type that would become very important in subsequent Hammer productions – the male professional authority figure. As a way of entering into and starting to think about Hammer horror as a distinctive aesthetic practice, we can now elaborate further on the role played by notions of professionalism in Hammer and how these related to and drew upon a wider social reality.

The professional

The figure of the professional is of key importance in Hammer horror throughout this period. Its Van Helsing is, arguably, horror cinema's first professional vampire hunter. Previously – in, say, the 1931 Universal version of *Dracula* (or to a certain extent in Bram Stoker's original novel) – this character was inclined to lengthy pseudo-scientific or quasi-religious speeches, the physical business of actually killing the vampire relegated to the sidelines. In Hammer, Van Helsing's statements concerning the vampire tend to be matter-of-fact instructions on how to destroy it. Hence his dictation into the phonograph in *Dracula* where the 'facts' about vampires are stated baldly and without fuss. When in this sequence he refers to the crucifix as 'symbolising the power of good over evil', neither he nor the film is underlining the religious or spiritual element of this. Instead the cross, garlic, running water and so on are given us as tools of the trade, so to speak, practical weapons against an all too physical threat.[13] The figure of Sherlock Holmes, the arch-professional of British detective fiction, in *The Hound of the Baskervilles* is another example, as, for that matter, is Hammer's Frankenstein, especially in his no-nonsense attitude to his business as opposed to the narrow-minded moralising of those around him.

One possible reason for the importance of professionalism to

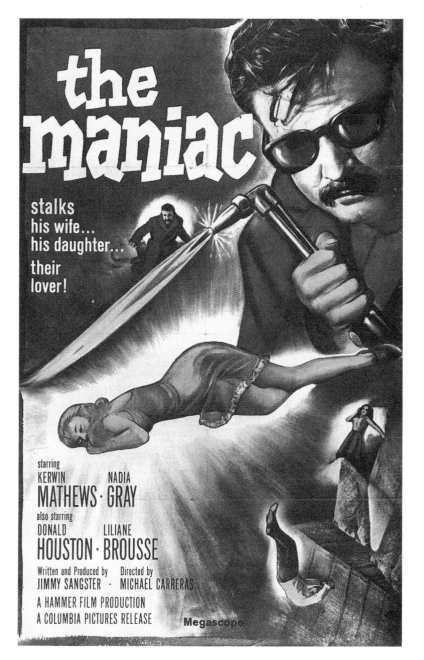

Director: Michael Carreras (US poster, 1963)

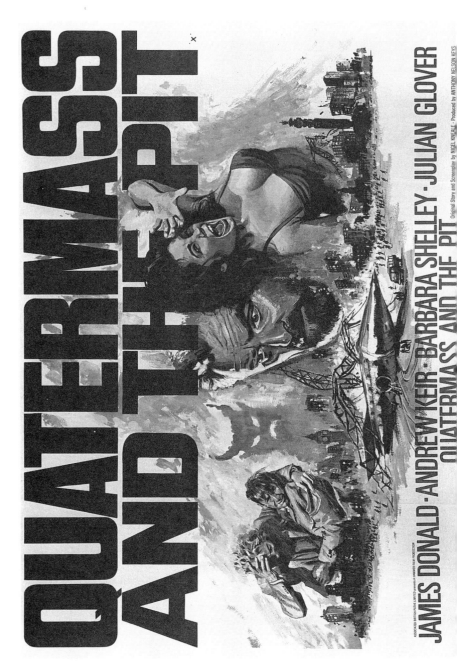

Director: Roy Ward Baker (British poster, 1967)

Hammer is revealed through a brief survey of its key creative personnel. What one finds is that, as far as the routes by which they had all entered the film industry are concerned, the filmmakers in question can be readily divided into two groups.

Firstly, family connections had brought producers Michael Carreras and Anthony Hinds into the Hammer company: the former was the son of chief executive James Carreras, the latter the son of William Hinds, cofounder with Enrique Carreras (James's father) of Exclusive Films, the distribution company from which Hammer had evolved. (William Hinds was also a music-hall performer whose stage name of Will Hammer gave the new production company its name.) Neither restricted themselves solely to the producer role: Carreras also wrote and directed while Hinds was a prolific screenwriter under the pseudonym of John Elder.[14]

Secondly, most of the directors who worked for Hammer, both during this period and after, had begun in menial posts in the industry and had usually worked their way up to the position of director by their mid forties. For example, Terence Fisher, Hammer's most prolific director (born in 1904, first film for Hammer *The Last Page* in 1952) and Freddie Francis (born in 1917, first film for Hammer *Paranoiac* in 1963) had both begun as clapper boys in the 1930s, with Fisher subsequently becoming an editor and Francis an award-winning cameraman. Similarly, John Gilling (born in 1912, first film for Hammer as screenwriter *The Man in Black* in 1950, as director *Shadow of the Cat* in 1961), and a later Hammer director Roy Ward Baker (born in 1912, first film for Hammer *Quatermass and the Pit* in 1967) had started out as, respectively, third and second assistant directors. Another key figure, Bernard Robinson, the art director for many important Hammer horror films, had also begun in the 1930s, this time as a draughtsman, joining Hammer in 1956 to work on *Quatermass II*. The one major exception to what was essentially a graduation to important posts after years of experience appears to have been screenwriter Jimmy Sangster (who in the 1970s would also direct and produce for Hammer). Here too, however, a similar career progression is evident, with Sangster joining Hammer as third assistant director in 1947, becoming production manager, and then writing the screenplay for *X – The Unknown* in 1956, although in Sangster's case this process was somewhat accelerated.

Two things are apparent from this. First, many of these people were working or had worked for Hammer before the inception of the colour horror films. Thus, not only was there a continuity of space and technical resources at Bray Studios (discussed in the previous chapter) but also a continuity in terms of creative personnel to facilitate what was by any standards a rapid move into horror production. Second, none of these individuals had entered the industry specifically to make horror films (unlike later directors such as Michael Reeves – see chapter 5), or for that matter any particular type of film. They owed their allegiance instead either to the family firm or to the film industry's standards of professional integrity and competence. It is in this context that the epithet 'journeyman', often applied pejoratively or condescendingly to Hammer filmmakers, takes on a different, non-evaluative meaning, describing a particular relationship between filmmaker and genre which stresses the former not as 'artist', someone whose work is imbued with originality and embraces serious themes, but instead as 'professional'.[15] Hence the lack of artistic pretensions which further aided Hammer's trans-formation into the 'horror factory': as James Carreras himself put it, 'I'm prepared to make Strauss waltzes tomorrow if they'll make money.'[16]

The designations of artist and professional are often located in a hierarchical structure, with 'art' at its pinnacle. What needs to be realised here is that these terms not only function within critical discourses but also operate within the film industry itself, and that Hammer's positive valuation of professionalism, in films, publicity and interviews, provided for it and its personnel a potent model of self-definition and worth. This in turn impinged upon the films themselves, all of which tend to endorse a no-nonsense approach to various manifestations of evil. (Of course, this did not mean that Hammer filmmakers possessed in any way a monopoly on profes-sionalism or that no other directors had ever worked their way up through the industry; however, the journeymen at Hammer can be contrasted with the 'artists' working concurrently in the British New Wave.)

It is also significant that in the years of Hammer's unquestioned dominance of British horror between 1956 and 1964 the designation 'professionalism' had a much wider social purchase, figuring as it did in debates about the nature of Britishness and British national identity. One can argue that in fact it was the resulting connection or correspondence between the inner workings of Hammer and the society within which it was located that bestowed upon Hammer's films a social relevance and potency which, in part at least, contributed to their success at the box-office. A sense of what this debate about national identity actually entailed can be gleaned from remarks made by Michael Frayn on the state of the country at the time of the Festival of Britain in 1951: 'for a decade, sanctioned by the exigencies of war and its aftermath, the Herbivores had dominated the scene. By 1951 the regime which supported them was exhausted, and the Carnivores were ready to take over'.[17]

For Frayn, the Herbivores were:

> the radical middle classes – the do-gooders; the readers of the *News Chronicle*, the *Guardian* and the *Observer*; the signers of petitions; the backbone of the BBC . . . gentle ruminants . . . who look out from the lush pastures which are their natural station in life with eyes full of sorrow for less fortunate creatures, guiltily conscious of their advantages, though not usually ceasing to eat the grass.

The Carnivores, on the other hand, were 'the members of the upper and middle classes who believe that if God had not wished them to prey on all smaller and weaker creatures without scruple he would not have made them as they are'. Frayn goes on to associate the Herbivores and their influence with what for him was by 1951 'the sad remnants of the once triumphant post-war Labour government', soon to be replaced by a Carnivore–Conservative administration.

As far as British cinema of this period was concerned, Herbivore values can be seen to have found their home in the Ealing comedies of the late 1940s and 1950s, which, as Charles Barr has noted, frequently dramatise a tension between what might be termed the herbivorous beliefs and attitudes of small businessmen and the carnivorous nature of big business, with the former invariably winning the day and seeing off the ruthless Carnivore–capitalists.[18] In Hammer, perhaps appropriately for a company whose most consistently successful product was its vampire films, this situation is neatly reversed, and now it is the authoritative upper- or middle-class male (usually middle-class), the Carnivore if you will, who is triumphant. The Herbivores, the decent but fatally narrow-minded and weak inhabitants of the Hammer world are either won over to the side of the no-nonsense authority figure or violently destroyed. If Ealing, under the benign dictatorship of Michael Balcon and harboured safely within the Rank Organisation, can be read as the archetypal Herbivore of post-war British cinema, then Hammer, independent of any major studio and hungry for finance and profit under the showmanlike guidance of James Carreras, can just as equally be read as the archetypal Carnivore.

However, the advent of Hammer horror some six years into a Conservative administration in no way involved an unequivocal endorsement by the films of all the values associated with that administration. Certainly there are distinctively conservative elements present in Hammer horror, particularly the stress laid throughout on the need for authoritative leadership. But at the same time, Hammer horror's impatience with any manifestation of what it saw as amateurism and the accompanying valorisation of professional activity immediately align it with further, contemporaneous shifts in the debate about national identity as it was developing through the latter part of the 1950s and into the 1960s.

To gain an insight into how the agenda for this debate about the nature of Britishness had changed since the early 1950s and the situation outlined by Frayn, we can look at an article written in 1963 by Henry Fairlie entitled 'On the Comforts of Anger'. In this he argues against the need for technological progress in industry: 'It is time that, against their evil doctrine, we reasserted our right to be inefficient.'[19] At one point he goes so far as to link the 'evil doctrine' of professional management with Nazism and deathcamps, and signals it as something completely alien to a British tradition. However, within the very book, *Suicide of a Nation?* (a special issue of *Encounter* magazine), that his remarks occurred, he was virtually a lone voice – one might even argue, a Herbivore voice – amongst many who, like Arthur Koestler, the book's editor, believed that 'The cult of amateurishness, and the contempt in which proficiency and expertise are held, breed mediocrats by natural selection.'[20]

Suicide of a Nation?, with its apocalyptic predictions of disaster unless 'amateurishness' was removed from British life, was published in the same year that saw Harold Wilson's keynote speech at the Labour Party conference on the potentially vast benefits of a new technology. As Stuart Hall has observed 'The whole aim of the Wilson propaganda leading up to the 1964 election was to put together an alternative, and more stable, historical bloc behind the slogans of "modernisation" and controlled and orderly "growth".'[21] Wilson won the election, a victory which was seen by many at the time as a managerial and professional takeover (albeit a shortlived one; in 1969 Dr David Granick, an American management expert, would call Britain 'the home of the amateur').[22]

It does seem from this that Hammer's privileging of the professional at this moment in social history enabled it, in an almost prescient fashion, to tap into a widespread feeling that British society was in transition. In this way Hammer offered itself to its audience as a particularly 'modern' intervention into British culture (in opposition to the traditional virtues extolled by many Ealing films from the 1950s). It is possible that the outrage of a handful of film critics over Hammer horror arose in part as a reaction against the relatively new ideas of British national identity proposed by the films. Certainly, one of their most disturbing qualities for these critics appears to have been their Britishness.

But a paradox still remains. While Hammer horror films need to be seen very much as addressing the social context within which they were fashioned, account also has to be taken of the fact that, despite their 'modernity', they were set in the past. Clearly the films' engagement with present-day matters was, at the very least, veiled or coded.

In a perceptive short piece on Hammer horror, David Robinson considers the reasons for the colour horror films being more successful than Hammer's black and white psychological thrillers. He argues that because the former are set apart from the present, they actually require less of a suspension of disbelief from an audience than do the thrillers with contemporary settings. The period setting, and the historical space thereby opened up between film and audience, enables a more fantastic, stylised acting out of events, unencumbered as it is with the suggestions of realism carried by modern locations.[23] This displacement ensured that Hammer was never as disturbing to audiences, most critics and the censors, as were more realistic horrors. It might also be the case, as I have already suggested, that the period settings permitted a conservative nostalgia for a fixed social order, one in which those who were powerless were legitimate prey.

Robinson's remarks underline the need to think about Hammer as, on the most basic of levels, an imaginative enterprise, one that is by its very nature distanced from the real world. While it might draw upon socially specific discourses associated with professionalism, while it might contain conservative elements, it is by no means reducible to any of these. In order to develop further an awareness of the way in which Hammer mobilises these various elements and the tensions that arise from them, to grasp in effect the aesthetic life of Hammer horror, it is worth considering how the figure of the professional is actually used within the films in question. How is his authority established and to what ends are his efforts directed?

Authority and masculinity

Valorised authority in Hammer horror of this period is always the property of the professional, the man (and it is always a man) who knows exactly what he is doing and why. It can be found in the attitudes and capabilities of, amongst others, Van Helsing and Holmes.[24] It is also apparent in a type of acting exemplified by Cushing and Lee, an economic and above all controlled performance style (which might profitably be compared with the flamboyance and nascent camp of Vincent Price's performances in Corman's Poe films).

In part, the authority of Hammer's two principal stars derives from their relative seniority. At the time of *The Curse of Frankenstein*, Cushing was forty-three, Lee was thirty-four (and Fisher fifty-two years old). Horror films are usually marketed to a younger audience, and Hammer was no exception to this.[25] Yet in these films (and this is a characteristic shared with other types of horror – Corman's Poe films, for instance) those members of the cast who most closely approximate the peer group of the film's intended audience tend to be the most ineffectual in terms of the power and authority that they wield. Clearly, they are not being held up as ideal figures for audience identification purposes. Neither, it can be argued, are Cushing, Lee or the characters they play. Rather, if one is to take audience identification into account, such identification must be with the power wielded by these authoritative characters. An appreciation of the certainty and unwavering capabilities expressed on every level of these films is an important, indeed necessary, element in an enjoyment of them.

Authority in Hammer horror also has a clear class dimension. Hammer's class structures are inflexible, with working, middle and upper classes remaining totally separate social strata. Despite the plethora of aristocratic titles in these films (Count, Lord, Baron, etc.) the figures of valorised authority (that is, Cushing or Lee) tend to be middle-class, if not in their actual social position then certainly in the values they espouse. The professionalism which, as we have seen, is an important aspect of their authority is dependent on their either having a profession in the conventional sense (the professor in *The Gorgon*, consulting detective in *The Hound of the Baskervilles*, archaeologist in *The Mummy*) or organising their obsessions in an ordered, methodical and altogether professional manner (Frankenstein and Van Helsing). The few members of the upper class – with the notable exception of the 'middle-class' Baron (who, as will be shown, is middle-class only in a limited way) – that do appear are invariably characterised, as they must be in a world which values a certain type of work ethic above all else, as parasitic and corrupt (Sir Hugo in *The Hound of the Baskervilles*, Lord D'Arcy in *The Phantom of the Opera*) or simply weak (Lee's Sir Henry in *The Hound of the Baskervilles*).[26] Further underlining the middle-class bias of these films, a bias which presumably arises from the fact that professionalism is itself a middle-class designation, one finds that on the few occasions the working class is seen in the form of a crowd (it usually appears only as comic relief or victims), it is always shown as ignorant and a force of repression. A useful comparison that can be made here is with the democratic torch-carrying crowds that are found in Universal horror films of the 1930s.

After age and class, the final significant dimension of the authority of Hammer's professional resides in his maleness. Authority is inalienably patriarchal in Hammer horror of this period; it also tends to be associated with celibacy. (Think, for example, of Van Helsing and Sherlock Holmes.) Male sexual desire is itself nearly always seen as either weakening or evil. In line with this, female characters have little or no autonomy in these films but are usually defined as an essentially sexual threat for male characters. Significantly, many of the Hammer leading ladies at this time are non-British – for example, Marla Landi in *The Hound of the Baskervilles* and Yvonne Furneaux in *The Mummy* – as if sexuality is in some way not a characteristic of the British woman and has to be imported. As will be shown later, the placing of the very British Barbara Shelley at the centre of *The Gorgon* signals a particularly intense crisis for Hammer horror.

While these are the attributes of the Hammer professional, our subsequent analyses of specific films will demonstrate that this professional is by no means the isolated, almost abstract figure that our earlier remarks might have implied. All of Hammer's authority figures exist and to a certain extent are defined in relation to particular dramatic and narrative contexts, with this in turn having distinct consequences for the ways in which professional authority is exercised. In this period, the unassailable confidence of Baron Frankenstein, Van Helsing and Sherlock Holmes (more on the first two of these in the next chapter) sits alongside slightly more troubled representations of professional activity. When viewed in this way, as a group of films which seek to reproduce in a compelling and credible fashion a particular set of values, rather than merely presenting them to us ready-formed, both the dynamism of Hammer's aesthetic and a sense of these professional values as themselves unstable, requiring constant reworking, become more apparent.

At this point, it is revealing to look briefly at some of the films that fall outside the relatively small Fisher–Cushing–Lee canon while still remaining a recognisable part of Hammer horror, namely *The Curse of the Werewolf*, *The Man Who Could Cheat Death*, *The Phantom of the Opera* and *The Two Faces of Dr Jekyll*. All four were directed by Terence Fisher, but Peter Cushing is absent from all of them and Christopher Lee appears only in supporting roles in *The Man Who Could Cheat Death* and *The Two Faces of Dr Jekyll*. All four were disappointing commercially. One possible reason for this lies in the way in which they deviate from ideas and themes that characterise the Fisher–Cushing–Lee collaborations. In fact, it can be argued that Fisher's work without Cushing and Lee in this period (although not later) is not as complex and intensely fashioned as his collaborations with those two actors. While there are some note-worthy setpieces in the films listed above, they tend to be effective but isolated moments rather than parts of an organic whole.

One only has to examine the central figure in each film to gain an awareness of how they differ from the authority figure embodied so well by, say, Cushing's Holmes. Leon (Oliver Reed) in *The Curse of the Werewolf* is born a werewolf, and as he grows to maturity is subject to frightening attacks and transformations. In *The Man Who Could Cheat Death* Dr Bonner (Anton Diffring), frantically attempting to keep old age at bay, is subject to violent fits if his medicine, the elixir of life, is kept from him. The Phantom (Herbert Lom) in *The Phantom of the Opera* also suffers from fits of rage and a wide range of nervous moods and twitches. Finally, Dr Jekyll (Paul Massie) struggles in vain against the monster within him.

All four, Leon, Bonner, the Phantom and Jekyll, have little or no control over either their bodies or their eventual fates. (Jekyll does succeed in eventually ridding himself of Hyde but only, inevitably, at the cost of his own life.) In their rages, fits and self pity, they stand opposed to the confidence and practical and professional abilities exhibited by Frankenstein, Van Helsing and Holmes. Bonner in particular, whose role as a pioneering searcher after scientific truth comes close to Frankenstein, is given us as little more than the conventional mad – that is to say, unprofessional – scientist. All four also embody what are seen as the debilitating effects of sexuality. This is most apparent in *The Curse of the Werewolf* where Leon's unwilled transformations into a ravening beast are linked with sexual desire, with one of these transformations actually taking place inside a brothel. Indeed the circumstances of his conception are also connected with a male sexual desire that is seen as animal-like and corrupting; this takes the form of both the degenerate beggar who rapes Leon's mother and the syphilitic nobleman who makes advances to her.

Bonner and the Phantom are both men who have sublimated their sexuality into an obsession with art, which is seen to be largely founded on the objectification of and control over the female figure. The final inability of these obsessions to contain the sexual drive is shown by these characters' involuntary lapses of control and the scars and marks that appear on their faces, visible testaments to a growing corruption within. Their respective downfalls are caused, inevitably, by their falling in love with a woman. *The Two Faces of Dr Jekyll* depicts a similar situation, with a staid and sexually repressed Jekyll directing his energies into obsessive scientific research, research which produces the highly sexualised evil of Mr Hyde.

Following on from this, the men in these films who do not fall prey to the evils of sexuality – Leon's friend in *The Curse of the Werewolf*, Harry Hunter in *The Phantom of the Opera*, the Christopher Lee character in *The Man Who Could Cheat Death* – are often shown to be in some way ineffective: one can note here as an example the helplessness of Harry Hunter, the notional hero, at the conclusion of the film in which he appears, as well as Lee's highhandedness and aloofness. In a process of identification already apparent in the earlier *The Quatermass Experiment*, male identity is shown as caught between monstrous, physically debilitating desire and a neutered ineffectuality.

It can be argued that *The Curse of the Werewolf*, *The Man Who Could Cheat Death*, *The Phantom of the Opera* and *The Two Faces of Dr Jekyll* are revealing failures or marginal texts in a wider project involving the construction of a significant relationship between professional action and a particular version of masculinity. That these four films are dealing primarily with the defeat of their central characters underlines the systematic control provided by a figure of professional authority elsewhere in Hammer horror.

In order to develop an awareness of the nature of this control and the 'evil' over which it is exercised, it is necessary now to look in some detail at specific films. First, *The Mummy* and *The Hound of the Baskervilles* (both from 1959) will be discussed in terms of their representations of authority, professionalism and gender. This will be followed by a discussion of *The Gorgon* (1964), considering it as a pivotal work that points forward to later developments in the horror field in the area of sexual identity while still remaining within the structuring tenets of the preceding Fisher–Cushing–Lee films.

It will be shown that the stress laid in these films on troubled father–son relationships is symptomatic of a view they all share that the transmission of patriarchal power from one generation to the next has become blocked. In order to represent this situation, each film mobilises distinctly oedipal elements, with a succession of male characters shown as inadequate in the face of demands emanating from a usually absent father and as troubled by a forbidden desire for the woman. Such a configuration – which the professional, himself a paternalistic figure, seeks to resolve – lends itself in a very potent way to an imaginative binding together of some of the social tensions and issues outlined above and in the previous chapter, in particular those to do with a problematisation of masculinity in the post-Empire, consumerist British society of the late 1950s. The authority of the absent Father stands in this sense for old definitional certainties that have become unattainable – perhaps even monstrous – but which Hammer is unwilling or unable completely to jettison.

The Mummy

As has already been noted, in the 1950s the British Empire was in the process of dissolution, with the Suez debacle offering itself as a symbol of this trend. In the face of such a historical situation, *The Mummy* portrays a nationalistic Egyptian priest with surprising sympathy, permitting him to present a considered argument against the cultural imperialism represented by the institution of the British Museum. The feebleness of the Cushing character's reply to this – that as an archaeologist he is only doing his job in collecting relics from overseas – indicates the especially troubled position of the professional within this film. One could add here that references to 'Egyptian relics' and representations of a threat to England emanating from Egypt would have had a particular relevance in 1959, a mere three years after the Suez affair.[27]

On one level, *The Mummy* does seem to operate as an interrogation of aspects of imperialism which conflates this with a representation of a troubled masculinity. In this, it can be aligned with a 1960 Hammer film (also directed by Terence Fisher), *The Stranglers of Bombay*. The latter, which tells of the Thuggee cult in British-ruled India, consists of what can only be described as a series of symbolic castrations (eyes put out, hands chopped off, legs cut open) committed in the name of the female god Kali. The important difference between the two films is that while *The Stranglers of Bombay* offers itself as little more than a forum for the playing out of castration anxieties, *The Mummy* comprises a more thoroughgoing investigation of a masculinity in trouble, an investigation which in the end goes beyond the effects of imperial collapse.

The form this investigation will take is apparent in *The Mummy*'s opening sequence which takes place at an archaeological dig in Egypt in 1895. An English expedition led by Stephen Banning (Felix Aylmer), his son John (Peter Cushing) and his brother Joseph (Raymond Huntley) is searching for the long lost tomb of Princess Ananka. By the end of this short sequence the tomb has been found, John is permanently crippled and Stephen has been driven insane. Already the confident world of the English middle-class professional – evident here in Stephen Banning's authoritative dismissal of the Egyptian priest who seeks to dissuade the English from disturbing Ananka's resting place – is shown as hubristic and inadequate.

John Banning's disabling leg injury is a direct result of his father's unwillingness to order his son to leave the site and go to a hospital. Here the father, the figure of patriarchal authority, is revealed to be weak (especially as played by the characteristically bumbling Felix Aylmer; later we discover that Stephen Banning is incapable of even managing his domestic affairs) and premature in relinquishing the power to make decisions to his son. The male inadequacy and impotence that this involves is signified by the array of male wounds and injuries that litter the film, most notably John Banning's own crippledness.   ·

The fate that Stephen Banning himself suffers is particularly

suggestive in this respect. While alone in the tomb of Princess
Ananka, reading the Scroll of Life, he is confronted by Kharis/The
Mummy (Christopher Lee) and promptly goes mad. This configuration – man discovered in the company of a dead woman by another,
older man (in this case, thousands of years older) – is reminiscent of
a similar scene in *Dracula* (1958), in which Dracula traps Jonathan
Harker in his tomb after Harker has just killed Dracula's bride. At
the moment of discovery, both Harker and Banning are shot from
above, this diminishing them in size before, respectively, Dracula
and Kharis. Under Dracula's gaze Harker drops the stake he is
holding, while Banning similarly loses hold of the Scroll of Life.

One thing that is apparent in both these scenes is the distinctively
oedipal qualities of Hammer's conceptualisation of male identity.
Many of its male characters, such as Stephen Banning and Jonathan
Harker, go in fear of a tyrannical father figure (who does not
necessarily have to be present for his baleful influence to be felt).
The role of the woman here – especially the ostensible love interest
in these films – tends in this context to be a thoroughly maternal
one: it is significant in this respect that the woman in both the scenes
described above is much older than the male victims. As is the case
in the classic oedipal scenario, the desire of the presumptive male
for this woman, who is characterised by maternal qualities, coexists
with and is inseparable from the punishment meted out by a jealous
father figure, punishment which usually takes the form of wounds
visited on the male body. In *Dracula* and *The Mummy*, the dropping
of the stake and the Scroll of Life, which are decidedly phallic both
in shape and in terms of their respective roles in the two dramas,
suggests that these moments function as yet more symbolic castrations. That there appear to be so many of these in Hammer
horror at this time underlines Hammer's obsessive identification of
masculinity as something which is unstable and liable to regression.

Under a distant Egyptian sky, a small group of men find themselves unwilling participants in an oedipal drama. These men have
travelled far only to come face to face with themselves and their own
troubled identity. Only in leaving England can they return to it
carrying this knowledge, the knowledge of the Mummy and all that
it represents. The way in which *The Mummy* then mobilises to
confront this knowledge shows us the figure of the professional under
pressure, complicit as he is here with a problematised male identity.
The fact that John Banning, the film's hero, is married, immediately

sets him apart from Hammer's celibate authority figures, Van
Helsing and Sherlock Holmes and brings him uncomfortably close
to the positions filled by the male leads of *Curse of the Werewolf*, *The
Man Who Could Cheat Death*, *The Phantom of the Opera* and *The Two
Faces of Dr Jekyll*. (This is underlined by the casting of Cushing –
who in Hammer horror plays Van Helsing and Holmes, both father
figures – in the role of the son.) Because of this, *The Mummy*, lodged
firmly within the Fisher–Cushing–Lee core of Hammer horror,
proves to be one of the more extreme tests for Hammer's professional
ideology to come out of its 1950s work.

After this opening sequence the narrative jumps three years and
moves to England. Quiet, pastoral music is heard on the soundtrack
as the camera slowly pans across a stretch of tranquil countryside
before, in a wonderfully apt moment, alighting on the leafy grounds
of a lunatic asylum. This peaceful looking location is at once an
integral part of this tranquillity and, because of its function, a
troubling, unstable element within it (as, in a different context, the
Glueman both belongs to and disturbs the English countryside that
provides the setting for Powell and Pressburger's 1944 film *A
Canterbury Tale*). *The Mummy* proceeds to elaborate upon the nature
of this instability by showing that inside the lunatic asylum, and by
implication at the heart of England, is Stephen Banning, a lone male
suffering, if one is to believe his doctor, from a persecution complex.
He thinks 'Mummy' wants to kill him. (This being Hammer, he is
of course proved correct.) 'The Mummy,' he says, to all intents and
purposes a paranoid child, 'it's waiting. It's always there.' The
possibility realised here of a psychological regression, of a collapse
into a fearful childhood, haunts the remainder of the film.

Within this situation, those people who refuse to open their minds
to the existence of the Mummy, to accommodate a knowledge which
in the end cannot be denied, are severely dealt with; most spectacularly
Joseph, killed by the Mummy shortly after denying that it exists.
The survivors are those who do preserve an open mind: John
Banning and an initially sceptical police inspector who at first only
wants 'the facts' but is willing to shift his position when these facts
do not fit with his own assumptions. The agency for this survival,
however, turns out to be not so much the professional and practical
abilities of Banning and the police inspector – Banning's attacks on
the Mummy are enthusiastic but ineffective – as it is Isobel, John
Banning's wife and the double of the Princess Ananka (both parts

are played by Yvonne Furneaux), the mere sight of whom stays the Mummy's hand. But the apparent power of the woman in this film needs to be seen as arising from a certain ambiguity regarding the identity of the Mummy itself.

Most obviously the Mummy is Kharis. Originally a high priest in ancient Egypt who is buried alive for attempting to resurrect the Princess Ananka, centuries later he is resurrected himself when Stephen Banning reads aloud from the Scroll of Life. He is the familiar bandage-wrapped figure that had already been established as a standard movie monster in a series of horror films made by Universal in the 1930s and 1940s.

However, there is another Mummy in Hammer's film, another cause for Stephen Banning's insane terror. That parallels can be drawn between Kharis and the character played by Cushing indicates that they might be similarly positioned in relation to this other mummy. Both suffer wounds before the tomb of Ananka – Kharis a ripped-out tongue, Cushing a damaged leg – with Kharis's fate also bearing a close resemblance to that of Stephen Banning insofar as both are caught in the tomb of Ananka by the delegates of Karnak and suffer because of this. Kharis is entombed alive for thousands of years; Cushing at one point remarks, 'It seems the best part of my life has been spent amongst the dead.' Finally, both Kharis and John Banning desire Isobel/Ananka.

This brings us to the other mummy in the film – Isobel/Ananka, the woman as maternal figure caught up in an oedipal struggle between men. Ananka is high priestess to and therefore the property of the god Karnak; Karnak himself is an essentially paternal figure before whom both Kharis and John Banning are emasculated (and whom a presumptuous Banning disparages at one point as a minor deity). Isobel is, quite literally, the double of Ananka; in marrying her, John Banning marries, as it were, the mother, a sign of regressive sexuality if ever there was one. When seen in this way, this marriage is analogous to the desecration of Ananka's tomb which opens the film and as a response to which Karnak's will demands the deaths of those involved. Both are transgressive actions which merit paternal punishment. Karnak's vengeance is realised largely by Kharis who in the latter part of the film, after his own disastrous defiance of the god and his subsequent mummification, is someone with little or no will of his own. Only the sight of Isobel, and presumably the memories it stirs of his own forbidden desire for

Ananka, prevents him from completing his mission and enables John Banning to survive. Significantly, within this oedipal configuration of fears and desires, female desire is notable only for its absence. Ananka herself remains silent – she is already dead when we first see her – and is eventually mummified. Isobel has very little dialogue in the film, her only real function being to appear as an image of Ananka.

What one finds in *The Mummy* is a complex set of parallels and analogies – at various points John, Stephen and Kharis, with their wounds and insecurities, are all compared and contrasted with each other as are the idealised figures of Ananka and Isobel – which in effect comprises a drama of male inadequacy and powerlessness, with a succession of men shown as incapable of fulfilling the demands of an inflexible patriarchal law. Even the film's ostensible professional John Banning, because of his emotional involvement in what is going on around him, finds it difficult to manage this situation as successfully as other Hammer professionals might have done.

The drama has to end, however, and *The Mummy* concludes with a blast of shotgun fire which terminates Kharis's living death. The Mummy is returned to the swamp from which, in a memorable haunting scene, it initially emerged after its arrival in England, dying, characteristically for Hammer, a physical rather than a spiritual death (with a large part of its chest graphically blown away). That this is in a sense a false ending, that this reassertion of a physicality and professionalism – with John Banning leading the shotgun-wielding rescuers – has to be tempered by our awareness of Banning's shortcomings, is indicated by the way in which the camera remains on the swamp as the end credits roll. This bottomless swamp is the last thing seen in the film. As a final image, it disturbingly suggests that this narrative closure can only be temporary, that the oedipal tensions which have propelled the narrative forward have not been resolved, that perhaps the monster is still with us.[28]

Finally, just to show how thoroughly *The Mummy* is bound up with the notion that male desire for the woman is ultimately something fearful, we can turn to one of the comic relief scenes. A poacher (played by Hammer regular Michael Ripper) has just seen Kharis walking through the wood. Understandably shocked, he stumbles into the local pub and asks for a drink to calm his nerves. When some other rustic character asks him what the matter is, he replies 'I've seen the likes tonight that mortal eyes shouldn't look at.' 'Ah,' the rustic notes wisely, 'You've been round to Molly Grady's again.' On one level, this functions as fairly uninspired low humour. On another, deeper level, it yet again points to the potential danger posed by women for men within the Hammer world of the 1950s.

The Hound of the Baskervilles

It is instructive to note the changes that Hammer made in its reworking of Sir Arthur Conan Doyle's classic 1902 Sherlock Holmes adventure, *The Hound of the Baskervilles*. The most significant occur around the position of women in the narrative. In Doyle's novel, the two women implicated in the mystery of the Hound are presented as merely the tools of John Stapleton, illegitimate heir to the Baskerville fortune and real villain of the piece. Hammer's film totally excludes one of these females, Laura Lyons, and turns Beryl Stapleton into Cecile Stapleton (played by Marla Landi), no longer Stapleton's wife and unwilling accomplice – in the novel, an image of quite literal bruised innocence – but instead his daughter, who is presented as a highly sexualised character. Stapleton himself is a working-class figure who in no way resembles the middle-class schemer envisaged by Conan Doyle. His daughter is rebellious and does not submit easily to his rule, and at the end of the film it is her hatred of the Baskerville family rather than his, her willing complicity in the attempt to murder Henry Baskerville (Christopher Lee), that results in the calling down of the Hound. The Hound itself, as was noted by critics at the time of the film's initial release, is unimpressive, being little more than a dog wearing a mask. While this could easily be put down to an inadequacy on the part of the filmmakers, one can also argue here that the shifting of Cecile from the margins into the centre of the Baskerville conspiracy registers a wider shift of focus within the film away from the male villain and Hound (hence their diminution) onto what is seen as the greater threat posed by the sexually attractive woman (although, as will become clear, the Hound still serves an important function). This makes it perfectly consistent with much of the Hammer product of this time and also makes for some interesting comparisons with what in many ways can be seen as its companion piece, *The Mummy*.

The Hound of the Baskervilles opens with a sequence which details the origin of the Hound and the terrible death of Sir Hugo Baskerville. This death scene bears a remarkable resemblance to those oedipal scenes already discussed from *The Mummy* – with both Stephen Banning and Kharis trapped and punished in Ananka's tomb – and *Dracula* – with Jonathan Harker trapped and punished in Dracula's tomb. Rapacious and cruel Sir Hugo has just stabbed a peasant woman to death. He then turns away from the body and sees the Hound (which we, the audience, do not see). Like Harker and Stephen Banning, he is shot from above as he screams; the knife falling from his hand also recalls Harker dropping the stake and Banning relinquishing his hold on the Scroll of Life.

This sequence, placed as it is at the beginning of the film, suggests that *The Hound of the Baskervilles* will deal with similar oedipal tensions to those found in *The Mummy*. However, a further comparison of it with equivalent moments in *The Mummy* indicates that these tensions are being posed in a different way and that, consequently, a more effective resolution of them is likely. In particular, attention has to be paid to the position adopted by each film's principal male authority figure in relation to these events.

It has already been argued that in *The Mummy* both Kharis's punishment and Stephen Banning's confrontation with Kharis parallel John Banning's own domestic situation. The fact that the sequences which depict these traumatic events occur in the film out of proper chronological order, in flashback form, with each flashback narrated by John himself, emphasises their closeness to and relevance for him. The events culminating in Sir Hugo's death, on the other hand, are narrated by a secondary character, Dr Mortimer. Sherlock Holmes, unlike John Banning, is not caught up personally either in this story or in the sexual tensions that it involves. As the film makes clear, he is celibate and lives in an all-male environment; there is no Mrs Hudson in this film. While both Holmes and John Banning are played by Peter Cushing, Cushing as Holmes, the uninvolved professional is much better equipped to deal objectively with the mystery posed within the narrative than he is as the weakened John Banning in *The Mummy*. Significantly in this respect, the leg injury suffered by Cushing's Holmes during the course of his investigation is a minor setback from which he has virtually recovered by the end of the film: it by no means carries the symbolic charge of John Banning's altogether more serious injury.

The story of Sir Hugo concluded, the narrative moves into the calmer confines of Sherlock Holmes's rooms at 221b Baker Street. As David Pirie has noted, this transition accentuates a division between the materialistic, eminently reasonable world inhabited by Holmes and the more irrational, mythic world of the Hound.[29] Holmes certainly is concerned to distance himself from mystical matters. 'There are many things in life and death that we do not understand, Mr Holmes,' says Mortimer at one point. 'Then I suggest you might have done better to have consulted a priest instead of a detective,' Holmes replies. 'Do you imagine I can influence the powers of darkness?' Like the police inspector in *The Mummy*, he states that he is interested only in 'the plain facts'. Unlike that inspector who is forced to relinquish this modus operandi, Holmes is able to hold to it throughout the film in which he appears.

However, such is the potency of the threat posed by the Hound and what it represents that even he, the most in control of Hammer's professionals in this, one of its most confidently authoritative films of the period, is compelled to modify his methods, although not his fundamental beliefs, before the film reaches its conclusion. That this shift is minimal when compared with the police inspector's wholesale abandonment of his scepticism in *The Mummy* is symptomatic of the wider differences between the two films. While *The Mummy* operates essentially through analogy, its oedipal drama played out obsessively across all the film's settings, Egyptian and English, ancient and nineteenth-century, *The Hound of the Baskervilles* restricts its portrayal of a troubled male identity to a particular finite geographical space, thereby rendering this trouble much more manageable. This enables the production of something lacking in *The Mummy*, a supremely rational narrative closure.

From the calm of Sherlock Holmes's rooms and some expository scenes in a London hotel, *The Hound of the Baskervilles* moves to the setting where the film's sexual tensions will be played out, namely the Moor. The precise nature of the threat posed by this wild, untamed place is made clear early in this section of the narrative when Dr Watson takes a walk across the Moor. The hostility of the environment is quickly confirmed when he nearly steps into a snare, only to be prevented from doing so by Stapleton, who then warns him of the dangers of being swallowed up by Grimpon Mire should he leave the safety of the path. A few minutes later, Watson encounters Cecile Stapleton. Without saying a word, she runs away from him. He follows, leaving the path, and promptly falls into the

Mire, to be saved at the last moment by Stapleton and his initially reluctant daughter. Here the figure of the sexually attractive woman is made equivalent with both the swamp and the lure of the snare, both deadly traps for men. Characteristically for Hammer, it is Cecile rather than Stapleton, the ostensible villain, who lures the male, be it Watson in this case or later Sir Henry, off the safe path, to be destroyed by either the Mire or the Hound.

In the middle of the Moor stands Baskerville Hall, which functions in this context as an evocative symbol of the current troubled state of masculinity (there are no female Baskervilles). It is a beleaguered, claustrophobic construction in the midst of a hostile wilderness, within which the male is safe. Significantly, when the Stapletons visit the Hall, only Stapleton enters. At no point in the film do we see Cecile inside it: she is of the Moor. But the line that holds the Hall is weak, suffering as it does from a congenital heart condition. Sir Henry is himself the last of the Baskervilles. This line is under attack, nominally by Stapleton but actually by Cecile, and it is to its defence that Holmes, unimplicated in the matter, springs.

A feature shared by both novel and film is the absence of Sherlock Holmes from the middle third of the narrative. In the novel, this gives Watson the opportunity to gather a considerable body of mystifying facts which Holmes can eventually illuminate with his customary conciseness. It also enables Holmes to form his reading of the case 'off-stage', so to speak, his mental processes hidden from us even more thoroughly than usual, so that his miraculous reappearance in the narrative coincides with a commensurately miraculous transformation of our understanding of the mysteries of the Moor.

While this is also true of the film, one also finds here that in this period of absence Holmes, as given us by Hammer, has shifted his position somewhat, so that now he tells Watson, 'There is more evil around us here than I have ever encountered before' (which can be contrasted with his earlier 'Do you imagine I can influence the powers of darkness?'). As if to underline this change, when he seeks the assistance of the local priest, he says 'I am fighting evil, fighting it as surely as you do', apparently contradicting the remarks he made at the beginning of the film. This shift brings Holmes closer to Hammer's Van Helsing insofar as the latter incorporates a positive moral force (as symbolised by the crucifix, light etc.) into a professional ideology of positive action. In solving this mystery, Holmes takes onto himself an authority over and above that which he demonstrates in his approach to more conventional and mundane problems; his deducing the reason for Dr Mortimer's initial visit, for example. Here the film is acknowledging the extremity of the threat posed by events on the Moor. This is a supreme mystery. The confidently made acknowledgment does not signal, however, any inadequacy on Holmes's part nor any insufficiency in his methods, but instead, in stressing how difficult and important the case is, prepares the way for the detective's triumph.

The case is thus. The male Baskerville line is threatened. The Moor, hostile to the male, is linked with the sexually attractive Cecile. She in turn is linked with the Hound. One can say that in fact the film gives us two Hounds. The first is the Hound of legend, firmly separated off from the rest of the film in its own sequence. We, the audience, do not see it but instead see Sir Hugo's reaction to it (dropping his knife, covering his eyes). It can be argued that this Hound serves an equivalent function in the drama to that served by the god Karnak in *The Mummy* insofar as both symbolise and guarantee an absolute male authority which underpins the narratives but is generally inaccessible to the men who appear in them (with the notable exception of the celibate Holmes). The second Hound – the dog in the mask – is the delegate of the first, as Christopher Lee's Kharis is the delegate of Karnak. The mask itself becomes significant as an image of role playing. This notion of role playing, of re-enacting via ritual a primal truth, is reinforced by the mutilation inflicted upon the unfortunate convict Selden by an antique dagger, this being the same dagger that Sir Hugo used to commit murder. (As with *The Mummy*, an array of male wounds greets us at every turn.) The identity of the person responsible for the mutilation of the convict is not made clear although circumstances (her vehement hatred of the Baskervilles) suggest that Cecile is the guilty party. On one level she is serving a similar function to Isobel/Ananka in *The Mummy*, with the desire for the woman associated with wounds and mutilation that emanate from Karnak or the Hound. At the same time, however, Cecile's aggressiveness and complicity with the conspiracy clearly distinguish her from the more passive heroine of that film. In this sense she is more like Kharis, herself the delegate of a patriarchal authority. Consequently, she suffers the same fate as Kharis – sucked down into a swamp.

What is at stake in both *The Mummy* and *The Hound of the*

Baskervilles is masculinity. An absolute, jealous, god-like male power – embodied in the absent Karnak and the Hound of legend, whose presences are so keenly felt throughout – operates in these films as an alienating force, with male characters in each weakened and/or crippled before it. The woman is also a powerful figure in this situation, although only insofar as she is identified as the property or delegate of these absent, essentially paternal figures.

There is a clear acknowledgement throughout both these films of a masculinity that is deeply troubled and anxiety-ridden. This can be seen as a representation of and response to the already-discussed changes in and disruptions of understandings of the roles and identities of men and women in the 1950s. But this situation is imagined here in such terms as make it impossible to see it as anything other than a tragedy for the male as he is unjustly and peremptorily refused the confidence and strength that, the films assume, is his rightful inheritance. The oedipal qualities of each narrative point in this respect to the films' overwhelming concern with what is viewed as a breakdown in the transmission of patriarchal power, with the filmmakers involved apparently feeling no need to question or in any way think about the nature of that power itself. The male-centredness of such an approach ensures that the objectification of the woman that occurs in both *The Mummy* and *The Hound of the Baskervilles* is taken completely for granted.

The breach between Hammer's troubled male characters and a god-like and self-sufficient patriarchal certainty – with both Karnak and the Hound placed inaccessibly in a distant past – is absolute, with no possibility of a final resolution of the tensions deriving from it. So, at the end of *The Hound of the Baskervilles*, masculinity remains in a parlous state, with a congenitally ill Sir Henry still the last of his line. (There is no romantic love interest in this film to promise a future regeneration of the Baskervilles.) However, Sir Henry's situation has certainly been ameliorated by the professional skills of Holmes who in solving the mystery of the Hound and thereby ensuring the death of Cecile has removed the most immediate danger. It is because of this that *The Hound of the Baskervilles* contains an element lacking in *The Mummy* – a coda, a moment of peace in Holmes's rooms before the film ends.

Like other Hammer professionals from this period, Holmes is working to manage and contain a problematic of male identity and male power rather than solving it once and for all. In the final

Fisher–Cushing–Lee collaboration, *The Gorgon* (1964), one finds this process of containment finally breaking down, with significant consequences for subsequent horror productions. In particular, the spectre of Cecile – of woman as object of terror – is revealed in *The Gorgon* to be an aesthetic strategy that is no longer viable.

The Gorgon

> To decapitate = to castrate. The terror of Medusa is thus a terror of castration that is linked to the sight of something. Numerous analyses have made us familiar with the occasion for this: it occurs when a boy, who has hitherto been unwilling to believe the threat of castration, catches sight of the female genitals, probably those of an adult, surrounded by hair, and essentially those of his mother.[30]

> Suppose we were to ask the question: what became of the Sphinx after the encounter with Oedipus on his way to Thebes? Or, how did Medusa feel seeing herself in Perseus' mirror just before being slain? . . . Medusa and the Sphinx, like the other ancient monsters, have survived inscribed in hero narratives, in someone else's story, not their own; so they are figures or markers of positions – places and topoi – through which the hero and his story move to their destination and to accomplish meaning.[31]

As the prologue roll-up of *The Gorgon* informs us, the film tells of 'a monster from an ancient age . . . No living thing survived and the spectre of death hovered in waiting for her next victim'. There are no revealing comic interludes and no reassuring codas in this film. It can be read in many ways as Hammer's most despairing, hopeless project. Its desolate conclusion, which takes place in a deserted castle and gives us the nominal hero and heroine (played by Richard Pasco and Barbara Shelley) along with Peter Cushing's character, the man of science, all losing their lives, is only the logical conclusion of a narrative in which nearly all the characters are seen as helpless and unable to control their own fates. However, this despair should not be viewed as a sort of existential angst but rather must be considered as a partial wrenching apart of some of the structuring tenets of the Fisher–Cushing–Lee canon.

What makes this film – a commercial failure and little valued in previous accounts of the horror genre – so important to the subsequent development of Hammer is that, while locatable within the same model of horror as earlier films, it is beginning to construct a way out of what is in effect a process of endless male denial. The despair and hopelessness which engulfs the formerly self-possessed

Hammer professional in *The Gorgon* arises in this sense from a collapse of certain patriarchal structures. A radical shift is thereby accomplished away from questions of masculinity and male subjectivity to a broader concern with sexuality and gendered identity in general. It is a break in Hammer horror that is, as will be shown, represented via the figure of the woman, significantly split in this film into two characters, Carla, the romantic lead, and the Gorgon, the film's monster. Arguably, this disruptive quality, the way in which *The Gorgon* set out to undermine certain expectations, contributed to the film's failure at the box office.

Perhaps the most striking difference between *The Gorgon* and the Fisher–Cushing–Lee collaborations discussed above is that *The Gorgon* lacks a powerful patriarchal figure like Karnak or the legendary Hound: in this film, the Gorgon, who has moved into the deserted castle that overlooks the town of Vandorf, serves no master but herself derives from ancient myth. Vandorf itself provides a characteristic Hammer setting, with its clearly defined class boundaries and men in charge throughout. As with previous Hammer films, these men are plagued by fears and anxieties. But in this film the close and forceful presence of the Gorgon serves to accentuate this 'man trouble' and, crucially, in so doing reveals and in part dispels its causes.

Peter Cushing plays Dr Namaroff, the head of Vandorf's medical institute. He spends the duration of the film attempting to protect Carla (Barbara Shelley), who works as a nurse at the institute (although from what he is protecting her only becomes clear at the film's conclusion). This romantically motivated, and ultimately unsuccessful, project is comparable both with the efforts of *The Gorgon*'s male romantic lead Paul Heitz (Richard Pasco) to win Carla's affections and, significantly, with Namaroff's imprisonment of a madwoman in his charge (a woman who is held in the same building which holds Carla). In each case, a male attempt to impose a particular role or function on the woman – whether it be lover, wife or prisoner – meets with resistance from the woman concerned, with Carla in particular providing the focus for many of the tensions that ensue from this.

This struggle over and for the female body is introduced in *The Gorgon*'s opening sequence. In this we find Bruno Heitz, Paul's brother, painting a nude portrait of his girlfriend, Sasha, in a room littered with similar pictures of her and other women. It is into this same room – a room which functions in this film nostalgically, almost as a shrine to the notion of the female figure as the object of a male gaze – that both the father Professor Heitz and later his son Paul move. That even this, and all that it represents, is no safe haven for the beleaguered males in the film (unlike Baskerville Hall) becomes apparent when the Gorgon appears uninvited in the grounds of the lodge in which the room is located.

Within this rather fraught situation, the two most likely candidates for the post of Hammer professional are Namaroff and Professor Heitz, both of whom are men of maturity and knowledge. Both of them prove resoundingly ineffective. While Cushing in this film retains from the Frankenstein cycle in particular his pragmatic attitude to physical and medical matters, he is shown to be dangerously, and in the end fatally, narrow-minded in his emotional refusal to confront the problem of the Gorgon. Professor Heitz is much more flexible and open-minded: 'I believe in the existence of everything which the human brain is unable to disprove,' he says at one point. Unfortunately, he is turned to stone before the film has run more than half its course.

In the latter part of the film, Professor Meister, yet another man of knowledge, arrives in Vandorf. A surrogate father to Paul and, as played by Christopher Lee, much closer to the decisive authority figure one expected of Hammer at this time, he does finally succeed in destroying the Gorgon. That this act does not function, however, as even a nominal restoration of patriarchal authority is suggested not only by the somewhat arbitrary way in which Meister is introduced into the narrative but also by the fact that at the end of the film every important male character – with the exception of Meister himself – is either dead or dying.

The Gorgon speaks then of a fairly comprehensive male defeat. But, importantly, this is entangled within the film with an unwillingness to project the cause of men's troubles onto either an idealised female (as was the case with Ananka in *The Mummy*) or a wicked woman (Cecile in *The Hound of the Baskervilles*). One can note in this respect the importance of mirrors and reflections in *The Gorgon*. This is part of the original myth of course – in order to guide his sword accurately, Perseus used the reflection of the Medusa on his shield. But it is taken up in this film in a more complex way. A mirror features prominently in the decor of the castle interior, the Gorgon's home, and reflected in it at one point or another, and always just before their fateful encounters with the Gorgon, are Professor Heitz, Paul Heitz and Dr Namaroff. Also, Paul's first glimpse of the monster occurs when he looks into a pool and sees its reflection next to his own. Here, explicitly, the Gorgon is given us as a 'male' problem, arising as it does from a man looking at himself.

Unlike Isobel/Ananka and Cecile, both of whom are tied inextricably to strong paternal figures, Carla, *The Gorgon*'s romantic heroine, is autonomous, with her own somewhat confused feelings and desires. Various men seek to control and possess her: they fail. But, crucially, Carla is unable to rid herself entirely of their attempts to objectify her, mainly because she herself is already possessed by the Gorgon (with this the knowledge from which Namaroff is attempting to shield her). The Gorgon functions in this respect as an ultimate symbol of female passivity and objectification. She does not actually do anything in the film. The horror deriving from her arises from a male reaction to her presence. Indeed she herself arises from a male reflection. It can be argued that she figures in the film as the logical endpoint of Namaroff's and Paul's desires – she is what they want Carla to become, the female as object, as an extension of their own being. But here the fearfulness of the objectified woman, something only implicit in *The Mummy*, has become an altogether more visible monstrousness.

This splitting – between woman as object and the nascent female subjectivity embodied by Carla – entails a recognition, both by the male characters in *The Gorgon* and in a sense by Hammer itself, that the woman as previously figured in the classic Hammer oedipal scenario was very much a male projection or fantasy, with this projection now perceived as itself a monstrous imposition. This recognition, coupled as it is in *The Gorgon* with the absence, so to speak, of the absent father provokes a collapse; that is the structure which has previously guaranteed a patriarchal order – within which representations of a troubled masculinity could be contained and managed – disappears. It is because of this that when, at the end of the film, Paul turns to look at the Gorgon, even though he knows he will die because of it, his look is particularly charged inasmuch as it is the most visible enactment within the film of that recognition; for Paul and, to a certain extent, for the classic Hammer horror, it is actually a kind of suicide.

After Meister has beheaded the Gorgon, he makes the dying Paul look at the severed head as it turns back into Carla. 'She's free now,' he says. Given that Carla is dead, this is a somewhat ironic statement. However, in symbolic terms if nothing else, Carla is free of the Gorgon, the object-woman. Meister's climactic act is the final moment of a particular patriarchal decisiveness. After *The Gorgon* an acknowledgement of female subjectivity, of female characters existing apart from or resisting male definitions of them, becomes a significant element in Hammer horror, not overnight of course nor in every film, but instead as a general mobilising concern. The 'man-problem' which powered *The Mummy* and *The Hound of the Baskervilles* has been brought to a moment of crisis and then dispersed.

Other horrors

The changes taking place in British cinema in the 1950s were not exploited by Hammer alone. Other companies and individuals, also seeing a potential new market opening up, moved into horror production in the mid to late 1950s (although none to such a great extent), with others following after Hammer in particular had proved that substantial profits could be earned in this area.

A survey of these films reveals that there was no alternative tradition that could have offered even the remotest challenge to the dominance of Hammer. Many of the non-Hammer horrors did in fact attend to issues also being dealt with by Hammer, although none succeeded in articulating as attractive an aesthetic formula as that devised by Hammer's filmmakers. What these films do represent, however, are various possibilities for the British horror genre which, while they might not have been taken up in any significant way, comprised an important part of British film production at this time. In particular, their existence testifies to the heterogeneity of the British horror genre in this period.

Monty Berman and Robert S. Baker, two producers working in partnership, were active in British horror in the latter part of the 1950s. Their films included *Blood of the Vampire* (1958, d. Henry Cass – featuring Barbara Shelley, later to star in *The Gorgon*, with a screenplay by Hammer writer Jimmy Sangster), *The Trollenberg Terror* (1958, d. Quentin Lawrence, taken, Hammer-style, from a TV play, with screenplay again by Sangster), *Jack the Ripper* (1958, d. Robert Baker from yet another Sangster screenplay) and *Flesh and the Fiends* (1959, the story of grave robbers Burke and Hare, directed by John Gilling, a frequent contributor to the genre). While these films all have some connection with Hammer, in terms either of creative personnel or of a vaguely equivalent period setting, one cannot detect any stylistic or thematic elements that bind them together into a coherent body of work. What is apparent in the first and last listed above, however, is a similar agenda to that addressed by Hammer's Frankenstein cycle, namely the abuse of the individual in the name of a presumptuous medical science. The figures of Donald Wolfit's Callistratus in *Blood of the Vampire* and Peter Cushing's Dr Knox in *Flesh and the Fiends*, no matter how differently they are played, signal a shift away from the monsters of the Universal period onto a more visibly human agency of evil.[32]

The producer John Croydon, who had been an associate producer on Ealing's *Dead of Night*, collaborated with director Robert Day (later to make *She* for Hammer) and British-born horror star Boris Karloff on two films shot back-to-back and released in 1958, *The Grip of the Strangler* and *Corridors of Blood*. In these one finds yet again an absence of the more traditional monster figure and a concern with the doctor-scientist. Perhaps *Corridors of Blood*'s closest companion piece in the Hammer canon is *Revenge of Frankenstein* (also 1958); in both the working-class patient functions as the object for the scientist's often very painful experiments; this in turn might be read as enacting a suspicion and fear of the notion of the nurturing Welfare State which, as our earlier analysis of *The Quatermass Experiment* has demonstrated, was apparent in many areas of British cinema in the 1950s.[33] The differences between the two films are quite striking, however. *Corridors of Blood* was (like *Grip of the Strangler*) shot in black and white and strives for a realism which rarely concerned Hammer. The operations – done without anaesthetic – in *Corridors of Blood* are painfully authentic; the image of Karloff frantically attempting to conduct the operation as quickly as possible stands poles apart from Cushing's cool relish of his surgical skills in the Frankenstein cycle.

It is in this difference between *Corridors of Blood* and *Revenge of Frankenstein* and the implications it has for the way in which their respective narratives develop that one can arguably locate a reason for Hammer's greater success in the genre. The Karloff figure in both of Day's films is a man crushed by the world in which he lives and works. Cushing's Frankenstein, on the other hand, effortlessly dominates the world through which he moves. His eventual and inevitable failure is caused not by any flaw or weakness in his own character but rather by the inability of the world around him to live up to the demands of his indomitable will. As we have already seen, this domination and mastery of the environment is one of the distinguishing features of 1950s Hammer horror. These non-Hammer films – *Blood of the Vampire*, *Flesh and the Fiends*, *Corridors of Blood* and *Grip of the Strangler* – certainly deal with issues that are also handled by Hammer: for example, the questionable authority represented by the figure of the scientist (in a nuclear age that saw the formation of the Campaign for Nuclear Disarmament) and the cruelty implicit in the medical objectification of the patient. But the stress laid by these productions on failure and defeat, especially in *Corridors of Blood*, immediately sets them apart from a more robust and assertive Hammer horror.

Commencing in the late 1950s, Anglo-Amalgamated produced three important horror films: *Horrors of the Black Museum* (1959, d. Arthur Crabtree), *Circus of Horrors* (1960, d. Sidney Hayers) and, perhaps most notoriously, *Peeping Tom* (1960, d. Michael Powell). All three had contemporary settings, utilised garish colour schemes and drew heavily on the iconography of 1950s pornography. All three have also been criticised (and praised) for their representation of 'sadistic' violence and have subsequently been dubbed by David Pirie 'the Sadian trilogy'.34

An awareness of these films as a constituent part of the horror genre is perhaps made difficult by the formidable presence of Michael Powell, a British cinema 'auteur' whose film has for various reasons come to be regarded in certain circles as one of the greatest British films ever made.35 Panned by critics on its initial release, it (and indeed much of Powell's earlier work with Emeric Pressburger) has played a key part in the critical remapping of British cinema that has taken place since the early 1970s and which, as has already been shown, has involved the recovery of fantastic elements from the margins of previous critical histories. Within this context, *Peeping Tom*'s belonging to one of the more disreputable of genres, as well as its self-reflexivity, the way in which it offers itself as a meditation on the nature of cinema, has marked it as a particularly charged example of a type of British filmmaking that can be used to challenge a critical privileging of the documentary tradition in British cinema.

While acknowledging the virtuosity and thematic complexity of *Peeping Tom*, it can in fact be argued that it fits in very tightly with the two other films that comprise this short Sadian cycle. The self-referentiality of Powell's film – in which a cameraman murders women as he photographs them – can be aligned with a self-reflexivity inherent in the cycle as a whole, and one that was becoming ever more explicit before Powell's entrance into the horror genre. The significance of *Peeping Tom* in this respect is that it accelerated and to a certain extent transformed a process or movement already in existence, providing a suitably accomplished endpoint to a group of films that were already heading, albeit in a far less distinguished and almost certainly unconscious manner, in that direction already.

An examination of the opening sequences of all three films is helpful here. *Horrors of the Black Museum* commences with a woman having her eyes gouged out by spikes that emerge unexpectedly from a pair of binoculars. *Circus of Horrors* begins with a screaming, horribly scarred woman (a victim of Dr Rossiter, an unscrupulous plastic surgeon) smashing a mirror, refusing to look at her own reflection. The first shot of *Peeping Tom* is a close-up of an eye which opens to the sound of a camera shutter. The following sequence, which depicts the murder of a prostitute, is seen almost entirely through the 'eye' of a handheld camera.

Two factors that work to bind this trilogy together, aside from the factors of colour and iconography mentioned above, are immediately apparent. The first is the repeated references to looking: the binoculars in *Horrors of the Black Museum*, the mirror in *Circus of Horrors* and the camera/eye in *Peeping Tom*. Only in the last is the link between looking and cinema spectatorship made explicit but this parallel is available in the other films, particularly in the way they conceive of the audience.

David Pirie has observed how *Circus of Horrors* plays on the dual response of a circus audience to see, on the one hand, success and survival, and on the other, death and disaster.[36] As the film progresses and the body count increases – the beautiful lion tamer mauled to death by her lions, the beautiful trapeze artist plunging to her death, the beautiful female 'target' for the knife-thrower receiving a knife in the neck – the circus, not surprisingly, becomes known as 'the jinxed circus' and consequently becomes more popular with its audience, who clearly have an appetite for such 'entertainment', for such horror. Similarly, in *Horrors of the Black Museum* Michael Gough plays a demented writer who engineers a series of particularly unpleasant murders and then writes books about them, books which inevitably turn out to be bestsellers.

In an important sense, both the circus-goers and Gough's avid readership stand in for us, the audience for horror cinema. Like us, they have come to see the violence and gore. It is as if we, that is the British cinema-going public of the 1950s, have actually been placed in the drama of each film. In this way, the films offer us a means of access into the horror, a position from which we can safely view gratuitous acts of violence, as well as providing for themselves a guarantee of a need or desire for this type of entertainment. Yes, *Circus of Horrors* and *Horrors of the Black Museum* seem to be self-reassuringly saying, there is a public demand for the horror product. On this level, these films are just as much about a new market for horror as they are about more traditional generic concerns.

The particular self-reflexivity of this approach is taken onto another level in *Peeping Tom*, where the audience that is literally in the drama disappears and the film's energies are directed instead

3 *Circus of Horrors*: Horror for (and before) the audience

towards an exploration of the nature of vision and looking in the cinema. The limited distancing from the intense death scenes given us in the first two films, their essentially exhibitionistic nature (most obviously in *Circus of Horrors* where all the victims are quite literally on show), is lost – hence the disturbing qualities of Powell's film. As spectators of *Peeping Tom*, the cinema audience becomes implicated in a way that the circus audience never does.

The second binding factor apparent from an appraisal of these three films' respective opening sequences lies in the aggression and violence against women represented therein, and particularly the independent woman. In *Horrors of the Black Museum* it is the woman gazing, appropriating the look to herself through the binoculars, who is punished by losing her eyes. In *Circus of Horrors* a woman before the mirror is forced to recognise herself, in what might be read as a sadistic reply to *Dead of Night*'s 'Haunted Mirror' sequence, as scarred, a woman moreover clad only in her underwear, inviting an audience to gaze at her semi-naked body while at the same time being repelled by the scar on her face. As a final turn of the screw, the image is juxtaposed within the frame with a photograph of the woman unscarred. In the photo she is passive and complete, in reality she is active (smashing the mirror) and mutilated. Finally, in *Peeping Tom*, the women who die, from the prostitute onwards, all break the first cinematic 'rule': they look directly at the camera, that is they resist being the objects of its voyeuristic gaze, and it is Mark Lewis, the psychopathic cameraman, who puts them 'back in place' with the assistance of a sharpened and decidedly phallic tripod leg. Here, as in so many other areas of cinema, to look is to be male and to be looked at female, with any attempted circumvention of this registering as a transgression.[37]

It has already been noted that the problem of identifying the role of women at this time revolved largely around a contradiction between the ideological placing of the woman within home and family and the economic necessity for women to work outside that institution in order to support it and the economy within which it was located. In dramatising this, these three films, and in particular *Circus of Horrors* and *Peeping Tom*, where all the female victims are working women, equate the figure of the working, independent woman with the woman actively looking. It is a condition of the undoubted powerfulness of these representations, and a limitation inherent throughout the cycle, that they are posed as threats to a male order that inevitably provoke acts of repressive violence. The sadism in these Sadian films is directed then almost entirely at women by men. This immediately problematises a reading of *Peeping Tom* which sees it purely and simply as a self-reflexive meditation on the nature of cinema. Certainly Powell's film exhibits a much greater awareness of the gender-specific issues with which it is dealing than do the preceding two films. But, as Linda Williams has noted, the fact that the only woman to survive Mark's murderous hobby is offered us as essentially non-sexual as opposed to the sexually assertive female characters found elsewhere in the film demonstrates that *Peeping Tom*, despite its undoubted cleverness and brilliance, is still to a certain extent caught up with some of the more questionable attributes of its companion films.[38]

If *Peeping Tom* provided the spectacular conclusion to this trilogy (and one doubts whether it could have gone any further, even without the hostile press reception to Powell's work), it did not staunch the flow of non-Hammer horror that had begun in the mid 1950s. However, a survey of the films produced in this period reveals no other approach that engages with a British social reality in as meaningful and significant a way.

Certainly there are further groupings to be found. For example, the influence of 1940s horror producer Val Lewton is felt in three films: *Night of the Demon* (1957, directed by onetime Lewton associate Jacques Tourneur), *Cat Girl* (1957, directed by Alfred Shaughnessy and featuring Barbara Shelley in her first British film) and *Night of the Eagle* (1962, d. Sidney Hayers), a tale of witchcraft on a university campus adapted from a Fritz Leiber novel by American writers Richard Matheson and Charles Beaumont. Lewton's horror films were often structured through an ambivalence regarding the existence of the monster: a real, independent entity, or an externalisation of a psychological state?[39] An equivalent ambiguity is reproduced within and provides much of the narrative drive in the three British 'Lewton' films. Such ambivalence, and the chiaroscuro lighting associated with it, was, like the disturbing and provocative self-reflexivity of *Peeping Tom*, alien to the Hammer approach. Again this suggests that one of the defining characteristics of Hammer period horror, that which separated it out from other horror films, was the sense of certainty that it projected.

More peculiarly British in the relation they bore to an indigenous strain of SF/horror developed in the 1950s, most notably by Nigel

Kneale (creator of Quatermass) and John Wyndham, were two film versions of Wyndham's 1957 novel *The Midwich Cuckoos*: *Village of the Damned* (1960, d. Wolf Rilla) and *Children of the Damned* (1963, d. Anton M. Leader) and their close companion piece, Joseph Losey's Hammer film *The Damned* (1961). All three, through representations of social violence directed against alien and/or mutated children, constructed a critique of a more general social repressiveness. However, the limitations inherent in their shared subject matter – children with unnatural powers – precluded any development of this approach into a substantial body of work.

One other film worthy of mention here is *City of the Dead* (1960, d. John Moxey), not only because it marked producer Milton Subotsky's entrance into the genre (he would later make a series of anthology horror films for the Amicus company) but also because of its bizarre expressionist style which seemed to have more in common with the contemporaneous Italian horror films of Mario Bava, Riccardo Freda and others. Lacking influence in itself, it is nevertheless symptomatic of the variety of approaches that characterised British horror production. To this can be added inert films like *Dr Blood's Coffin* and *Konga* (both released in 1960), whose existence at the very least testified to the currency of horror as an established category of production in the British film industry.

Conclusion

The Hammer horror films from this period bound together within a distinctive and original aesthetic form ideas about national identity and gender. While some horror films with contemporary settings, most notably *Circus of Horrors* and *Peeping Tom*, were clearly working with similar issues, registering the contradictory position of women in relation to broadly patriarchal definitions of their role in Britain of the late 1950s and early 1960s, Hammer, liberated from such settings although equally locatable within a particular socio-historical context, concerned itself far more systematically with the psychological consequences of certain shifts in gender position for a male identity. The male wounds and symbolic castrations around which it constructed its oedipal narratives functioned then essentially as metaphors, permitting in the interests of entertainment a coded engagement with the social reality within which Hammer found itself.

It was the metaphor of castration, and the male-centred view of the world that it involved, that both enabled and, on another level, blocked off the Hammer text, acting both as the fulcrum around which it revolved and the point beyond which it could not see. The Hammer films from this period offered a variety of responses to it, but it was not until *The Gorgon*'s recognition of the repressiveness at the heart of Hammer horror that Hammer (and, one can argue, British horror in general) was set free to progress and develop.

That this decisive shift occurred in the very year of Harold Wilson's coming to power had about it a certain degree of irony. This is not only because Wilson, responsible in the late 1940s for the government's dealings with the film industry, had expressed a dislike of the sensationalist trend in British cinema that was later exemplified so well by British horror, but also because it was at the commencement of the premiership of Wilson, the 'professional manager', that the discourse of the professional within Hammer horror became much less effective.[40] In subsequent years, there were to be further substantial shifts in the ways in which male and female identity were commonly understood. Later chapters will detail how the post-1964 British horror film, through responding to these and other social and economic changes, ensured its continued aesthetic vitality and commercial success. Before this, however, we turn to the two principal stars of British horror whose careers in British cinema endure, in varying degrees of health, through the 1950s, 1960s and 1970s: namely Baron Frankenstein and Count Dracula.

Notes

1 The three would be reunited in 1967 for Planet's *Night of the Big Heat*. Cushing and Lee would not appear together in a Hammer horror film until *Dracula AD 1972* in 1972, although they would both feature in the non-horror *She* in 1965.

2 In my judgement only ten British horror films were produced between 1945 and 1955 while in the next nine years seventy-two were released. These figures are necessarily approximate and none of the points I make in this chapter rely on their absolute accuracy. This is because that while there is a body of work in British cinema that clearly offers itself as horror, certain films have an ambiguous status; for example, Hammer's own psycho-thrillers. Some of these I have included in my grand total while others, which I have judged less important, have been excluded. However, these marginal cases are only few in number, and neither their exclusion nor their inclusion causes the figures for British horror production to fluctuate to any great extent.

3 Robert Hewison, *In Anger: Culture in the Cold War 1945–1960*, London, 1981, p. 127.

4 'The spring of 1955 was the zenith of Britain's post-war boom and it seemed legitimate, after all that had gone before, to the average Englishman to feel entitled to relax and anticipate the fulfilment of Butler's prophecy of a dramatic and imminent rise in the standard of living.

'Any such mood of complacency was to be rapidly dissipated during 1956, one of the most momentous years in post-war history and one which sharply and uncomfortably upset many of the attitudes and assumptions established in the ten years we have been examining.' T. E. B. Howarth, *Prospect and Reality: Great Britain 1945–1955*, London, 1985, p. 237; for an account that is more ambivalent about the 'shock' to Britain of 1956, see Stuart Hall et al., *Policing the Crisis: Mugging, the State, and Law and Order*, London, 1978, pp. 233–4.

5 John Hill, *Sex, Class and Realism: British Cinema 1956–1963*, London, 1986, p. 25.

6 Ibid., pp. 20–7.

7 D. E. Cooper, 'Looking Back in Anger' in V. Bogdanor and R. Skidelsky (eds), *The Age of Affluence: 1951–1964*, London, 1970, p. 257.

8 Hill, *Sex, Class and Realism*, p. 25.

9 Stuart Hall, 'Reformism and the Legislation of Consent', in National Deviancy Conference, *Permissiveness and Control – the Fate of Sixties Legislation*, London, 1980, p. 23.

10 Hall et al., *Policing the Crisis*, pp. 235–8.

11 Hammer produced a series of 'psycho-thrillers' from 1961 onwards – in the period under discussion: *Taste of Fear* (1961, d. Seth Holt), *Maniac* (1963, d. Michael Carreras), *Paranoiac* (1963, d. Freddie Francis) and *Nightmare* (1964, d. Francis). These were usually filmed in black and white and, more often than not, written by Jimmy Sangster. Clearly designed – in their short, emotive titles and their concentration on themes related to insanity and mental illness – to exploit the enormous success of Hitchcock's *Psycho*, in fact the plot variations played out in each bore a closer resemblance to Henri-Georges Clouzot's classic French thriller from 1954, *Les Diaboliques* (although, to be fair to Hammer, they can also be seen as deriving from that company's own *The Man in Black* – 1949, d. Francis Searle, with Jimmy Sangster in the production team – which was itself adapted from the famous BBC radio series). The central character in a Hammer psycho-thriller is usually made to doubt his or her sanity as he/she witnesses a series of apparently inexplicable occurrences. After a number of complicated plot twists, these are shown to have a perfectly natural explanation, one that is rooted firmly within the criminality or psychopathology of one character or a group of characters. (*Fanatic* – made in 1965 – is one exception to this.)

12 Vincent Porter discusses the influence of Hammer's studio set-up on its working methods in 'The Context of Creativity: Ealing Studios and Hammer Films', in James Curran and Vincent Porter (eds), *British Cinema History*, London, 1983, p. 194.

13 Raymond Durgnat on Hammer's Dracula: 'Count Dracula becomes then the "soul" of erotic egoism, at bay in a Victorian era which, far from being characterized as, in contrast to ours, puritan and repressive, is opulent, materialist and rationalist (very like ours). Even the cross which destroys the vampire is despiritualized. It's used like a special kind of hypodermic needle, a ritual prophylactic.' *A Mirror for England*, London, 1970, p. 224.

14 Anthony Hinds has been acknowledged by many Hammer personnel as a key creative figure at the studio. For example, Michael Carreras: 'I suppose Tony [Anthony Hinds] was really the major force, particularly in the horror field. He wrote a lot of them under another name (John Elder), he produced most of them and he had a marvellous relationship with Terry Fisher. I think you'll find that

on all the so-called classic Hammer horror films it was a combination of Tony Hinds and Terry Fisher.' Quote taken from John Brosnan, *The Horror People*, London, 1976, p. 116.

It is not easy to ascertain the importance of Hinds's creative input into Hammer horror. His writing pseudonym appears both on some of Hammer's most interesting films (*Frankenstein Created Woman*, for example) and on its least successful (*The Evil of Frankenstein*); much the same can be said for screenwriter Jimmy Sangster, who after writing *The Curse of Frankenstein* and *Dracula* went on in the 1960s to write some uninspired psycho-thrillers.

The biographical material on Hammer filmmakers in this chapter is largely drawn from Brosnan's book and *Little Shoppe of Horrors*, 4 (April 1978).

15 David Thomson's well-known designation of Hammer filmmakers as 'decent men who did the garden at weekends' (Thomson, *A Biographical Dictionary of the Cinema*, London, 1975, p. 191) can be read in this sense as a backhanded acknowledgement of Hammer's professional/journeyman identity.

16 Quoted in *Variety*, 28 May 1958.

17 Michael Frayn, 'Festival' in Michael Sissons and Philip French (eds), *Age of Austerity 1945–1965*, Harmondsworth, 1964, p. 331.

18 Charles Barr, *Ealing Studios*, Newton Abbot, 1977.

19 Arthur Koestler (ed.), *Suicide of a Nation?*, London, 1963, p. 24.

20 Ibid., p. 14.

21 Hall, 'Reformism and the Legislation of Consent', p. 37.

22 Quoted in David Childs, *Britain Since 1945: a Political History*, London, 1979, p. 105.

23 *Financial Times*, 7 January 1966.

24 The authority of Hammer's Dracula is of a different, although related, nature and will be discussed in the next chapter.

25 For examples of some of the marketing gimmicks used by Hammer to attract young audiences, see David Pirie, *Hammer – a Cinema Case Study*, London, 1980.

26 Again Count Dracula, the greatest parasite of all, will be discussed in the next chapter.

27 *The Mummy* stands at the end of a tradition of narratives dealing with objects removed from the far-flung corners of the empire causing destruction within Britain: for example, see Wilkie Collins's classic novel of 1868, *The Moonstone*.

28 *The Mummy* can to a certain extent be aligned with another horror film in which a swamp plays an important part, namely *Psycho* (1960, d. Hitchcock). Both comprise highly complex explorations of gender identity within different national contexts (although some critical accounts of *Psycho* tend to universalise or 'de-nationalise' its content).

29 David Pirie, *A Heritage of Horror: the English Gothic Cinema 1946–1972*, London, 1973, p. 55.

30 Sigmund Freud, 'Medusa's Head', *Standard Edition – Volume 18*, London, 1955, p. 273.

31 Teresa De Lauretis, *Alice Doesn't: Feminism, Semiotics, Cinema*, London, 1984, p. 109.

32 Clearly the scientist is also an important figure in Universal horror, but there he usually features as 'the mad scientist', someone whose project is marked from its inception as insane. Perhaps the most disturbing thing about British horror's scientists is that their motives tend to be, initially at least, quite humane. What is questionable are their methods and the usually disastrous outcome of their experiments.

33 A 1950s newspaper review of *The Revenge of Frankenstein* made this connection in the headline, 'Will Dr Frankenstein join the Health Scheme?' (*News of the World* 31 August 1958).

34 Pirie, *A Heritage of Horror*, pp. 99–106.
35 In *A Night at the Pictures: Ten Decades of British Film* (Gilbert Adair and Nick Roddick, London, 1985, pp. 140–3), a number of critics selected their top ten British films. *Peeping Tom* came second in the aggregate list (with *Kind Hearts and Coronets* coming first). For a discussion of Powell's work see Ian Christie (ed.), *Powell, Pressburger and Others*, London, 1978, and Christie, *Arrows of Desire*, London, 1985.
36 Pirie, *A Heritage of Horror*, pp. 102–3.
37 See Laura Mulvey, 'Visual Pleasure and Narrative Cinema' in Bill Nichols (ed.), *Movies and Methods – Volume 2*, Berkeley, 1985, pp. 303–15.
38 See Linda Williams, 'When the Woman Looks' in Mary Ann Doane et al. (eds), *Revision: Essays in Feminist Film Criticism*, Frederick M D, pp. 83–99.
39 For a discussion of Lewton's work, see Joel Siegel, *Val Lewton: the Reality of Terror*, London, 1972, and J. P. Telotte, *Dreams of Darkness: Fantasy and the Films of Val Lewton*, Urbana and Chicago, 1985.
40 See Charles Barr 'Amnesia and Schizophrenia' in Barr (ed.), *All Our Yesterdays: 90 Years of British Cinema*, London, 1986, pp. 1–29 for a discussion of some of the critical implications of Wilson's likes and dislikes in British cinema.

Frankenstein and Dracula 4

Frankenstein (or the Monster that often goes under his name) and Dracula are without doubt the two 'stars' of the horror genre as well as being the most influential and widely known products of literary gothic. This fact raises the question of how Hammer's Frankenstein and Dracula cycles relate to the earlier novels and films which originated and developed these figures. To put it another way, how can one conceive of Frankenstein's and Dracula's historical passage from their nineteenth-century literary origins to their entrance into British cinema in the 1950s?

In an essay on the various adaptations of *Frankenstein*, Paul O'Flinn remarks, 'There is no such thing as *Frankenstein*, there are only *Frankensteins*, as the text is ceaselessly rewritten, reproduced, refilmed and redesigned.'[1] If this is true, what needs to be considered is whether relating the various film Frankensteins directly to Mary Shelley's original 1818 novel, or for that matter to a broader eighteenth- and nineteenth-century gothic sensibility, has any explanatory force.

It has already been noted that in many ways the horror film genre in the form that we understand it today was founded by Universal in the early 1930s. This company established various monsters (Dracula, Frankenstein, the Wolfman, the Mummy) within cycles of films, with their destruction and subsequent reconstitution built into a particular generic pattern that commanded the movement from one film to another. It was this model with which Hammer was working when it commenced its cycles. It invoked a structure, a set of expectations (which involved the names of monsters, aspects of iconography) in order that its audience, for whom Universal horror was in many ways the norm, would recognise Hammer's films as belonging to that genre. However, at the same time Hammer worked to differentiate its product from American horror, directing its films at a particular audience.

Hammer's Frankenstein and Dracula films exist then not as one of a number of historically specific variants or interpretations arranged around an originating literary text or cultural myth, but rather as part of a chain of interpretations which runs through particular social and historical contexts. Clearly this works against any notion of an unbroken continuity that links either literary gothic or a more diffuse gothic sensibility directly to British horror cinema. (While Hammer's filmmakers might on occasion rescue elements which had been lost in earlier stage and film adaptations of either Mary Shelley's or Bram Stoker's work, such activity needs to be located within this broader project of product differentiation.)

Bearing this in mind, what we need to look for in our account of these films is, first, the ways in which Hammer established its own versions of the Baron and the Count, how it differentiated them from earlier versions; and second, how these figures were developed throughout the cycles in which they featured. As far as the latter is concerned, one often finds – particularly in the Frankenstein cycle – that there is rather more innovation and rethinking than one might have supposed.

For example, one of the more obvious elements that bind Hammer's Frankenstein and Dracula films together is the presence of Peter Cushing as Frankenstein and Christopher Lee as Dracula (Lee does not appear in *The Brides of Dracula*; Cushing is replaced by Ralph Bates in *The Horror of Frankenstein*; Cushing also appears as Van Helsing in *Dracula*, *The Brides of Dracula*, *Dracula AD 1972* and *The Satanic Rites of Dracula*). However, the attitude adopted towards them by the various films is never fixed but, on the contrary, is constantly being modulated and reworked in relation to changes going on both within the genre and in society in general. In fact, the eventual fate of each cycle can be traced to the degree to which it can sustain such a reworking and rearticulation of its constitutive elements.

Frankenstein

Critics dealing with the novel *Frankenstein* and subsequent theatrical and cinematic versions often seem to be searching for elements which link all the works together. For David Pirie, writing about Hammer's early Frankenstein films, continuity is provided through relating these to a gothic tradition which is seen as permeating the last two hundred years of British culture (although elsewhere he displays a clear awareness of the historical specificity of Hammer's films): 'Terence Fisher and his collaborators transformed the Baron into a magnificently arrogant aristocratic rebel, in the direct Byronic tradition, who never relinquishes his explorations for one moment.'[2]

For other critics, there is a continuity in the meanings (psychological and cultural) that run beneath what are in this case seen as historically specific variants of the Frankenstein myth, which itself symbolises and crystallises a modern consciousness of the world.

In an essay on stage and film versions of *Frankenstein*, Albert Lavalley attempts to establish what exactly these various adaptations have in common with Shelley's novel: 'they share a vision of man as victim and outcast, innately good and open to the joys of nature and human society, but cut off from positive emotional responses and severed from society, a tormented and pitiful creature'.[3] However, at the same time he also identifies a problem in the adaptive process from book to stage/screen which, regardless of the degree of its faithfulness to the story, ensures that each adaptation of *Frankenstein* can be only partial and incomplete:

> Almost any visualising of the Monster makes him the focal point and a point that is perforce primarily physical. The book may gradually present us with a fully formed human psyche whose feelings, yearnings, and logic are often more profound than those who reject its outward husk, but the stage and film must fix that outward appearance from the very start . . . the problem of make-up in dramatizing *Frankenstein* would remain both an occasion for drama and spectacle and a barrier against the deeper themes of the novel.[4]

What Lavalley recognises (although he does not develop this insight in his article) is that the visibility of the creature that results from theatrical and cinematic adaptation is necessarily destructive of much, if not all, of the novel's distinctive identity. In particular, what is lost is the way in which in the novel the Monster functions as a sort of tabula rasa, a blank space (descriptions of it are conspicuously lacking in detail) within and around which various moral and political debates can be staged.[5] In both stage and film versions the Monster or creature is more visibly, materially present, leading its own independent existence, the nature of its monstrosity fixed, there for all to see. Connected with this, a fascination with its physical appearance and especially with its creation and destruction becomes far more important than in Shelley's work:

it is no accident that the most 'spectacular' and intricate – the most arresting – mobilisation of 'trucage' centres so frequently either on the initial appearance of the monster or on its ultimate destruction; or even more tellingly, on its birth, the process of its construction 'there before our very eyes', an essential ingredient of the Frankenstein films, of the Jekyll and Hyde versions, the werewolf films and Hammer's *Dracula* series.[6]

One does indeed find in Universal's 1931 version of *Frankenstein* (based on Hamilton Deane's stage play rather than Mary Shelley's novel) and its 1935 film *The Bride of Frankenstein* moments of visual spectacle associated with the creation of both male and female monsters. This does not mean, however, that it is in the nature of film versions of *Frankenstein* to be less complex or worthwhile than Shelley's novel. Rather, we need to be aware of and sensitive to the different ways in which literature and cinema go about the production of meaning and significance.

As has been noted by many critics, the Universal Frankenstein cycle centred on the Monster rather than on Frankenstein himself, a Monster whose appearance was fixed from the beginning by Jack Pierce's now famous make-up (the large forehead, the bolts through the neck, etc.). This Monster, which survived across a range of films with ersatz mid-European settings, is signalled – through its hobo-like costume and its position within the various narratives – as a proletarian figure, this of course having a particular signifying force during the American Depression, and each film in the cycle can be seen as exhibiting an ambivalent attitude towards this proletariat–monster. On the one hand, the working class is, literally, monstrous, destructive and dangerous; in this sense, the films adopt a reactionary position, warning as they do against positive class action. On the other hand, however, the Monster is also a figure of sympathy and pathos, mutely (although temporarily acquiring some basic linguistic skills in *Bride of Frankenstein*) suffering social injustice, a potential locus for an audience identification which is essentially masochistic.

In the Universal cycle as a whole, the fixing of the Monster's appearance mainly in class terms results in an approach in which gender-based issues – interwoven with a class discourse in the first two films, *Frankenstein* and *The Bride of Frankenstein* (with Frankenstein's wife and a female monster mediating between the scientist and his male creation) – are marginalised or excluded as the cycle progresses. Significantly in this respect, it is the male monster which survives the explosion that concludes *The Bride of Frankenstein* while the female monster, defined through her gender rather than through her class, perishes.

Between 1957 and 1973 Hammer released seven Frankenstein films: *The Curse of Frankenstein* (1957, d. Terence Fisher), *The Revenge of Frankenstein* (1958, d. Fisher), *The Evil of Frankenstein* (1964, d. Freddie Francis), *Frankenstein Created Woman* (1967, d. Fisher), *Frankenstein Must Be Destroyed* (1969, d. Fisher), *The Horror of Frankenstein* (1970, d. Jimmy Sangster) and *Frankenstein and the Monster from Hell* (1973, d. Fisher). Peter Cushing starred as Baron Frankenstein in six of these productions, and his presence was obviously important in binding the films together into a recognisable unity. To this can be added those formal properties which characterised the work of Terence Fisher, who directed five of the seven, and, more generally, what might be termed a studio 'house style' – which included the use of particular settings, actors, etc. – that emerged from the formative activity of the 1950s (and towards which both Cushing and Fisher were extensive contributors).

Hammer's construction of a Frankenstein cycle takes on elements of the pre-existing Universal cycle; most notably, the foregrounding of the name of 'Frankenstein', which is widely recognisable as a generic category, a marketable horror 'star'. In addition, as the cycle develops, a movement or pattern from (re)constitution to destruction becomes evident both within and between films, although in Hammer it is Frankenstein himself, rather than the Monster, who is caught up in and defined through this constitutive–destructive process (but, importantly, not always destroyed at the end of any film). This change of emphasis is connected with and contributes to a wider shift of focus away from concerns of class towards a set of historically determined and specific gender problematics, thereby aligning the Frankenstein cycle with the characteristic concerns of the British horror genre in the 1950s.

The process of product differentiation, of negotiating with a pre-existing version of Frankenstein, is most apparent, as one would expect, in the earliest part of the cycle. In fact it is in *The Curse of Frankenstein* and *The Revenge of Frankenstein* that, through this negotiation, a conceptual and thematic framework is established upon which subsequent productions are founded. What these films are doing is articulating the figure of Frankenstein within and making it relevant to a particular socio-historical context, bringing him back to Britain, so to speak.

The opening sequence of *The Curse of Frankenstein*, in which a priest visits the Baron in the prison where he is awaiting execution for a murder (which, we later learn, was actually committed by his Creature) and the Baron proceeds to tell him his story, has a two-fold function. First, it invokes memories of the moralistic dimension of the early Universal horror films, the stress laid there on the dangers of straying outside social and moral norms (which, of course, is also an important aspect of the original novel). Second, it explicitly announces a rewriting of the Frankenstein myth, a return to and reworking of origins which will result – as is hinted by the fact that it is Frankenstein himself who tells his own story – in the privileging of the creator over the monster. In this sense, the priest's 'Perhaps you'd better start from the beginning' refers as much to Hammer as it does to the Baron.

This combination of pre-existing and innovatory generic elements

4 Peter Cushing in *The Curse of Frankenstein*

is reiterated in the relationship between Frankenstein and his tutor then friend, Paul Krempe. On one level, this reproduces the moralistic element present in Frankenstein's encounter with the priest, with Paul frequently arguing for the social responsibility of the scientist and Frankenstein supporting an idea of 'pure', socially uncommitted scientific research. There can be no doubt that this debate had a particular resonance in the period which saw the birth of the Campaign for Nuclear Disarmament.[7]

In this sense, Victor Frankenstein operates as yet another of Hammer's male authority figures. As was the case with the Hammer films discussed in the previous chapter, this authority manifests itself in the organised, professional manner in which the Baron pursues his scientific activities; clearly he is a very different sort of scientist from the more melodramatically emotional Frankenstein portrayed by Colin Clive in the first two Universal Frankenstein films.

But Hammer's Frankenstein exhibits only a limited number of the bourgeois-professional virtues, as is demonstrated by his eventual alienation from the far more conventionally (and literally) bourgeois Krempe. The latter's wishing to take Elizabeth, Frankenstein's wife, away from the scene of the Baron's experiments displays a bourgeois concern with separating out work from domesticity which Franken-stein resists and challenges. One can note in this respect the several occasions on which the Baron goes happily from his gory work to a scene of domesticity and the moments where, first playfully and later seriously, he considers inviting Elizabeth to be his assistant as examples of this non-bourgeois mobility.

Christopher Lee's Creature, mindless, without speech, malevolent and destructive from its first moment of life (when it attempts to strangle its creator), functions in this respect as a symbol of the anti-social nature of Frankenstein's ambitions. (Of course this is true for Frankenstein films generally, although the forms which this anti-social behaviour takes in Hammer, the deployment of notions of class and gender therein and the way in which all these elements are valued, are specific to Hammer itself.) The dramatic conflict posed here goes beyond any concern displayed in the film about the social responsibility of the scientist, caught up as it is with the more characteristic Hammer preoccupation with male authority. The sort of male authority represented by the Baron – powerful and attractive but also anachronistic and disruptive – is shown to be at odds with the more socially viable but far less authoritative and less attractive masculinity embodied in this case by Krempe.

That Frankenstein's experiments involve the displacement of the woman from the processes of biological reproduction suggests – as, more obviously, does the near-contemporaneous *Dracula* – the possibility of a non-reproductive female sexuality, although this possibility is ruthlessly circumscribed by a male authority which is dependent upon the woman's silence or submission. So in *The Curse of Frankenstein* Elizabeth is never aware that Krempe and the Baron are struggling over her, never sees the Creature, never even suspects its existence. In this, as well as in some of its other attributes, *The Curse of Frankenstein* can be aligned with other Hammer period horror films, although, as will be shown, the absence of any distinct oedipal structures in *Curse* ensures a different, potentially more questioning approach to this placing of the woman.

The defining opposition between different forms of masculinity is elaborated and refined in *The Revenge of Frankenstein*. In this film, the Baron confronts the medical council. This, with the exception of Hans who quickly defects to Frankenstein, comprises respected members of the bourgeoisie in a society characterised by immutable class boundaries. That Frankenstein moves freely from his middle-class practice to a working-class hospital, while the council members who at one point visit him in the latter location seem distinctly uncomfortable in the presence of the proletariat, underlines the Baron's separateness from social structures. At the same time these same council members are shown as being weak as regards their domestic authority over their wives who continue to visit the fashionable Baron Frankenstein despite the council's disapproval of him. (A similar moment occurs in *The Curse of Frankenstein*, where the burgomeister, a symbol of male social authority, is given us as a hen-pecked husband when he appears at the Baron's eve-of-wedding reception.)

In this context, Frankenstein becomes an ambivalent figure. On the one hand he is signalled as monstrous; his first appearance after his 'execution' (from which he escapes by bribing the executioner to execute the priest accompanying him) scares a grave robber to death; he ruthlessly uses the bodies of the poor for his own ends and appears largely indifferent to his creature Carl's suffering;[8] and at the end of the film, when his brain has been transplanted into another body, he becomes his own creation, his own monster. But on the other hand he is also given us as a heroic figure. He represents a male authority that is no longer socially viable – hence his anti-social status, his exile to the outskirts of society – but which remains enormously attractive when placed alongside either the hypocritical, petty and ineffectual maleness of the medical council or the degraded brutality of the working-class hospital patients. Also, while the medical council is a professional body, its members clearly embody the gentlemanly amateurism – particularly in their unquestioning acceptance of the status quo – so derided by Hammer films of this period. It is instead the Baron who approaches his work in a professional fashion, Cushing's meticulous performance aligning itself with Fisher's ordered mise-en-scene to privilege that figure in the narrative.

As with *The Curse of Frankenstein*, the heroine Margaret is a troubling element in the relationship between Frankenstein and his male assistant. Like Elizabeth in the earlier film, Margaret tempts the assistant away (although only temporarily in this case) as well as intruding into spaces where she is not made welcome by the Baron (the laboratory in the first film, the hospital in this). However, the Creature is substantially different, human and articulate, serving a different end, for here, in a fully realised urban and non-feudal setting (which can be contrasted with the feudal castle that provides the main location for *Curse*) the humanness of the 'creature', the way in which, initially at least, it (and the monsters from *Frankenstein Created Woman* and *Frankenstein Must Be Destroyed*) looks no different from human beings, functions both as an expression of the Baron's need to disguise himself and his research – the Baron acquires a variety of false identities throughout the cycle – and as an eloquent commentary on the Baron's own inhumanity, the impossible demands he makes upon the human body. In line with this, Hammer's 'monsters' are often more human than their creator. The scene in which Carl, his body deteriorating, bursts into a party and screams out Frankenstein's name, thereby revealing his identity to the members of the bourgeoisie present, perhaps shows most clearly the key element in Hammer's version of Frankenstein, the necessary and inevitable exclusion of the Baron from the essentially bourgeois social order that he, through his nature and his experiments, disrupts and threatens (although, as already noted, the films' attitude to this disruption is decidedly ambivalent, part fascinated, part appalled).

By the end of the 1950s, Hammer had succeeded in establishing an identity for the Baron. This was in part signalled through Peter Cushing's authoritative performance, but, crucially, it also involved the construction of a set of class and gender relations, within which the actions of Frankenstein were positioned, defined and valued. The Baron's aristocratic title served to place him in relation to the invariably bourgeois society within which he was compelled to live and work (with *The Revenge of Frankenstein* responsible for introducing him into this world). He was a patriarch, a confident, sardonic, dandyesque figure who, while displaying some of the professional attributes favoured by Hammer, also threatened a bourgeois social order: in this he shared some of the characteristics of Hammer's more obviously parasitic aristocrats from this period (Lord D'Arcy in *Phantom of the Opera* and, of course, Count Dracula).

The Hammer Frankenstein formula as sketched out here, with the Baron defined in relation to the monster, the woman and other men, does seem to offer more opportunities for development than does the Universal Frankenstein cycle. In the latter, the Monster, 'a shambling goon with a forehead like a brick wall and a bolt through his neck',[9] its appearance and status fixed from the start, stumbles from one film to another. In Hammer's cycle, however, there are substantial changes of emphasis from film to film, with these changes signalled through the different ways in which each film identifies the creature (more often than not human) and the woman (increasingly foregrounded). This in turn permits an increasingly eloquent interrogation of all the values that the Baron represents, one which ensures the cycle's continuing vitality and social relevance.

The third film in the cycle, *The Evil of Frankenstein* (directed by Freddie Francis) was released in 1964 – a year already identified as marking the end of what we have designated the classic period of British horror – and seems content merely to reproduce pre-existing formulaic structures, infusing them with a sense of defeat which can be seen to arise from the disintegration of the authority of the male professional apparent in other Hammer films of the period (in particular *The Gorgon*). Again Frankenstein is opposed to a society dominated by bourgeois values and characterised as petty and hypocritical, having as his companions a faithful male assistant who seeks after knowledge and a servant girl whose muteness underlines her passivity. However, this Frankenstein appears to be experiencing an identity crisis. Relinquishing his grand ambitions, he has become instead petty, concerned more with the possessions stolen from him than anything else (and foolishly revealing his identity to the local burghers in his attempts to retrieve certain items). In addition, his pride and hubristic arrogance have been replaced by self-pity: 'Why won't they leave me alone?' he asks at one point. Throughout the film he lacks substantial motivation, even stumbling across his Monster, a left-over from a previous experiment, by accident. The Monster itself is the least human of all in the cycle, a return to the lumbering creature of Universal horror, with no sense of any relation or complicity between creator and his creation. The film's conclusion, in which this listless Baron is destroyed by unsympathetic burghers – 'They beat him at last,' comments his young assistant – only underlines the lifeless, uninspired quality of the film as a whole.

But Hammer's Frankenstein was by no means as exhausted a figure as *The Evil of Frankenstein* suggested, as would be demonstrated by Terence Fisher's triumphant return to the cycle. His *Frankenstein Created Woman* (1967) and *Frankenstein Must Be Destroyed* (1969) together mark one of the creative highpoints of the British horror genre, systematic and uncompromising explorations of the potentialities and limitations of Hammer's conceptualisation of Frankenstein.

Frankenstein Created Woman opens with an ominous low-angle shot of a guillotine. The execution which follows – throughout which the liveliness of the condemned is favourably contrasted with the meaningless words of an accompanying priest and the brusqueness of the guards – suggests that the social order which provides the film's setting is a particularly repressive one. In line with this, in the later trial scene, in which Hans, Frankenstein's young assistant, is accused of a murder of which he is innocent, those in positions of social authority, most notably the police chief, are shown as vindictive, petty, self-important and ignorant. (One partial exception to this is the judge who wants to help Hans but because of his position within this unforgiving court is compelled to pass the death sentence on him.)

Perhaps not surprisingly when located within such a context, Frankenstein becomes a more sympathetic figure than he is at any other point in the cycle; indeed many of the police chief's undesirable qualities are made apparent through Frankenstein's resistance to them in his appearance before the court. However, these sympathetic qualities need to be seen as arising from a weakening of that absolute and arrogant male authority which previously in the cycle had characterised Frankenstein's actions. That such a shift has taken place is made clear by the nature of the Baron's first appearance in the film. He emerges deep-frozen from a coffin-like box, a willing object of one of his own experiments (which can be contrasted with his medical objectification of other people elsewhere in the cycle), with the gloved hands that cover his face signifying an uncharacteristic degree of passivity and subjection.[10] Consequently the Baron is far less threatening to a social order than he is elsewhere. He seems more concerned to create a space for himself where he can work undisturbed, showing little interest in money (as opposed to the previous film in the cycle, *The Evil of Frankenstein*), supported financially by his two associates, neither of whom is the knowledge-hungry acolyte who accompanied him in *Revenge* and *Evil*. Significantly, this work – soul transplantation – is not physically orientated but instead to do with the spirit.

So while a familiar opposition between aristocratic decisiveness and bourgeois pettiness and ineffectuality is reiterated here, much of the pre-existing mutual animosity has been siphoned away. A key factor behind this change, which is also an engagement with a possibility already present within Hammer's Frankenstein cycle, is the transformation of the woman from passive object to problem–subject. Her being moved centre-stage causes other elements in the film to be revised, so that what previously had been a contest between different forms of masculinity becomes an investigation of the basis upon which masculinity in general is founded – namely sexual difference, itself understood in terms of a particular masculine positioning of the woman.

Christina, the only woman of any importance in the narrative, daughter of the local innkeeper, is scarred, and, as the film makes clear, this scar – conventionally a sign of castration, especially when used to mark the female body in horror films – does not stand for castration and sexual difference *in itself* but rather signifies only in relation to a male perception of it.[11] This is clear from the response of the town 'cads' to Christina, which is part fascination, part repulsion, their apparent need constantly to return to her suggesting that their own masculine identities are (re)established through an awareness of the difference represented by her.

Later, after Christina has witnessed her lover Hans's execution and has herself committed suicide, Frankenstein resurrects her minus the scar (and, incidentally, transforms her from brunette to blonde), making her 'whole', so to speak. But, crucially, the condition of this wholeness within this patriarchal world is that she now has a male soul (transplanted from Hans's dead body).

'Who am I?': the resurrected Christina's question is never answered by any man in the film, and the attempts she makes to assert her own identity, to establish a coherent subjectivity for herself, are doomed from the beginning, precisely because she can only speak from a male position (and on occasion with a male voice), with all her efforts inevitably leading her back to that starting point. For example, in her murderous encounters with those men responsible for the crime for which Hans was executed, she, as David Pirie has noted, becomes a fatal woman or Lamia, which is here figured, through Fisher's mise-en-scene, as, like the Gorgon, an externalisation of male fears, another object in a male discourse. The film discovers a dilemma for the constitution of female subjectivity which has more recently been theorised by Luce Irigaray:

> The masculine can partly look at itself, speculate about itself, represent itself and describe itself for what it is, whilst the feminine can try to speak to itself through a new language, but cannot describe itself from outside or in formal terms, except by identifying itself with the masculine, thus by losing itself.[12]

Throughout this, Frankenstein remains largely a passive and, at the film's conclusion, helpless spectator. While it is his soul transplant that facilitates an investigation of gender identity, the Baron himself seems unaware of the implications of his actions. (At one point he, 'creator' of woman, brusquely asks Christina to make him breakfast.) In a sense, he becomes a peripheral figure, servicing a narrative which centres on Christina rather than himself. A significant detail in this respect is that his hands, nearly always covered by gloves, have been injured in a past experiment. This impairing injury marks a diminution in his power and authority which must now be seen as a condition of and consequent upon the entrance of woman-as-subject into the cycle at this point. However, the conceptual framework which defines the cycle and sets the terms for and thereby limits this female incursion (and which is connected with the indispensability of Frankenstein, the way in which his presence is required to bring in an audience familiar with Hammer's earlier

Frankenstein films) is made clear at the end of the film when Christina throws herself off a cliff while Frankenstein looks helplessly on. The camera, instead of following the woman into the waterfall beneath the cliff, stays fixed on the Baron as he walks away from the cliff's edge. Like the Baron, the filmmakers cannot save Christina. Having provided a sensitive and sympathetic portrayal of her plight, with this involving a representation of the difficult existence of female subjectivity in a patriarchal world, they are in the end unable to transform their insights into the more radical investigation of gender identity and definition that Christina's survival would have necessitated. To do this would involve a questioning and perhaps abolition of Frankenstein himself and the fixed identity and absolute authority he represents (which would mean effectively the end of Hammer's Frankenstein cycle). It is the defining presence of Frankenstein then that both enables and encloses the possibilities for Christina – permitting her to speak but only in a male voice – so that the only autonomous act left open to her is suicide. In this sense, the title *Frankenstein Created Woman* contains a bitter irony, pointing as it does to what for the cycle is quite impossible.

Like *Frankenstein Created Woman*, *Frankenstein Must Be Destroyed* opens with a decapitation, although in the first film this is a socially sanctioned act, against which the Baron to a certain extent stands opposed, while in the second it is Frankenstein himself, in search of fresh body parts, who is responsible. The change of attitude towards the Baron thereby registered – also apparent from the film's title, which transforms him from what was previously a creative subject to an object requiring destruction – is underlined by Frankenstein's first appearance after the decapitation when, wearing a disguise, he grapples violently with a burglar who has strayed into his laboratory. Here Frankenstein himself, through the grotesque mask that is his disguise, is seen as monstrous. Moreover, the physicality of the fight, with glass smashing and, at the end, a human head being kicked across the floor, signals a move away from the poetic abstraction of *Frankenstein Created Woman* to a more characteristic (for Hammer) physically orientated realism; here the transference of souls has been replaced by the gorier business of brain transplantation.

As has already been noted, Hammer's Frankenstein is defined in relation to particular understandings of society, the monster and the woman; and it is through shifts in this network of relations (alongside subtle modifications in Cushing's performance and appearance – an increased iciness and darker hair, the latter signifying here a renewed vitality) that the Baron is repositioned and revalued. One change that is significant in the light of Frankenstein's 'monstrousness' is that the society in which the film is set, while not presented uncritically, contrasts favourably with the vindictive and ignorant lawgivers of *Frankenstein Created Woman*. In the later film the figures of social importance are doctors (Thorley Walters's policeman is a blustering bully who proves to be completely ineffectual and disappears before the film's conclusion) who, despite their narrow-mindedness, exhibit a degree of humanity. This is most apparent in the scene in which the director of the asylum gently advises Ella Brandt to cease her distressing visits to her incurably ill husband. Compared to this, Frankenstein is progressive and effective (he does cure Brandt), seeing beyond the cry of 'Absolutely impossible' with which Karl, the young doctor who becomes his unwilling assistant, greets his plans. However, in this film to go beyond these limits is to become inhuman, monstrous. In line with this, Richter/Brandt, the film's ostensible 'monster', is extremely articulate, bestowed with complex emotions and in every sense more human than its monstrous creator.

A consideration of the position of the woman in *Frankenstein Must Be Destroyed* shows that the film has a twin focus. On the one hand, it is the story of Frankenstein's endeavours in the field of brain transplantation, his authoritative search after knowledge. But on the other hand, it is also about Frankenstein's subjection of the film's heroine Anna (with the romance between Anna and Karl providing the link between these two aspects); and it is in the relation between these two strands, which are only tenuously connected within the narrative itself, that the film establishes its position regarding the particular type of authority represented by the Baron. At this point one can in fact argue that while the earlier *Frankenstein Created Woman* presented a tentative exploration of the possibilities – and eventual impossibility – of female subjectivity within the cycle's constitutive structures, *Frankenstein Must Be Destroyed* stands as a reaction against this, a self-destructive implosion by which the certainty and sense of professional purpose which had characterised earlier Hammer productions (and especially the work of Terence Fisher in the 1950s), and which had been largely dissipated in *The Evil of Frankenstein* and *Frankenstein Created Woman*, is restored, but only at the cost of the explicit destruction of the woman, an act

which enables the hero/professional to come into being and at the
same time marks him as completely, irredeemably monstrous.

Unlike Christina in *Frankenstein Created Woman*, Anna is, initially
at least, permitted a degree of autonomy in running her own house,
in which all the guests are, significantly, given us as stereotypically
weak men, weak, that is, in relation to the decisive Baron. That this
autonomy – the space in which Anna is able to move freely – is
extremely limited is underlined by Fisher when he cuts from Anna
in her home to a woman screaming in an asylum. But even this
limited domestic space, which represents a tacit and partial acknowledgement of a femininity separate from male definitions, is intoler-
able within Frankenstein's mission in the film, which is nothing less
than the reconstruction of an unquestioned patriarchal authority
previously disrupted, as we have seen, by the female subject. His
incursion into and destruction of Anna's space begins shortly after
his installation as paying guest in her house when he blackmails her
into evicting her other guests, the weak men who accept Anna's
ownership of the property in which they live. As a demonstration of
his mastery of the house, the Baron then appears, Dracula-like, in a
commanding position at the top of the stairs during the eviction.
Later he will rape Anna and later still stab her to death, events which
at an early stage are hinted at in his reply to Karl's questioning of
his need for Anna's assistance, a reply, mundane in itself, which
represents the beginnings of an eventually murderous subjection: 'I
need her to make coffee.' Significantly, both the rape and the murder
are excluded from the official plot synopsis issued by Hammer. They
do not substantially further the narrative of Frankenstein's medical
experimentation – that is the more conventional plot which the
synopsis centres on as a selling point – but they are inextricably
linked with it, a necessary condition of Frankenstein's activities
elsewhere.

The conclusion of *Frankenstein Must Be Destroyed* – with Anna
dead, Karl either dead or unconscious and the Baron carried
screaming into a burning house by his own creation – exhibits a
nihilism which, as with the near-contemporaneous *Witchfinder General*,
signals simultaneously a recognition of the destructiveness of a
particular type of masculinity, the negative qualities of which are
largely defined through the representation of relations between
Frankenstein and the female, and an inability to find a credible
alternative within the cycle's terms of reference.

Frankenstein Created Woman and *Frankenstein Must Be Destroyed* can be placed as one half of an unofficial quartet of late-1960s British horror films, the other half consisting of *The Devil Rides Out* and *Witchfinder General* (for a discussion of these, see the next chapter), which addresses in a variety of imaginative ways the introduction of notions of female subjectivity into pre-existing generic structures. (If nothing else, the fact that three of these were directed by Fisher confirms, if such confirmation is needed, his importance to the genre.)

In a sense, the Frankenstein cycle as a whole can be read as a paradigm for much wider changes in the genre that were made as a response and contribution to a historical transformation of gender identities. The instability of the figure of Frankenstein in the late 1960s – from progressive creator in one film to a monstrous, destructive force in the next – results then from an instability within generic structures as their ideological foundations begin to crumble. One can go on from this to argue that *Frankenstein Created Woman* and *Frankenstein Must Be Destroyed* – both of which combine a questioning of the old certainties of the 1950s with an inability finally to jettison these – function as a bridge between British horror of the 1950s and the 1970s version, which would prove to be more open ended, less dependent upon an absolute male authority. Frankenstein's destruction at the end of *Frankenstein Must Be Destroyed* can be read in this way as a symbolic and necessary casting out, opening the way for a potential distancing from a patriarchal authority conceived by this stage as utterly monstrous.

The final two films in the cycle, *The Horror of Frankenstein* (1970, d. Jimmy Sangster) and *Frankenstein and the Monster from Hell* (1973, d. Fisher), only confirmed the redundancy of the Baron within the context of 1970s horror production. Indeed, *The Horror of Frankenstein*, which returned for its subject matter to the Baron's initial experiments and replaced Peter Cushing with the younger Ralph Bates, clearly demonstrated an awareness on the part of Hammer of a need for a reorganisation within the cycle. However, the film itself, a commercial failure, was marred aesthetically by an unevenness of tone and attitude (with lurches from horror into the characteristic camp humour of much of British horror of this period). Hammer's final Frankenstein film, *Frankenstein and the Monster from Hell* (also Terence Fisher's final directorial project) was

Director: Terence Fisher (British poster, 1973)

DRINK A PINT

CHRISTOPHER LEE

Screenplay by JOHN EL

Directed by PETER SAS

Director: Peter Sasdy (British poster, 1970)

OF BLOOD A DAY

Warner Bros presents A Hammer Film Production

TASTE THE BLOOD OF DRACULA

TECHNICOLOR®

Produced by AIDA YOUNG
Released through WARNER-PATHE

Director: Alan Gibson (British poster, 1972)

not as ambitious, contenting itself with a representation of the Baron as a senescent figure trapped within an asylum, his ineffectuality coming to stand for the irrelevance of those cyclical structures which define him and once bestowed on him enormous power.

Dracula

As with Hammer's Frankenstein cycle, the first film in its Dracula cycle – *Dracula* (1958, d. Terence Fisher) – both responded to and differentiated itself from the commercially dominant Universal approach. Fisher himself describes this process when he discusses how he went about introducing Hammer's version of Dracula:

> In my film, when Dracula made his first appearance, he took a long time to come down the stairs but it seems a short time because you're waiting to see what he's going to look like. Because, the first time, everybody was ready to laugh their bloody heads off – I've seen it in cinemas again and again – they thought they were going to see fangs and everything. They didn't, of course. Instead they saw a charming and extremely good-looking man with a touch, an undercurrent, of evil or menace.[13]

The mise-en-scene described by that director stresses the physicality of Dracula: the shot under discussion is structured around the decisive movement from the mysterious first appearance of its principal figure to a revealing close-up of his physical features. One can contrast this with the carefully composed oneiric images to be found in *Nosferatu* and *Vampyr* (for example, in the first of these the vampire is filmed emerging slowly from darkness). At the same time, however, the effect of this sequence relies on an audience's expectation of seeing something *different*.[14] What is involved is a transformation of what in the Universal version was foreign and alien – one can note here the 'foreignness' of Bela Lugosi's performance, deriving most of all from his Hungarian accent – into a figure that is at once familiar and much closer to home. This is achieved not only through Christopher Lee's conventional attractiveness but also through his having an impeccable English accent.[15] (In Fisher's *Dracula*, unlike the Universal *Dracula*, the vampire's castle is only a short ride away from the home of the bourgeois family he threatens, and the customs office which separates them is ineffective and presented comically.)

Another important difference, as David Pirie has remarked, is that Jonathan Harker is no longer the unsuspecting innocent he is in Stoker's novel.[16] Instead he is a knowledgeable and fully prepared,

although in the end ineffectual, vampire hunter. In fact, his failure
points to some of the innovative work done by Hammer filmmakers
in order to make their version of the myth connect with the social
reality of Britain in the latter part of the 1950s. As has been noted
in a previous chapter, Harker's death scene, in which he is caught
in the presence of a woman he has just staked by the Count, contains

5 Christopher Lee in *Dracula*

distinctively oedipal elements. It is as if Harker – who is framed from above, his size thereby diminished – has been found in the bed-chamber of an older woman (the mother) by an older man (the father). In this sense, the stake which Harker drops becomes a symbolic castration before the father's punishing gaze.

Such an oedipal configuration immediately places this film along-side others produced by Hammer in this period. But in these other films (most notably, *The Mummy* and *The Hound of the Baskervilles*, both released in 1959), the oedipal elements constitute a narrative which moves towards a resolution (sometimes imperfectly or half-heartedly realised) whereby male authority and an accompanying objectification of the female are restored or reinforced. In *Dracula*, however, there does not appear to be any such clear-cut narrative progression. Rather, the oedipal quality of Harker's death underlines the way in which throughout the film masculinity is seen (with two notable exceptions) as arrested, in a permanently weakened state. In this respect, Harker's ineffectuality – even with knowledge of the vampire, he fails – can be aligned with the inability of Arthur Holmwood, another of Van Helsing's assistants, to defeat Dracula by himself. Initially Arthur is, like Joseph Whemple in *The Mummy*, a Hammer unbeliever, unwilling at first to face something that is, within the terms of the film, palpably real and urgently needs to be recognised. Significantly, his marriage with Mina is childless; the only child in the house – who is often treated as if she is their child – actually belongs to the housekeeper. His impotency is further signalled by his helplessness in the face of his sister Lucy's vampiric attack on him (an attack which has decidedly incestuous qualities) and in his reaction to her death; as she is staked he clutches his chest, his identification with her at this moment, when she is restored to a passivity which is conventionally feminine, suggesting a femininity within him which the film equates with weakness.[17] Moreover, the only two representatives of legitimate social authority in the film – a policeman and a customs official – prove completely ineffective.

In its response to this weakened masculinity, Hammer recovers an aspect of Stoker's novel which had been lost in the Universal version, and that is the correspondence and similarity (often implicit) between Dracula and Van Helsing, authority figures who in this case can be seen as two faces of the symbolic father, guarantor of a patriarchal system: 'the existence of two fathers, Dracula and Van Helsing, is a kind of wish fulfilment, allowing the hunters both to kill and to obey the father at the same time'.[18] In the novel, this recognition, albeit an unconscious one, signals an awareness of how the threat posed by Dracula, the acquisitive patriarch with three wives, arises from within those patriarchal assumptions and structures which guide the actions of the band of good vampire-hunters.[19] In Universal's *Dracula* the Count is completely isolated from the world of social normality and the role of Van Helsing is downplayed; in Hammer's version, because of the way in which masculinity is represented elsewhere in the film, these two figures embody essentially the same male authority, their conflict arising from the uses to which this authority and power are put.

Clearly Van Helsing is a consummate Hammer professional, with the appropriate skills and knowledge with which successfully to combat the vampire. It is he who authoritatively 'names' Hammer's version of the vampire in the sequence in which he dictates details of the laws surrounding its existence into his recording machine. These laws are in fact broken in later films: what is important is that there has to be an authoritative recognition of the vampire's existence. Moreover, it is an authority which is reinforced by Fisher's distinctive mise-en-scene which through editing and framing often stresses Van Helsing's dominating control – for example, his appearance during Lucy's attack on Arthur when his hand is thrust in suddenly and decisively from the side of the frame. It is a dominance which, significantly, is also on occasion assigned to Dracula (his already discussed first appearance, for example). Notionally celibate, nevertheless the condition of Van Helsing's authority is a potency which has decidedly sexual implications. Throughout, only he and Dracula are accomplished penetrators of the female body, an act which is invariably symbolic – Dracula with his teeth, Van Helsing with a stake. (Jonathan Harker tries but dies in the attempt.)

Like Van Helsing, Dracula is a figure who exists on the periphery of a world characterised by a normative masculine weakness (and is also, apparently, monogamous, with only one wife at the beginning of the film) and whose actions are defined in relation to this. What he does is prey on this world, and more particularly on its women. That both Mina and especially Lucy are not unwilling victims demonstrates the ineffectiveness of a male hold over them, and involves an acknowledgement of female desire, most notably in the scene in which Lucy waits longingly for Dracula. However, it is important to realise that Dracula does not represent liberation per se but rather that he attempts to place these women within a different power hierarchy, where they have power over mortal men but are subservient to him. (His first act of violence in the film is directed against a woman, his first bride, when he throws her across the room.)

This defining structure – in which Dracula attacks and Van Helsing defends, against a background of a widespread masculine ineffectuality – has particular relevance to the way in which understandings of gender were shifting in the 1950s. As has already been noted, the growth of consumerism in this period was often seen as a feminising process which threatened masculine authority and identity. At the same time the main social roles available for women – the housewife and the working woman, the former the locus of consumption, the latter helping to fund the consumer boom – were contradictory insofar as many individuals had simultaneously to fill both. This real contradiction registers in *Dracula* in the perceived and (within the terms of the film) inexplicable uneasiness of the females within the bourgeois household; this can also be read as a projection of male anxiety over the detachment of the female from her traditional social position.

In this context, Dracula and Van Helsing, each in his own way, guarantee a system of male power which is elsewhere seen as weakened. This situation is symbolised through the Holmwood house, in which Arthur, the nominal head is weak and unable to prevent Dracula's incursions and from which the women are beginning to wander. In this sense, defending the women is equated with defending the house. One can note in this respect the resonances of the scenes in which Mina is lured away from the Holmwood house and subsequently introduces the Count into the cellar. Dracula's disturbing project is to restore male authority over women by taking the latter away from the weak men, establishing himself as immortal, sole patriarch (an early version of the greedy fathers of 1970s British horror, who are not willing to share their patriarchal power with other men) while Van Helsing's task consists of protecting these same men but without, crucially, doing anything to restore their strength and authority.

Hammer's *Dracula* thus establishes a narrative pattern – as well as a distinctive iconography to do with Dracula's physical appearance – which because of a perceived *inherent* weakness in the male and the general absence of fully-fledged oedipal elements cannot lead to a final resolution. Dracula attacks and is defeated by Van Helsing, but the situation from which the vampire arises and to which he is responding is left unchanged. Arthur Holmwood does very little to help in the tracking of the Count and during the climactic battle he does not even enter Castle Dracula. The conclusion of the film, in which Arthur is reunited with his wife, must be seen – even outside of our knowledge of the sequels that were to follow – as only provisional.

Comparing this with Hammer's version of Frankenstein (where Frankenstein often undergoes a symbolic rebirth at the narrative's beginning and is in each film inserted into a different set of dramatic relationships, with, in particular, the growing prominence of the woman in the cycle altering our perception of the Baron), there seems less potential in the Dracula formula for either development or modulation. Hammer's Dracula and Van Helsing are deeply conservative figures insofar as their actions work to buttress a patriarchal system that appears incapable of supporting itself without their presence. Perhaps the splitting of male authority into good and evil, and the repeated ritualistic punishment of one by the other, encouraged in those filmmakers working within the cycle a complacent, less questioning attitude in regard of those patriarchal power structures which enabled the cycle to come into being. Even the wavering, uncertain position of the woman – because of the absence of oedipal elements she is not as rigorously objectified as she is in other Hammer films of this period – is finally circumscribed by her constantly being defined in relation to the activities of either Dracula or Van Helsing.

The next two films in the cycle, *The Brides of Dracula* in 1960 (d. Terence Fisher) and *Dracula – Prince of Darkness* in 1965 (d. Fisher), can be seen to reproduce these structures, enriching them with innovative and elaborative detail but not questioning their determining ideological parameters. That is to say, the battle between vampire and savant–professional over the woman within a weakened patriarchy is restaged twice over, with no sense of the increasing redundancy of this formula as the cycle moves into the 1960s. For example, in *The Brides of Dracula* an ineffectual male social authority is again apparent, represented here by the blustering but ineffective head of the girl school and the bumbling doctor who attends one of the vampire's victims; it is this state of affairs that Van Helsing has to defend. The film lacks even a notional male romantic lead with whom the heroine can finally be united, so that at the film's conclusion she is simply led away by Van Helsing.

One of the film's innovatory elements lies in its presentation of the vampire, for here Count Dracula has been replaced by a Baron Meinster, a decadent aristocrat who has contracted vampirism and has been locked away by his mother. However, despite this difference he does serve much the same function as his predecessor in his relation both to Van Helsing and the world of 'normality'. The theme of incest which lurked beneath the surface in *Dracula* is here made more explicit when, released by the unsuspecting heroine, the Baron attacks and vampirises his own mother. In the earlier film, Lucy's incestuous attack on her brother showed his weakness: the attack in *Brides* displays the Baron's power. (Later in the film Van Helsing stakes the mother, a perverse enactment of his function elsewhere which is to destroy a sexuality which, according to patriarchal definitions, is misplaced, usually in the body of the marriageable woman but here in the Baroness's old body.) Like Dracula, Meinster proceeds to vampirise or attempt to vampirise a series of young women, thereby placing them in a new social order with himself at the head. In this film, with a degree of irony, this process is seen as a rebirth from the constraints of an old way of life equated with death to the joys of a new subservience: the peasant girl scrabbles up from her grave, urged on by the Baroness's housekeeper, now a monstrous midwife, and as Gina, the heroine's friend and one of the Baron's victims, awaits her 'liberating' resurrection, the locks slowly fall away from her coffin/womb.

Dracula himself returns in *Dracula – Prince of Darkness*, Terence Fisher's final contribution to the cycle. However, the role of savant–professional is filled not by Van Helsing (who appears only briefly in the film's precredit sequence which reprises the ending of *Dracula*) but instead by a Father Sandor, a monk whose earthly qualities and practicality is signalled by, amongst other things, the gun he carries. Like Van Helsing, his notionally celibate status allows him to be a non-vampire penetrator of the female body, most notably in the scene in which Helen, the film's sole female vampire, is staked.[20] It is a privilege which he jealously guards: the film begins with his preventing a group of villagers from staking the body of a woman they mistakenly believe to have fallen victim to a vampire. Their blind superstition – which is also their impotency – is contrasted with his superior practical knowledge, just as in earlier films Van Helsing stands opposed to the weakness and narrowmindedness of those around him.

The major instance of elaboration is the film's restoration of the normative heterosexual (and middle-class) couple and its doubling of it. Two brothers and their wives stray from the safe world of normality represented by the map upon which Castle Dracula does not appear. One couple, Helen and Alan, is victimised and destroyed, the other, Charles and Diana (in retrospect, a rather unfortunate pairing of names), with the aid of Sandor, survives. This doubling – which is underlined by the fact of the couples sharing the same surname – enables an enactment of the threat posed by the vampire, with the husband killed and the wife sexualised and made strong under the authority of the Count, while at the same time permitting the institution of the couple, and the broader social relations it implies, to remain safely intact at the film's conclusion. (The scene in which Alan's blood pours onto Dracula's ashes and revivifies the vampire – the heterosexual male victim is in a sense resurrected as Dracula – underlines the way in which the vampire 'stands in' for weak men.) In Fisher's hands, this never becomes schematic, however. The couples are subtly differentiated, so that, for instance, Helen's abrupt transition, never fully explained, from scoffing at superstition to an apparently irrational fear suggests an unease in and unhappiness with her socially assigned role which is not apparent in the other wife, Diana. Significantly, only the latter survives.

In *The Brides of Dracula*, Van Helsing destroys the vampire by causing it to stand in the crucifix formed by the shadow of a windmill while in *Dracula – Prince of Darkness* Sandor shoots a hole in the ice upon which Dracula is standing so that the vampire is drowned. Both of these actions display the same qualities that were seen in the actions of the vampire hunter in *Dracula*, namely knowledge (of what will destroy the vampire), skill (physical agility in *Brides*, marksmanship in *Prince of Darkness*) and an ability to improvise. Significantly, in these and subsequent productions it is the means of destruction rather than the fact of destruction itself which appears to be of central importance and is the source of much innovation on the part of filmmakers. (Compare this with Frankenstein, who is not compelled to die at the end of each of his films.) One can connect this with the role played by ritual throughout the cycle, which rather than being a religious one involves the outlining of a network of laws and conventions which determine the conditions of the vampire's existence. This can be seen to serve a two-fold function. First, the vampire-hunter's specialist knowledge of it, an absolute structure which permits no ambiguity (if one applies the correct procedure, the vampire will inevitably be destroyed), is the source of his certainty and authority. Second, it provides a degree of stability, a set of assumptions about vampire behaviour (aversion to light and the crucifix etc.) within which the limited degree of innovation necessary for the preservation of the cycle can take place.

As will be seen, the latter function becomes increasingly important as the discourse of male professional authority disintegrates in the mid 1960s. Later films are more concerned with the mechanics of the vampire's resurrection and destruction: instead of the professional defining himself through laws which are at the same time a sign of his authority, the 'naming' of the vampire becomes largely arbitrary, detached as it is from any overarching thematic structure. Innovations around the accepted rules – for example, the need for an assertion of faith simultaneous with the act of staking in *Dracula Has Risen From the Grave* or the deadly powers of the hawthorn bush in *The Satanic Rites of Dracula* – are made mainly to permit moments of distinctive spectacle or frisson at either the beginning or end of particular films.

This process is already apparent to a certain extent in *Dracula – Prince of Darkness* in the elaborate ritual by which Dracula is resurrected. While in this film the sacrifice of Alan does make a thematic point, the form which it takes, the casual blasphemy of the inverted crucifixion – Dracula as son of the devil is certainly not developed by any of the films in the cycle – seems to work more on the level of spectacle and dramatic effect (which can also be connected with a testing of what was permissible in terms of censorship).[21] The fact that Dracula has no dialogue at all further indicates the growing subjection of the vampire to the demands of this type of spectacle, and perhaps provides an explanation for the actor Christopher Lee's increasing dissatisfaction with the role as the cycle developed through the 1960s and 1970s.

Hammer's Dracula formula – with vampire and vampire-hunter mutually defining an endangered male authority, and the woman functioning in part as the site of their struggle – was forged within and responded to British social reality of the middle and late 1950s. When this situation changed, and the horror genre as a whole had to deal in particular with the 'problem' of female subjectivity, the elements which constituted the cycle – the vampire, vampire-hunter, (weak) hero and heroine – and which up until then had been in dynamic interaction, became detached from each other. The resultant lack of coherence coincided with an increasing concern with what might be termed mechanical, non-thematic innovations within the formula.

This is apparent in *Dracula Has Risen From the Grave* (1968, d. Freddie Francis), in which the authoritative 'good' man, the Monsignor, is narrow-minded, bombastically rejecting the hero Paul's honest announcement of his own atheism. He displays little specialist knowledge of the vampire and eventually falls easy prey to one of Dracula's followers. As far as Paul is concerned, he proves as ineffectual as had been previous Hammer heroes in his dealings with Dracula, and yet, significantly, his relationship with the heroine Maria seems very much to embody a reassuring, untroubled hetero-sexual norm. This immediately sets him apart from earlier troubled men like Arthur in *Dracula* and Alan in *Dracula – Prince of Darkness*. It also makes a nonsense of the stress laid by the film on Dracula's supposedly transforming Maria from child to woman. As the Count bites her for the first time, the camera closes in on a doll, offered here as a symbol of childhood and innocence, which Maria pushes away from her. However, it is elsewhere made clear that, like Paul, she is quite at home within sexual and social norms. This couple's only problems are conventionally romantic ones.

It would seem from this that the film's interests lie elsewhere. Perhaps the most noteworthy sequence in this respect is the one which shows Dracula able to remove a stake that has been embedded in his chest because it was placed there by a non-believer. Clearly, the intention behind this sudden overturning of audience expecta-tions is to provide a moment of frisson. But equally clearly this moment lacks a coherent thematic function, for the Dracula cycle as established by this date does not deal with religion and faith in themselves but rather utilises these as a means of defining and supporting an essentially secular male authority, so that, for example, Father Sandor is first a savant–professional, only second a priest.

By the end of the 1960s then, innovation within the cycle was increasingly focusing upon the provision of variation in the rituals involved in the resurrection and destruction of the vampire rather than on the representation of what by this stage was a largely defunct disturbance in gender definitions. At the end of *Dracula Has Risen From the Grave* Dracula is staked by a giant cross and cries tears of blood, a conclusion that relates not so much to the somewhat confused thematic framework of the film as it does to our expectations of how vampires are conventionally made to die. (Appropriately enough for a film in which a savant–professional does not appear, this comes about more or less by accident.)

One of the results of this tendency, and an accompanying disintegration of a network of relations which assigned the vampire a particular place, is the marginalisation of Dracula. When in his presence, hero and heroine tend to react as they did in previous films, but this behaviour tends not to arise from their lives elsewhere. Because then the conditions of the vampire's existence – his motivations and reason for being – no longer stand in organic relation with the social norms reproduced by the film in question, he becomes a peripheral, often mute figure.

The next film in the cycle, *Taste the Blood of Dracula* (1969, d. Peter Sasdy) was released in the same year as *Frankenstein Must Be Destroyed* and to a certain extent can be aligned with that film in its rejection of paternal authority as irredeemably monstrous. However, while *Frankenstein Must Be Destroyed* exhibits the conceptual clarity which one associates with the best of Fisher's work, *Taste the Blood* is characterised by a degree of confusion and even contradiction in its handling of Dracula, and this can be seen to arise from that cycle's inbuilt inflexibility in the face of social change, in this instance expressed in the film's attempted movement away from an obsessive concern with masculinity to a consideration of the relations between the generations.

Taste the Blood contains many of the important themes of late 1960s and early 1970s British horror: in particular, a concentration on the repressiveness of familial structures and the notion of innocent youth corrupted and destroyed by monstrous father figures. (See chapter 6 for a fuller discussion of this.) In this context Dracula functions as a catalyst. His intervention causes the film's oppressed young people to turn on their own parents – all three fathers are weak and hypocritical – and destroy them. But then, in order to ensure their own survival and freedom, those children left alive must turn on Dracula, the ultimate patriarch, and destroy him too.

Dracula's resurrection within the body of the decadent aristocrat Lord Courtley would at first appear to be a logical part of this programme, underlining – as does Alan's sacrificial death in *Prince of Darkness* – the way in which Dracula emerges from *within* social tensions. Yet when reborn, Dracula's motivation for his murderous actions, which is to obtain revenge on the three men who inadvertently caused the death of Courtley, is simplistic (if not incredible, even within the film's own terms) when compared to the subtle psychologising that is found elsewhere in the film, most notably in the presentation of the Hargood family. Dracula's intoning of 'The first' and 'The second' after the appropriate deaths both underlines the minimal quality of this motivation as well as serving as a near parody of the narrative process itself. A further example of his estrangement from normative structures, be they social or narrative, can be found in the way in which, while clearly related to the 'bad', hypocritical fathers, he exists in relation to the young people very much as an external, alien threat. A misalignment or absence of desire within a conventional heterosexual relationship which had in the past enabled Dracula to intervene, in a sense to feed through complicity, is absent here.

If one returns to Dracula's resurrection in this light, one can see how to all intents and purposes it forms part of another narrative – the story of Dracula's destruction, reconstitution and final destruction – which runs alongside and is distinct from the drama of generational conflict, with only occasional intersections of the two. *Taste the Blood* begins with a slightly revised version of the final sequence of *Dracula Has Risen from The Grave*, with this in turn followed by the inevitable resurrection and then, finally, after the hero's resanctification of the church in which the Count is hiding, an equally inevitable destruction. Like *Dracula Has Risen*, *Taste the Blood* lacks a savant–professional, relying instead on one of the fathers reading up on the subject of vampires; its fascination with the means of destruction does not signify an exercise of professional male authority, but rather demonstrates a concern to provide the audience with *original* forms of reconstitution and destruction. In fact one can argue that this bipartite structure represents a tacit recognition of, to use Robin Wood's term, the 'obsolescence' of Count Dracula, the impossibility of his existing within the same dramatic space as those individuals whose actions embody the characteristic generic themes of the period.[22]

The final three films in the cycle only accelerate tendencies already apparent in *Dracula Has Risen from the Grave* and *Taste the Blood of*

Dracula. *Scars of Dracula* (1970, d. Roy Ward Baker) returns the Count to Transylvania and gives him, apparently at Christopher Lee's insistence, more speech than usual. But again the young lovers' relationship is 'healthy' and unquestioned, and the lovers themselves are kept apart from Dracula, who remains a marginal figure and dies another accidental death, on this occasion struck by a bolt of lightning.

Much the same can be said for *Dracula AD 1972* (1972, d. Alan Gibson) and *The Satanic Rites of Dracula* (1973, d. Gibson), both of which move Dracula to contemporary London and match him against Cushing's Van Helsing. As might be expected by this stage, the first, and less interesting, rigorously separates Dracula from the lives of the youths upon whom he preys. Dracula is seen only in the grounds of a desacralised church while the young people congregate in nightclubs and parties. Again Dracula is assigned what is in effect a secondary narrative beginning with his destruction in Hyde Park at the end of the nineteenth century, followed by his resurrection in 1972 and concluding with his destruction at the hands of Van Helsing. In *The Satanic Rites* Dracula adopts, tantalisingly, the disguise of the capitalist D. D. Denham and, it is suggested, his own death wish leads to his attempt to destroy the whole world through unleashing a deadly bacillus upon it: this would indeed be a suitable epitaph for Hammer's Dracula. However, the film as it stands is over-plotted, incoherent and fails even provisionally to develop any of these potentially fascinating ideas. Instead, as was the case with *Frankenstein and the Monster from Hell*, it serves only to confirm the ultimate redundancy of its central figure and the inability of the filmmakers to rejuvenate the Count any further.

Notes

1 Paul O'Flinn, 'Production and Reproduction: the Case of *Frankenstein*' in Peter Humm et al. (eds), *Popular Fictions: Essays in Literature and History*, London, 1986, p. 197.
2 David Pirie, *A Heritage of Horror: the English Gothic Cinema 1946–1972*, London, 1973, p. 70.
3 Albert J. Lavalley, 'The Stage and Film Children of *Frankenstein*: a Survey', in George Levine and U. C. Knoepflmacher (eds), *The Endurance of Frankenstein: Essays on Mary Shelley's Novel*, Berkeley and London, 1979, p. 224.
4 Ibid., p. 249.
5 For example, David Punter has noted the ambiguous nature of the Creature: he sees this as arising from an unreconciled conflict within the novel between

Rousseauistic and Godwinian theories of innate human 'innocence' and a repulsion from what is perceived as non-human: 'Principally, there is an intense fear of the ugly, the unpredictable, the disruptive, which prevents the author from dealing fairly with the monster. Frankenstein may have committed a heinous sin, or a social crime, but in the end he is "one of us": the monster may not be wholly blameworthy, even for his later acts of violence, but nonetheless he is *different*, and must be chastised as such.' Punter, *The Literature of Terror*, London, 1980, p. 125.

6 Steve Neale, *Genre*, London, 1980, p. 45.

7 While Pirie acknowledges the ways in which nuclear power becomes an issue in Hammer SF/horror, somewhat surprisingly he does not explore this issue in relation to Hammer's Frankenstein films: *A Heritage of Horror*, pp. 30–4.

8 This dehumanising objectification of the patient within a medico-scientific discourse is also apparent in a film discussed in a previous chapter, *Corridors of Blood* (1958, d. Robert Day) and can possibly be connected with anxieties arising from the growth of the National Health Service. See also my analysis in chapter 2 of *The Quatermass Experiment* (1954, d. Val Guest).

9 O'Flinn, 'Production and Reproduction', p. 212.

10 On one level, this is a moment of self-reflexivity, as the filmmakers remove the Baron from cold storage for another profitable adventure.

11 See Carol J. Clover, 'Her Body, Himself: Gender in the Slasher Film', *Representations*, 20, autumn 1987, pp. 187–228; Linda Williams, 'When the Woman Looks' in Mary Ann Doane et al. (eds), *Revision: Essays in Feminist Film Criticism*, Frederick MD, 1984, pp. 83–99.

12 Luce Irigaray, 'Women's Exile', *Ideology & Consciousness*, 1, May 1977, p. 74: quoted in Mary Ann Doane, 'Film and the Masquerade: Theorising the Female Spectator', *Screen*, 23, no. 3–4, Sept.–Oct. 1982, pp. 74–87.

13 John Brosnan, *The Horror People*, London, 1976, p. 113.

14 Roger Dadoun has argued that the first appearance of Dracula – the play between absence and presence that this involves – connects with a disavowal of lack/castration/the archaic mother: see Dadoun, 'Fetishism and the Horror Film' in James Donald (ed.), *Fantasy and the Cinema*, London, 1989, pp. 39–62. However, Dadoun's remarks, while intriguing, are perhaps too general. In their concentration on an 'archaic' level of meaning, they fail to take account of the way in which the figure of the Count is caught up in and transformed by different social contexts.

15 The first part of the film contains several equivalent effects; for example, the close-up near the film's opening of Dracula's grey tomb which is suddenly spattered with blood signals the transition from black and white horror to a 'full-blooded' colour variety: see Gregory Waller, *The Living and the Undead: from Stoker's Dracula to Romero's Dawn of the Dead*, Urbana and Chicago, 1986, pp. 113–23.

16 David Pirie, *The Vampire Cinema*, London, 1977, p. 74: as Gregory Waller has noted, the fact that Harker is forewarned, forearmed and yet is defeated underlines his ineffectuality; Waller, p. 114.

17 Significantly, in the novel it is Arthur himself who stakes Lucy, there his fiancée rather than his sister. In Hammer's film he is unable to do this, and Van Helsing performs the task for him.

18 Richard Astle, 'Dracula as Totemic Monster: Lacan, Freud, Oedipus and History', *Substance*, 25, 1980, p. 102.

19 See Christopher Croft, '"Kiss Me with Those Red Lips": Gender and Inversion in Bram Stoker's *Dracula*', *Representations*, 8, autumn 1984, pp. 107–33.

20 S. S. Prawer has discussed this sequence at some length (*Caligari's Children: the Film as Tale of Terror*, Oxford, 1980, pp. 240–69). He notes its 'rape-like'

qualities but does not extend this remark into a consideration of the film's sexual politics.

21 For the British Board of Film Censors' remarks on Alan's death scene in *Dracula – Prince of Darkness*, see David Pirie, *Hammer – a Cinema Case Study*, London, 1980, item 27.

22 Robin Wood, 'Burying the Undead: the Use and Obsolescence of Count Dracula', *Mosaic*, 16, no. 1–2, pp. 175–87.

1964–69: Horror production   5

1964–66

By the mid 1960s the British horror film, largely because of Hammer's unprecedented success, had become firmly associated in the public's mind with period settings. What one finds between 1964 (the year of *The Gorgon*) and 1966 is a cluster of films which seek, presumably in the commercial interests of product differentiation, to relocate horror in a recognisable present-day world while at the same time appealing to the already established market for that period horror.

One of the first of these 'modernising' films is *Witchcraft* (1964, d. Don Sharp), the plot of which revolves around a longstanding feud between two families, the Whitlocks and the Laniers. In the seventeenth century the Laniers burn one of the Whitlocks, Vanessa, as a witch and move into the Whitlocks' mansion where they are still living when the film opens. As far as they are concerned the feud is over, but for Morgan Whitlock (played by an aging Lon Chaney Jnr), who is later revealed as a warlock, the enmity still stands. During the course of the film, Vanessa Whitlock is revived and causes two deaths – Bill Lanier's aunt and his business partner – before perishing along with Morgan and Morgan's niece, Amy. The film ends with the destruction by fire of the Whitlock/Lanier home.

This plot exhibits a degree of self-consciousness, especially in its opening, about its attempt to rework and modernise British horror. The assault of the new upon the old represented by contractors bulldozing aged gravestones at the beginning of the film promptly leads to a debate between Lanier and Myles Forrester, his business partner, as to the advantages and disadvantages of progress and modernisation. Lanier, who is a planner/architect, wants to respect the past: 'We can still make money without desecrating a cemetery,' he says. An exploitative Forrester, on the other hand, has no such scruples. The warlock Morgan Whitlock, the conservative, is rooted firmly and irrationally in the past – his costume could have come from a Hammer period horror film – and is against modernisation of any kind. In this context, Lanier, trying to bring together Forrester and Whitlock, could conceivably operate as a stand-in for the filmmakers insofar as both are here attempting to negotiate between pre-existing horror conventions and the need for profitable innovation. However, in the end, *Witchcraft* does not make much of this promising dramatic situation. Instead, after its opening scenes, it falls back onto one of the more traditional of horror scenarios, that of the dead hand of the past reaching out into the present. It is appropriate then that for its conclusion it relies on yet another staple of the horror genre, namely fire.

Don Sharp, the director of *Witchcraft*, has been identified by David Pirie as one of the stylists of the British horror genre.[1] Indeed his horror films from this period and before – *Kiss of the Vampire* (1962), *The Curse of the Fly* (1965) and *Rasputin – the Mad Monk* (1965) – do contain moments of stylistic innovation. For example, *The Curse of the Fly* begins with a slow-motion (and voyeuristic) sequence depicting the escape of its heroine from a mental home clad only in her underwear. The mannered sluggishness of her flight might be read as suggesting the illusory nature of her escape. Significantly, however, as Pirie has noted, such a reading is not at all developed in the remainder of the film, which is much more concerned with depicting some of the disastrous consequences of a series of teleportation experiments: 'there is no question here of an organically successful film.'[2]

It arguably makes more sense to place moments like this, and Sharp's work in general, within a broader generic context, to see them as comprising just one part of a more pervasive concern with updating some of the conventions of British horror at this time. This reworking, certainly up until 1966, takes place largely in the area of style rather than theme. So, to provide another example from a film not directed by Sharp, in Hammer's *The Plague of the Zombies* (1966, d. John Gilling), in a much-quoted, often-imitated dream sequence, zombies rise up from their graves in a misty cemetery. Thematically the sequence has little to do with the rest of the film, which centres upon the exploitation of the 'dead' labour of the working class by the wicked squire. Its oneiric qualities, like those found in the opening sequence of *Curse of the Fly*, remind one instead of certain pre-1960s European horror films (for example, *Vampyr*); but here these qualities do not connect in any meaningful way with the broader thematic preoccupations of the British horror productions in which they appear.[3]

The modernising impulse evident in *Witchcraft* was also apparent in two films also released in 1964, *Devils of Darkness* (d. Lance Comfort) and *Dr Terror's House of Horrors* (d. Freddie Francis). *Devils of Darkness* was the first British-made vampire film with a contemporary setting (and, other than that, it is insignificant in terms of the influence it has wielded over the genre). The second, *Dr Terror*, in which five men assemble in a railway carriage and are shown prophetic stories about themselves by the mysterious Dr Schreck (played by Peter Cushing), was much more significant on several accounts.

First, it was made by Amicus Productions, which rapidly became Britain's number two horror production company. Second, it initiated a series of portmanteau horror films – which included *Torture Garden* (1967), *The House That Dripped Blood* (1970), *Asylum* (1972), *Tales from the Crypt* (1972), *From Beyond The Grave* (1973), *Tales that Witness Madness* (1973) and *Vault of Horror* (1973). Most of these were produced by Amicus and based upon the work of American writer Robert Bloch or EC horror comics of the 1950s and can be seen as constituting a recognisable type within British horror. Third, like *Devils of Darkness*, *Dr Terror's House of Horrors* was a horror film with contemporary settings that was made in colour. There had been such films in the early 1960s (the Sadian trilogy – discussed earlier – and *Dr Blood's Coffin*, for example) but these had usually been filmed in the garish tones of an Eastmancolor system. However, the move into a more 'realistic' use of colour can be seen as a part of a wider technological and aesthetic shift within cinema that had important implications for the development of the horror genre.

As Steve Neale has noted, it was not until the mid-1960s, 'when television had converted to colour, that the use of colour in the cinema became virtually universal'.[4] He goes on to trace some of the aesthetic consequences of this: 'the overwhelming association of colour with fantasy and spectacle began to be weakened: colour acquired instead the value of realism'.[5] The historical development of colour as aesthetic spectacle, he argues, has often been associated with the visual representation of the woman, with the female functioning as the object around which certain colour effects were organised.[6] Significantly in this respect, *Horrors of the Black Museum* (1959) and *Circus of Horrors* (1960), the first two films of the Sadian trilogy, were largely centred upon an unabashedly voyeuristic gaze at the female body while in *Dr Terror*, in which all the tales centre on and are told for the benefit of men, this is not the case. Clearly the aesthetic judgement implied by Hammer's decision to film its period horror films in colour and its more realistic contemporary psychothrillers in black and white was no longer tenable. (*Fanatic*, released in 1965, was the first of Hammer's psychothrillers to be made in colour.)

The most obvious connection that can be drawn as far as *Dr Terror* is concerned is with the earlier portmanteau horror film *Dead of Night*. However, as has already been demonstrated, in that film the separate stories are complexly interrelated, while in *Dr Terror* one finds instead a simple accumulation of short, discrete narratives dealing, respectively, with werewolves, killer plants, vampires, voodoo and a reanimated severed hand. Each segment consists of an already-familiar monster or theme inserted into a 15–20 minute narrative, with this relatively short length enabling an avoidance of some of the credibility problems that the use of such monsters within a colour contemporary setting might entail at a time when colour itself was beginning conventionally to signify realism. (Of course, all these monsters are, on a very basic rational level, incredible: however, an audience's willing suspension of disbelief seems to have been easier at this time in relation to distant, period settings.) The film's strategy regarding the maintenance of a sense of credibility in this context can be seen to reside in its carefully constructed joke-like qualities. Each segment sets out a situation, initiates a short narrative and ends with an ironic twist which functions as a kind of punchline. In some of the stories this is quite literally a line of dialogue: examples include a triumphant doctor–vampire saying (to the camera), 'This town isn't big enough for two doctors – or two vampires,' and, at the conclusion of the severed hand segment, as an art critic is pulled alive from a car wreck, someone cheerfully remarking 'Could have been worse. He's lucky. There's a lot of things a blind man can do nowadays.' These moments of irony are part of a broader play with belief and disbelief. In the vampire story, for instance, the drama and humour is generated not through the more traditional and conventional themes of vampire movies but instead almost entirely from the sheer incredibility of the vampire's actual existence. Much the same can be said of the werewolf and voodoo episodes.

This connects with the stress on storytelling evident throughout *Dr Terror*, where this vacillation between belief and disbelief is reproduced in the reactions of the characters to Dr Schreck's stories, both as they listen to Schreck and as they act out their own encounters with the monstrous and the supernatural within the stories themselves. It can further be argued that inasmuch as the audience for the film is encouraged to identify with these characters – in a sense, it is as much Dr Schreck's audience as are the characters – it too is caught up in this process.

The ending, in which the five main characters discover that they are dead and that Schreck the storyteller is Death himself, finally closes down this play, but it is an arbitrary intervention, something arising from outside the film's world – the figure of Death ensures that the film is the requisite ninety-minute length – rather than emerging dramatically from within it. This arbitrariness is made necessary because *Dr Terror*'s narrative structure, in which a play around questions of belief is repeated in slightly different forms both within the stories told by Schreck and in the film's framing story, does not proceed logically towards a final resolution. In this it can be contrasted with its portmanteau predecessor *Dead of Night*, the framing story of which enables a much more complex and charged narrative.

1967–69

David Pirie has identified this period as decisive in the history of the genre, with an influx of young, new talent which transformed and regenerated British horror:

> by the middle of the 1960s the horror genre was just about the only part of the British film industry vital enough to really have a chance of sustaining new directorial talent at grass roots level. This does not mean that it was the only possible sector for promising young directors, or that it gave countless opportunities ('Swinging London', for one, provided more of these), but it did represent an established cinematic field in Britain, where almost for the first time the aspiring filmmaker could work within a tentative cultural tradition. What was more, it was a tradition that by about 1966 had lost some of its original rigidity and was beginning to hunt for new talent and new ideas.[7]

Our reading of this stage in the genre's history will be different. Undoubtedly, new talent was to be found in the genre; for example, the brilliant young director Michael Reeves. But older hands, in particular Terence Fisher, were still producing significant work. Neither can the films of this time be seen as simply moving on from the outmoded and inflexible certainties of previous horror productions. Instead, their relation to earlier horrors is decidedly ambivalent.

Three of the major horror films produced in this period – namely *The Sorcerers* (1967, d. Michael Reeves), *Witchfinder General* (1968, d. Reeves) and *The Devil Rides Out* (1968, d. Terence Fisher) – although operating from different perspectives, are simultaneously drawn towards and repelled by figures of absolute male authority. (In this they can be aligned with both *Frankenstein Created Woman* and *Frankenstein Must Be Destroyed*.) It was surely no accident that these films were produced at a moment in British social history when the ways in which both youth and gender – very much fixed categories in 1950s Hammer – were understood in society were becoming increasingly contested. As Stuart Hall et al. have noted:

> 1964 was . . . the year of the Beatles' rise to cultural pre-eminence; of massive record sales and the 'beat' boom; of 'mod' styles, the flourishing artisan capitalism of the Kings Road boutiques, and the whole phenomenon of 'swinging London'.[8]

An incipient counter-culture, whose membership was largely drawn from middle-class youth, was becoming visible: a study of post-war youth subcultures lists 1965 as the first year in its chronology of the counter-culture.[9] The historical passage of various youth groupings through the revolutionary activities of 1968 and their subsequent, although intermittent, connections with radical politics has been discussed elsewhere.[10] Importantly, as far as horror is concerned, out of this arose the Women's Liberation Movement in the late 1960s and early 1970s.

Within this context, the formal innovations of the 1964–6 years were incorporated (especially by younger filmmakers) into a more or less coherent, on occasion deeply felt, response to these social shifts (shifts which, of course, impinged most upon horror's predominantly youthful target audience). Two of the key figures caught up in and contributing to the genre's development at this time were the young Michael Reeves and the somewhat more senior Terence Fisher. A comparative study of their work in this period reveals some striking differences and also, surprisingly, significant similarities.

Generations apart? Michael Reeves and Terence Fisher

> After all, in this age of Youth, when young actors and actresses are
> coming forward in such great numbers, why not directors too? (Michael
> Reeves)[11]

Michael Reeves was born in 1944. After a British public school
education, he worked in minor capacities in the American and
British film industries. From there he went to Rome where he
rewrote some scripts and in 1964 was hired as a second unit director
for a film starring Christopher Lee, *Il Castello dei Morti Vivi* (*Castle
of the Living Dead*). By some accounts, he ended up directing almost
half of the film himself. There followed in 1965 his first complete
feature, another horror film by the title of *La Sorella di Satana*
(*Revenge of the Blood Beast*), which starred Barbara Steele and Ian
Ogilvy. Returning again to Britain, Reeves spent a year trying to set
up various projects before completing *The Sorcerers* with Boris
Karloff in 1967, which was followed in 1968 by *Witchfinder General*.
He was to direct *The Oblong Box* but fell ill and was replaced by
Gordon Hessler. In February 1969 Michael Reeves died of a drug
overdose.

The contrast between the career paths of writer–director Reeves
and director Terence Fisher is striking. While the latter worked his
way up slowly and methodically through the British industry, and
as a director made films in a variety of genres before specialising in
horror, Reeves's experience of the industry was both international
and rapid – with his first feature completed in Italy by the time he
was twenty-one – and from the beginning he appeared committed to
the horror genre. He can in fact be located within a growing
cosmopolitan and counter-cultural fascination with Hollywood and
genre cinema. (*Time Out*, a voice of this counter-culture, was first
published in 1968.)[12] We have already seen how with Fisher, and
indeed with Hammer in general, a particular notion of professionalism
provided a potent image of self-definition. In the case of Reeves, a
different, altogether more ambitious and provocative understanding
of horror was proposed.

The difference between the approach of Reeves and that of
Hammer is apparent in an exchange of views between the critic–
writer Alan Bennett and Reeves himself that took place in the pages
of *The Listener*. In a brief review of the recently released *Witchfinder
General* (Reeves's third and, as it turned out, final feature film)

Bennett listed some of the acts of violence contained within that film and went on:

> Of course blood and guts is the stuff of horror films, though, as with Victorian melodramas, what makes them popular and even healthy are the belly laughs which usually punctuate them . . . There are no laughs in *Witchfinder General*. It is the most persistently sadistic and morally rotten film I have seen. It was a degrading experience by which I mean it made me feel dirty.[13]

In the next week's edition, a response from Michael Reeves was published. It concluded:

> Surely the most immoral thing in any form of entertainment is the conditioning of the audience to accept and enjoy violence? Is this not exactly the attitude that could lead to more and more *casual* indulgence in violence, starting with individuals, and thence spiralling nauseatingly upwards to a crescendo of international blood-letting? To sit back in one's cinema seat and have a good giggle between Mr Bennett's bouts of 'healthy' violence, as he so strangely advocates, is surely immoral to the extent of criminality. Violence is horrible, degrading and sordid. Insofar as one is going to show it on the screen at all, it should be presented as such – and the more people it shocks into sickened recognition of these facts the better. I wish I could have witnessed Mr Bennett frantically attempting to wash away the 'dirty' feeling my film gave him. It would have been proof of the fact that *Witchfinder* works as intended.[14]

Bennett's views replay the critical response to the earlier *The Curse of Frankenstein*, where the critics standing against the film were on the whole appalled by the increased verisimilitude of Hammer horror. While for them the type of horror to be laughed at would presumably have meant Universal horror films of the 1930s and 1940s, for Bennett, one assumes, it is Hammer, so vilified ten years previously, which has become safe and non-threatening. Reeves's approach, on the other hand, is quite different and original insofar as he is attempting to mark his work as 'art'. *Witchfinder General*, he argues, has something important to say, something that might shock its audience, an experience that will change them in some way. These are hardly the terms used by Hammer personnel in discussing their work. Yet, paradoxically, Reeves was working within – and, as his letter testifies, was committed to – a genre which was at that time generally held to be of little, if any, artistic value. As far as Reeves's films are concerned, one finds that while their preoccupations are characteristic of British horror generally at this time, the director's treatment of his subject matter, both its sheer energy (which no written analysis can hope to capture) and the particular aesthetic and thematic strategies deployed therein, marks his work as a significant new departure in the genre.

The Sorcerers

A pavement. A pair of feet walk into the frame. A handheld camera moves shakily back and it is revealed that the feet belong to an aged Boris Karloff. One might want to compare this with the opening shot of Terence Fisher's 1958 film of *Dracula*, a smooth, magisterial camera movement up to the entrance of Dracula's tomb which signifies on a formal level a clarity and certainty which manifests itself on other levels throughout this and other Hammer films of the period. *The Sorcerers*, on the other hand, begins with an image that is, quite literally, unstable. Although, as was the case with Lon Chaney Jnr in *Witchcraft*, Karloff inevitably stands for an earlier horror cycle, the film places him firmly (especially through his contemporary costume) within this grey, urban world. This is developed in the next two short scenes, the first of which takes place in the seedy, claustrophobic newsagent's where Professor Monserrat, the character played by Karloff, advertises his trade of hypnotist and the second in the cramped Monserrat flat which appears as aged and faded as its inhabitants.

The transition from this opening sequence to the next, which takes place in a nightclub full of young people dancing to live pop music, is sudden and shocking. It involves an abrupt movement from quiet – the only sound in the Monserrat flat other than the couple's voices is the ticking of an unseen clock – to loud, grey to bright colours, old to young, stasis to movement; with the violence of this contrast suggesting that these two different lifestyles can be related only antagonistically.

These two worlds – that of the old and that of the young – can in fact be read as a representation of a contradiction or fissure in mid- to late-1960s British society:

> This was an altogether different – puzzling, contradictory – world for the traditional middle classes, formed in and by an older, more 'protestant' ethic. Advanced capitalism now required not thrift but consumption; not sobriety but style; not postponed gratifications but immediate satisfaction of needs; not goods that last but things that are expendable; the

'swinging' rather than the sober lifestyle. The gospel of work was hardly apposite to a life increasingly focussed on consumption, pleasure and play . . . The counter-cultures were born within this qualitative break inside the dominant culture.[15]

The Monserrat flat can be seen as representing the Protestant work ethic. The furniture it contains signifies thrift; it is old, used, 'made to last' and it can be compared with the briefly glimpsed interior of Mike Roscoe's flat which is functionally bare, decorated with throwaway posters. The meat and two veg. meal which Estelle, Marcus's wife, serves Marcus on his return to the flat in the opening sequence also testifies to a domestic economy that structures their lives. Again this separates them from the young characters in the film who, when they do eat, consume convenience food outside the home. The bitterness of the Monserrats' situation lies in the fact that Marcus's work has come to nothing, that their thrift and diligence has been a waste of time when time, as symbolised by the quietly ticking clock always heard in the background, is now short. Their planned escape from this involves taking control through hypnosis of a young person's mind. In what turns out to be the film's central plot device, they will then be able to command that person from a distance and share in his or her physical experiences.

The other world given us in the film is that which belongs to and is symbolised by youth, which is seen in terms of consumption, sensation and instant gratification. As Marcus and Estelle characterise it in describing the intended outcome of their own experiments: 'Dazzling, indescribable experience. Complete abandonment with no thought of remorse . . . Intoxication with no hangover. Ecstasy with no consequence.' Very little time is spent on showing the young characters – the hero Mike Roscoe, his girlfriend Nicole, their friend Alan – at work. Mike shuts his antique shop whenever he wants (we only see him with a customer once) and Alan takes time off from the garage where he works to go and see Nicole at a moment's notice. For most of the film these characters are presented as consumers, not only of food and drink but also of lifestyle and experience.

Bearing in mind the relative youth of the film's director, one might argue for the following reading of *The Sorcerers*: the innocent young, represented here most visibly by Mike, enjoying a lifestyle that is free and centred on pleasure and consumption, are threatened and eventually destroyed by the jealous, repressive older forces in society. In this way the film might be seen as predicting the increasing repression directed against various aspects of youth culture as the decade progressed.

However, a closer examination of *The Sorcerers* reveals that in fact the film is much more ambivalent than this. The Monserrats, rather than being destroyers, are themselves destroyed by this sensational world. On one level, this destruction involves a critique of the lifestyle and values of a consumption-centred youth culture which is seen to encourage a desire for sensation that can never be satisfied. On another, more submerged level, what one also finds is a concern with shifting understandings of gender, and in particular female sexuality

Taking the question of the youth lifestyle first, the film suggests that a barely hidden violence lurks beneath the colourful hedonism. It can be found in some of the songs heard during the narrative. Pirie has already indicated this in respect of the sequence in which Reeves cuts from Roscoe stabbing a woman to death with a pair of scissors (intercut with Estelle's reaction to this) to a female nightclub singer singing 'Boy, you're coming on strong now'; another lyric relevant to Mike's increasingly schizophrenic actions is 'You're tearing me apart.' It can also be located in some of the tensions arising from the triangular Mike–Nicole–Alan relationship. This is apparent from the beginning when Mike rudely leaves Nicole behind in the nightclub; later he will be repeatedly rude to and contemptuous of Alan. In this sense later developments – such as a hypnotised Mike yet again standing up Nicole or fighting with Alan in the garage – are only extensions of elements that were already present before the Monserrat intervention.

The notion of the Monserrats as preying upon youth culture is further undercut by the fact that their principal victim, Mike, is clearly shown as an untypical representative of that way of life. He exists on the periphery of the world of normality that is represented by Alan and Nicole. At the beginning of the film he sits alone in the nightclub, excluding himself from social interaction, an observer looking in. In this way he is in a similar position to the Monserrats. 'How long do you think all this can last?' he asks as he surveys the club – his remark ostensibly directed at female fashion but having distinctly apocalyptic undertones – and then announces his boredom and his intention to go for a solitary walk. Alan's response to this moodiness is significant. 'Bloody artistic temperament,' he retorts. This connects with other remarks directed against Mike, mainly in jest by Alan – for example, when he refers to him as both a Boy Wonder and a 'poor misunderstood lad' – and suggests that Mike Roscoe is supposed to be viewed as a youthful artistic figure, albeit a non-productive one. To a certain extent, he functions as a stand-in for Reeves himself (another Boy Wonder), Reeves, that is, as an artist–director. This is announced not only through the similarity of names but also by the presence of Ian Ogilvy in the role. This actor, a close friend of the director who bears a distinct physical resemblance to him, is used in a similar way in the later *Witchfinder General*. It should be stressed here, however, that what is being constructed in this instance is a particular image of the artist which functions figuratively within the text, and we actually need to know very little about Reeves's personality, about Reeves the real person, to understand how this image works.

For Roscoe, the sensitive artistic personality, the excluded observer, the youth culture of the day is ephemeral, superficial, without substantial meaning. He moodily wanders the streets in search of an indefinable something. In this sense he fulfils the requirements the Monserrats have of their first guinea-pig. 'He must be someone whose mind is pliable, someone who is basically willing . . . A boy who is bored, out looking for something.' The hypnosis which will render Mike the tool and surrogate of the Monserrats takes place in Marcus's laboratory – its psychedelic visual and aural presentation connoting a drug experience – and Mike becomes an extension of the Monserrats, who are eventually destroyed by Estelle's increasingly monstrous desires for new sensual experiences.

It has been argued that within contemporary industrial society, where art exists on the margins, the artist only has two choices: 'to refuse the marginalised position allotted to artists and organise with other artists to make a political intervention into society; or to accept the futility of artistic production and continue to work entirely for his or her own sake, a retreat from politics into solipsism'.[16] These remarks occur in a discussion of the work of Ingmar Bergman but are applicable, despite the different generic context, to *The Sorcerers* inasmuch as the figure of the artist, the Romantic (or rather romanticised), politically uncommitted artist, is shown as having no way forward.[17] More particularly, the film can be seen as speaking from Reeves's class position, operating as both a variant of and a response to one of the two pathways available within the essentially middle-class counter-culture of the period. 'The two most distinctive strands flow, one way, via drugs, mysticism, the "revolution in lifestyle" into a Utopian alternative culture; or, the other way, via community action, protest action and libertarian goals into a more activist politics.'[18] While *The Sorcerers* – with its psychedelic imagery – clearly refuses the overtly political route, neither does it produce a Utopian answer to social ills. Instead, society is seen as incurably sick and destructive, polluted by a contagious violence that leaves the artist impotent.

Beneath this despairing response, however, there lies a more literal impotence connected with the possibility of an active female desire, a desire which resists male definitions and thereby threatens and undermines male identity. In many ways, this constitutes the real issue around which *The Sorcerers* is constructed and to which it is a response. One can in this respect point to the weak men who appear throughout the film: Mike, Marcus Monserrat (crippled, dominated by his wife) and the policemen, conventional figures of male authority but here quite ineffective.

Predictably, one can place alongside these representations of a troubled heterosexual masculinity the presence of several independent women. The most obvious example of this is Estelle, a character who dominates her husband Marcus both mentally and physically through most of the film and is increasingly driven by her own selfish desires (which stand opposed to Marcus's avowed humanitarian aims in initiating their experiment); her demands for more intense experience lead to Mike's committing socially transgressive acts on her behalf, first theft and then murder. Eventually this results in her own and Marcus's death when Mike, fleeing from the police, is burned to death in a car crash and the Monserrats, still bound to his physical sensations, suffer the same fate. (The crash is in fact willed by Marcus in order to stop his wife. It is one of his few effective acts in the film, albeit in this case a suicidal one.)

Significantly, the two women murdered by Mike are also shown as independent. The first of these, Audrey, an old friend, apparently lives alone. When she lets Mike in, she is only partially dressed and yet she stands before him quite unselfconsciously, an image of autonomy (albeit limited – the bedsit is very small). The second murder victim is a nightclub singer whom Mike lures to her death by pretending to have found her a job. Just before he strangles her, he taunts her professional aspirations: 'Sing for us. Sing!' he shouts.

A ribald joke made by Alan's boss is revealing in this respect. As

Alan leaves for a date with Nicole, he calls after him 'Make sure she's on the pill.' The oral contraceptive, introduced in Britain in the late 1950s, had transformed the lives of many women. As Jeffrey Weeks notes:

> it opened up more decisively the possibility for the incorporation of the active, if male-defined, sexuality of women into the repertoire of public debate, including advertising and publishing. The eroticisation of modern culture could focus on the female body without most of the consequences which in earlier days had been feared and expected.[19]

The 'male-defined' part of this statement is important for as Weeks notes elsewhere: 'There was little in the original American or British counter-culture that indicated any rejection of stereotypes of women and gays.'[20] In fact, one can go further and argue that the figure of the sexually active woman was to function as a symbol of the permissive society, just as the mother in the domestic household had come to symbolise much of consumerist society in the 1950s; and that the women's movement arose within this context in part as a reaction against this objectification.

That there is a cruel, secondary punchline to this 'joke' becomes apparent when Reeves cuts from the garage to a close-up of Estelle's aged face. The non-reproductive sexuality associated with the oral contraceptive is thereby given us in two contrasting ways. First, it is seen as enabling the sexual availability of women to men (Alan, in this case) in what is essentially a restructuring of male-centred discourses of femininity. Second, through an image of a woman who is because of her age 'non-reproductive', Reeves points to the potential for a disruption and undermining of these discourses that a shift away from reproductivity might entail; significantly in this respect, the first command Estelle gives to Mike is to break an egg. Estelle is the only character in *The Sorcerers* who exhibits decisiveness and ambition. Consequently, the film very much centres on and is driven by her desires; and it is the prospect of a woman actively desiring rather than being the desired object that it finds alternately so appalling and so enthralling, and which it works both to signify and manage. It is a condition of this recognition that Estelle is old and conventionally unattractive, so that what is a gender problem can be displaced onto a generational division. But it should now be clear that to all intents and purposes, Estelle's desires – which lead to theft and then murder – constitute the dark, transgressive possibilities of a particular male-centred definition of gender which has also produced the young, sexually available women found elsewhere in the film (two of whom are murdered by Mike).

The prospect of femininity breaking the bounds of male discourses – subsequently materialised in the various forms of the Women's Movement – is the crisis which the film identifies and with which it is working. In this sense, Mike's repeated acts of violence against women are more an expression of his own male fears than they are the result of Estelle's commands. For example, at a moment when his mind is temporarily free of the Monserrat influence, he refers to the nightclub singer as a 'slag'. That Estelle is notionally in charge of Mike when he commits his murderous acts does not undermine such a reading, although importantly it does reveal that a condition of the film's (often disguised) insights into contemporaneous shifts in gender definition is its inability to develop these in any potentially radical direction. Estelle does not recognise herself in the murdered women; this failure of recognition, and the rigorous separation of Estelle's situation from that of other females it involves, effectively depoliticises the film in which it appears.

Also contributing to a process of displacement is the tendency of the film – which it shares with *Witchfinder General* – to lapse into an all-encompassing, nihilistic despair, with this providing a useful and reassuring escape route from more disturbing, necessarily political considerations. The film concludes with the simultaneous deaths of Mike and Estelle. Mike dies very publicly in a car crash, with Nicole and Alan looking on; Estelle, by way of a contrast, lies dead alongside her husband in the privacy of their home. Her death is secret and hidden, just as the threatening female desire she represents is, in a sense, the film's secret, that which is hidden behind the more visible story of an artistic sensibility despairing in a corrupt world.

Witchfinder General

Witchfinder General is a fictionalised account of the activities of real-life witchfinder Matthew Hopkins (played in the film by Vincent Price), who operated in East Anglia during the English Civil War.[21] The film's hero is Richard Marshall (Ian Ogilvy), a soldier in Cromwell's army who swears revenge against Hopkins after the witchfinder has hanged as a witch the uncle of Sara Lowes, Marshall's fiancée, and slept with Sara herself; the narrative is concluded by a bloody scene in a torture chamber where Hopkins is brutally attacked by an axe-wielding Marshall and is then shot dead by another soldier.

Despite the move from the contemporary London settings of *The Sorcerers* to the seventeenth-century English countryside that provides the locations for *Witchfinder General*, both films can be seen as dealing with the same issue: namely, the difficulties involved in the maintenance of a male authority that is largely dependent upon female submission in the face of an increased female resistance to this submissive role. In the case of *The Sorcerers*, a representation of violent generational conflict to a certain extent works to cover over an awareness of shifts in the ways in which gender identity was understood at the time of the film's production; the prospect of the desiring woman is simultaneously invoked and hidden away within the film. In this way the film seeks to legitimise the despair of Mike Roscoe, the 'Romantic' artist figure over what is offered, on one level at least, as an irredeemably corrupt world.

A similar situation is evinced in *Witchfinder General*. On the one hand, there is in this film an even more powerful and wide-ranging investigation of issues relating to gender, particularly in its representation of a violently repressive male denial of a female subjectivity. But on the other hand, one also finds attempts to construct a 'despairing', i.e. non-gendered reading of this situation, one in which the pain and suffering so clearly in evidence are not marked as specifically 'male' or 'female' but instead seen in toto as 'human' and existential. In this way, the film, like *The Sorcerers*, seeks to avoid some of the more disturbing implications of its own insights. However, the analysis of *Witchfinder General* that follows will demonstrate that these attempts to contain or efface gender-related issues are not as effective as they were in *The Sorcerers*. Consequently *Witchfinder General* is an extremely fractured, disturbed film. In this it can be aligned with Hammer's *The Gorgon*; both offer a recognition of the female's separateness from male-centred definitions and placings of her which threatens a male authority and identity upon which the films are themselves founded. A crucial difference between the two is that Reeves's film – faster-paced than Fisher's and a great deal more violent – comprises a more complex and troubled acting out of this situation.

An examination of the opening minutes of *Witchfinder General* reveals some of the tensions – which in the end will prove irreconcilable

– operative within the film. The first shot of the film gives an initial impression of tranquillity: the sun shines through tree branches while hammering and sheep bleating are heard on the soundtrack. After a near-complete scaffold is shown (the source of the hammering sound), there is a cut to the village where the 'witch' is being dragged screaming down a street. These unsettling transitions – from an image of nature to an image of social violence, from the quiet of the countryside to the woman's screams, from peace to violence – occur throughout the film and can be aligned with Reeves's juxtaposing the opposed worlds of young and old at the beginning of *The Sorcerers*: in this sense, the violence in these films is as much an effect of mise-en-scene as it is a result of characters' actions.

Perhaps more importantly, this strategy also involves the juxta-position of images of a society seen as endemically violent with images of a pacific Nature, with the natural world providing a calm and indifferent backdrop to the events of the drama.[22] One of the possible effects of this is to render the violence in the film, most of which is actually directed against women, a general factor of this 'alienation' from nature; that is, humanity *as a whole* is marked as brutalised. (In support of this, one can note that the crowds who provide the audience for this and other public executions in the film comprise both men and women.) The gender-specific qualities of violence are thereby avoided or hidden. Having said this, however, it is questionable whether such a strategy succeeds to any great extent in the opening sequence, or for that matter at any other point in the film. Much of the undoubted impact of the film's various hangings and other atrocities arises from the helplessness and terror of the *female* victim (which can be contrasted with the more restrained reactions to torture later in the film of John Lowes, a male victim.)

This tension between vivid and shocking images of women oppressed and suffering and attempts to universalise (i.e. 'degender') this suffering is further elaborated in *Witchfinder General*'s striking credit sequence (which follows immediately on from the hanging of the 'witch'). In this one finds an assertion of a particular mystificatory notion of authorship and the artist akin to that embodied by the character of Mike Roscoe in *The Sorcerers*. This credit sequence consists of distorted, grainy photographs of various individuals, male and female, suffering and in pain (with one image of Stearne, the witchfinder's assistant, laughing). The final image shown is that of a human face – it is difficult to say whether it is male or female –

contorted into a scream. Over this face appears Michael Reeves's directorial credit. The statement thereby implied could not be clearer. The artist is in despair, a despair which is existential, outside history, ungendered, beyond analysis.

While such a reading of the credit sequence is available if one views it in isolation, this visualisation of generalised, universal despair becomes questionable when seen in the context of the sequence that has preceded it, a sequence that so obviously centres on the victimisation of the woman. Indeed this is the case throughout the film, as 'despairing' moments (often associated with the representation of an indifferent Nature) constantly give way to a compelling portrayal of the repressions involved in a male objectification of the female.

This portrayal – which can be seen as the film's other project, that which sits alongside and threatens to overwhelm the artist's despair – is developed in the sequence that follows the credits. Like the hanging sequence, it relies for much of its effect on counterpointing an act of human violence – in this instance Richard Marshall's killing of a sniper – with an incongruously beautiful Nature.[23] The essential difference between these two sequences, that is underlined precisely by these similarities, arises from the social spheres within which the depicted actions take place. In the first sequence this is the civil world whereas in the second the setting is one of military conflict. What this suggests is that the collapse of social order attendant upon the Civil War is not only played out in a conventional military fashion – with Cromwell (who, played by Patrick Wymark, makes a brief appearance in the film) as the new symbolic father, the father of the nation, leading the fight – but also has disturbing implications for social definitions and understandings of gender, with Matthew Hopkins, the Witchfinder, as the authority figure in this case.

Perhaps the most important point to note about the scenes dealing with military life is that they are exclusively male. Women do not even appear as extras. What one finds instead is a male bonding that exists within, and is legitimated by, a tightly organised power structure (with an authoritative but fair Cromwell at its head), with all this reminiscent of certain British war films from the 1950s. In this case it would be going too far to argue, as Andy Medhurst has done for those war films, that:

> In the same way that the Western foregrounds intense relationships between men, the war film could be seen as occupying an equivalent

position in British cinema, a licensed space for the otherwise inexpressible. Both genres depend on assumptions of masculinity that protected their characters from 'accusations' of homosexuality.[24]

The military scenes in *Witchfinder General* are too perfunctorily done for that (this might have something to do with extreme budgetary restrictions, but could also reflect the film's lack of faith precisely in those institutions it desires to value). Nevertheless, the existence of an all-male space that is separate from civil society is important for the progression of the film as a whole, operating as it does as a place of relative safety where the only danger comes from other men and from which Marshall ventures at his peril. Within the army he is a hero, outside he becomes psychotic. This is made clear when, on returning from the army on leave, he embraces Sara. 'The army has taught you rough manners,' she exclaims as she pushes him away, a temporary act of resistance which marks the separateness of Sara's world from that of the male militia and the need for modified behaviour therein.

Connected with this, and achieved in much greater detail, is the relationship between the Witchfinder and his assistant Stearne, which, while having distinct homo-erotic qualities, can also be seen as a parody of a heterosexual union. This is apparent in the incessant, semi-comic 'rowing' that goes on between them. More particularly, Hopkins's affair with Sara clearly provokes Stearne's jealousy – 'I hear tell you've been a-wandering, Matthew' – which is directed principally at Matthew rather than at the woman. Stearne's subsequent rape of Sara, when seen in this light, is a tactic designed to win Matthew back to him more than a display of lust and male power (although it is also that). The threat to this male couple then and also, implicitly, to the relationship between Marshall and his fellow soldiers, that which threatens to break the male bond, is the female. At the same time, it is the woman – the woman as object – through whom these relationships, and male identity in general, are often figured. One thinks here of a short scene near the film's beginning where Marshall and a fellow soldier Swallow discuss the absent Sara; later Marshall and John Lowes and then Hopkins and Stearne will also talk of Sara in her absence. In these moments, the figure of the woman is used to bind together and support male relationships, but she does not herself actively participate in this. (Significantly, Sara is never seen talking to another woman.)

The way in which *Witchfinder General* positions itself in relation to this exclusion and objectification of the woman becomes clearer when one turns to its presentation of its one developed female character, Sara Lowes, later to become Sara Marshall. Sara is presented to us – through script, direction and most of all through Hilary Dwyer's sensitive performance – as intelligent and articulate, sufficiently strong willed to resist some of Richard's rougher advances, quick witted and worldly enough to negotiate her uncle's remission from torture through offering herself sexually to Hopkins. One can also note in this respect the scene of her lovemaking with Richard, with its stress on her pleasure as well as his. However, she is surrounded by men who objectify her in various ways. Her uncle sees her as an innocent young woman, unaware as he is of her physical relationship with Richard and her obvious knowledge of the ways of the world as displayed in her scenes with the Witchfinder. For Hopkins, she is first a sexual object, then an object of a thwarted romantic fantasy (implied by the sadness on his face after being informed of Stearne's rape of Sara) and then an object of torture, a weapon to be used against her husband. Finally, for Richard, after Hopkins's intervention, she becomes that upon which his desire for revenge is constructed. This is apparent in the wedding ceremony when, after having solemnly declared their union and without pausing for breath, Richard swears a bloody oath of vengeance. For him, Sara and his own wild justice are inextricably connected. (The expression on Sara's face indicates that she is disturbed by this but, traumatised as she is, she remains silent throughout the ceremony.) This reaches its logical conclusion when, towards the end of the film, Richard allows Sara to be tortured before him rather than confess to the hated Witchfinder.

The final tableau of the film – which takes place in a torture chamber – comprises a particularly charged enactment of those irreconcilable tensions that structure the film as a whole. Stearne is on the dungeon floor, one of his eyes kicked in by Marshall's spur. Hopkins is dead, victim of Marshall's axe attack and Swallow's merciful bullet. Sara is lying face down on a slab, tortured, almost certainly insane. Richard too is mad, shouting at an uncomprehending Swallow who has just shot Hopkins 'You took him from me. You took him from me.'

Throughout its running length, *Witchfinder General* has represented male identity as essentially a narcissistic construct, a meeting of men in which the woman as object is central but the real woman, woman as subject, is absent. This situation, hardly a desirable one, is reiterated in the physical configuration of the final scene. Two soldiers staring at each other, with another dead man between them. The woman is to one side, excluded from this drama (although it is because of her – or rather Hopkins's and Marshall's emotional investment in her – that all this has happened). It is another male-centred world in which women are troubling objects/subjects within the relationships between men. By this time Sara has more or less ceased to exist for Richard, whose sole concern is the prolongation of Hopkins's suffering, as if it is only through this that he can achieve a degree of completeness.

But this, extraordinarily powerful in itself, is by no means the whole story, for this scene also brings about a final undoing of the other project of the film, namely the construction of a discourse of 'despair' – expressed via the film's mise-en-scene, the insistence therein on the intractable division between the beauty of Nature and a degraded humanity – by which woman-as-subject and the disruption of the genre she brings can be effaced. At the end of *Witchfinder General* the camera cuts away from a close-up of Sara screaming to shots of the interior of the castle. It then cuts back to her. The image freezes and the end credits and music begin, with Sara's screaming continuing in the background. The scream functions on one level as a sign of Sara's final traumatic objectification. On another, however, it resists the directorial control marked by the freeze frame. The existential, despairing scream in the credit sequence has here become a real scream, that is a scream arising from a vividly portrayed male violence, a violence which seeks to preserve a certain masculine stability and power. It is a sign of the irrefutable presence of the woman-as-subject within this world, and it marks a recognition on the film's part that the reinstatement of certainty in gender definition around which classic Hammer horror had been structured involves the violent (re)objectification of the woman. Of course, such a recognition was already present in *Witchfinder General*'s depiction of the monstrously repressive actions of certain male characters – most notably Hopkins and Stearne but by the film's conclusion Marshall as well. But at this concluding moment, the moment of Sara's scream, *Witchfinder General*, unlike *The Sorcerers* at its conclusion, relinquishes its hold on even the possibility of returning to the certainties embodied in an earlier type of horror film. The despair of the conclusion in this sense arises from an inability to go further, to put something else, something more positive, in its stead.

The reasons behind this urge to return to classic Hammer have already been noted in our discussion of *The Sorcerers*; in particular, the shifting position of the woman and definitions of femininity within 1960s Britain, the contradiction between her desire and her as symbol of the permissive society. It is significant in this respect, although one cannot suppose a direct, causal connection, that *Witchfinder General* is produced at the very beginning of the women's movement, which itself arose in part as a reaction against the male-centredness of certain permissive discourses.[25] It can be argued that Reeves, in making *Witchfinder General*, exhibited both a sensitivity to strains and tensions within British society at this time and an awareness of the challenge these presented for a type of filmmaking to which he was artistically committed, and the film that resulted from this is an intensely imagined struggle – and eventual failure – to pull these elements together into a coherent whole.

One can speculate endlessly on how Reeves might have proceeded, if indeed he could have, from the apparently intractable blockage that his final film identifies and which it is unable to transcend. However, as a partial antidote to such speculation, we can now turn to a director who in *The Gorgon*, made four years before *Witchfinder General*, had engaged with a similar problem, albeit in a less charged and violent way. The director is Terence Fisher, whose Hammer film *The Devil Rides Out* was released in the same year as *Witchfinder General*.

The Devil Rides Out

At first glance, Terence Fisher's *The Devil Rides Out*, a notable product of the old school, appears to have little in common with Reeves's *Witchfinder General*. Indeed it would seem to represent a type of horror film against which Reeves and other young filmmakers were reacting. Made by an older director (Fisher was sixty-four in 1968), with many of the creative personnel responsible for Hammer horror from the mid-1950s onwards, it embodied all those qualities associated with Hammer in the 1956–64 period, and, in particular, films directed by Fisher himself. Devices which characterise Reeves's work – particularly the use of zooms and a handheld camera – are alien to Fisher's approach: indeed he has openly expressed his dislike of such techniques.²⁶ His films are characterised instead by compositional balance, smooth tracks and symmetrical editing patterns, with these in turn linked with a moral certainty whereby good (represented in this film by the Duc de Richleau/Christopher Lee) and evil (represented by Mocata/Charles Gray) are implacably and unambiguously opposed. Nevertheless, it can be argued that *The Devil Rides Out* is engaging with socially and historically specific issues and causes for concern which overlap with those identified by *Witchfinder General*. That each offers a different treatment of these issues can be ascribed to the different ideologies (of class, gender and cultural production) within and through which they are produced.

Some structural parallels are immediately apparent. Both films centre upon a young man and woman – Richard and Sara in *Witchfinder General* and Simon and Tanith in *The Devil Rides Out* – who are caught between two father figures, one good and the other bad – Cromwell and Hopkins in *Witchfinder General*, Richleau and Mocata in *The Devil Rides Out*. Differences arise from the way in which these young characters are treated and valued. Reeves, the young director, invests them, initially at least, with a degree of psychological autonomy, although, as has been shown, this is by no means an unproblematic support for a youth revolution. Fisher's younger characters, on the other hand, are viewed as weak and unstable, requiring the steadying assistance of a benevolent father figure. Both Simon and Tanith are susceptible to the evil influence of Mocata, and whatever Richleau and his assistant Rex do to them is for their own good. These actions range from simple commands through hypnosis – Richleau hypnotises Simon and controls Tanith's spirit via a hypnotised Marie (a sort of hypnosis by proxy) – to physical violence – Simon knocked unconscious by Richleau, Tanith tied up by Rex.

However, the view of Richleau as an essentially benevolent figure is consciously undermined by the film through the stress it puts on similarities between Richleau and Mocata. Both are well-dressed, knowledgeable figures of authority. Both make extensive use of hypnosis, with each hypnotising Simon, Tanith and Marie during the film. Both talk of Simon as a son; Richleau, who promised Simon's father he would look after his son, on discovering Simon's involvement with black magic remarks 'I feel like a father who sees his child trying to pick live coals out of the fire'; Mocata on Simon's return to the coven greets him with 'Welcome back, my son.'²⁷

What both Richleau and Mocata represent is a clarity and force of vision, a certainty lacking in the younger characters. It is interesting in this respect to note the changes that Hammer made to the character of Mocata. In Dennis Wheatley's original novel he is described by Richleau thus: 'He's a pot-bellied, bald-headed person of about sixty, with large, protuberant, fishy eyes, limp hands, and a most unattractive lisp. He reminded me of a large white slug.'[28] In the film he is transformed through the casting of suave Charles Gray in the part; handsome in appearance, precise in diction, his power and authority stressed as is that of Richleau by Lee's characteristically authoritative performance.

Both Tanith and Simon oscillate helplessly between the Satanists and Richleau. At the same time Marie Eaton, Richleau's niece, and her husband Richard (especially the latter) exhibit scepticism in the face of Richleau's learned warnings against demonic forces. In the climactic scene within the circle, it is Simon, Marie and Richard who are pressured by Mocata while in each case it is the knowledgeable Richleau who leads the resistance. This clear vision is, appropriately, often signalled through a visual play on eyes and looking, most obviously in the various hypnosis scenes but also elsewhere. For example, when Richleau first appears he is looking through a pair of binoculars. Later two important scenes take place in an observatory with a telescope clearly visible in the background. In the second of these, a demon appears whose power seems to emanate from its eyes. Richleau orders Rex not to look, as later he will instruct the Eatons and Simon not to look. Only he has the requisite knowledge, the visionary ability, to dispel the power of evil.

Both good and bad father figures exhibit an absolute authority, the film implies, but in the right hands that power over the young, which on occasions takes the form of physical violence, is necessary. Needless to say, it is an equation which leaves youth incapable of self-determination, and in this the film is clearly supportive of a paternalist ideology that is perfectly in keeping with both the age and gender of the filmmakers and the positive valuing of the social authority deriving from the male professional which, as has been demonstrated, characterised Hammer production in the late 1950s and 1960s.

It is reported that Fisher chose actress Nike Arrighi for the part of Tanith in the face of resistance from the studio.[29] Certainly she is an unconventional Hammer lead with her fragile features and deep voice. This break with tradition can be seen as marking a shift in the position of the woman within Hammer horror that can be linked to shifts observable in *The Sorcerers* and *Witchfinder General*, and some of the implications of this can be traced in the penultimate sequence of *The Devil Rides Out* which takes place within the Satanist temple. Richleau, Rex, Marie and Richard enter and look on helplessly as Mocata prepares to sacrifice Peggy, Marie and

Richard's young daughter. Marie implores Richleau to speak the magical words which saved them before, but Richleau, afraid of the consequences of such an action, refuses. At this point Marie speaks with the voice of the recently deceased Tanith: 'Only those who love without desire shall have power granted them in their darkest hour'. She then says the magical words herself, Peggy repeats them, the temple crumbles, the satanists are destroyed and, in the next sequence, Tanith is restored to life.

The important thing to note here is that Tanith's spirit is not summoned by Richleau, as it is earlier in the film when the Duc's commands to her are particularly forceful. Instead it comes of its own free will. It is her first free action in the film, that is, one not ordered by Mocata or Richleau, or arising as a direct consequence of their actions. A 'speaking union' of three women is thereby formed in order to protect Peggy and destroy Mocata. In this way

6 *[facing] and* **7** The Duc de Richleau (Christopher Lee) and Mocata (Charles Gray) in *The Devil Rides Out*. Two well-dressed, knowledgeable figures of authority

the film creates a space for the exercise of a female power and desire and the acknowledgement of woman as an independent speaking subject (posited earlier in *The Gorgon* but not there achieved), something that an anguished *Witchfinder General* could only imagine in the form of a scream. That *The Devil Rides Out* is by no means as disturbed a text as *Witchfinder General*, that it can accommodate with apparent ease an acknowledgement of these shifts within a progression to a satisfying narrative conclusion (as opposed to *Witchfinder*'s collapse into insanity) can largely be put down to the film's unwavering faith in and identification with an essentially patriarchal power and authority. So, at the film's conclusion, Richleau can reveal that the events in the temple took place in another time, their transportation to this other place being caused by his own utterance of those words which later he dared not repeat. The space in which the female exercises power and from which the ethereal Tanith speaks is thereby marked as an illusory space *outside* the dramatic world of the film. 'Only those who love without desire shall have power granted them in their darkest hour'; in assigning these lines to Marie/Tanith the film authoritatively sets limits. Desire – that which made Estelle so threatening, Sara Marshall so appealing – is, quite simply, magicked away.[30]

The Sorcerers, *Witchfinder General* and *The Devil Rides Out* (as well as *Frankenstein Must Be Destroyed*) all articulate a situation in which a securing of a fixed male identity depends upon a violent objectification of the woman that previously in the genre had been taken completely for granted. In each, this produces an ambivalence regarding figures of male authority: on the one hand, guarantors of a reassuring security; on the other, monstrously repressive. The intense and charged qualities of each film arise from the complex imaginative strategies adopted by Reeves and Fisher, which, in the main, hold together in a dynamic relationship tensions that are unresolvable within the films' terms of reference. Hence the violent contrasts in Reeves's mise-en-scène; hence too the clear parallels drawn by Fisher between Richleau and Mocata.

Notes

1 For a discussion of Sharp's 'authorship', see David Pirie, *A Heritage of Horror: the English Gothic Cinema 1946–1972*, London, 1973, pp. 114–19. For an

interesting account of the opening of *Kiss of the Vampire*, see V. F. Perkins, *Film as Film*, Harmondsworth, 1972, pp. 176–7.

2 Pirie, *A Heritage of Horror*, p. 116.

3 John Gilling's companion piece to *Plague of the Zombies*, the similarly Cornish *The Reptile* (1966), falls into the same category, although here taking as its central theme the 'alienness' of female sexuality within a British setting.

4 Steve Neale, *Cinema and Technology: Image, Sound, Colour*, London, 1985, p. 143.

5 Ibid., p. 144.

6 'The role of the female body within the regime of representation inaugurated by the introduction of Technicolor was one both of focusing and motivating a set of colour effects within a system dependent upon plot and narration, thus providing a form of spectacle compatible with that system, and of marking and containing the erotic component involved in the desire to look at the coloured image.' Ibid., p. 155.

7 Pirie, *A Heritage of Horror*, pp. 155–6.

8 Stuart Hall et al., *Policing the Crisis – Mugging, the State, and Law and Order*, London, 1978, p. 237.

9 Stuart Hall and Tony Jefferson (eds), *Resistance through Rituals: Youth Subcultures in Post-war Britain*, London, 1976, pp. 58–9.

10 See David Caute, *Sixty-Eight: the Year of the Barricades*, London, 1988 and Ronald Fraser et al., *1968: a Student Generation in Revolt*, London, 1988.

11 Quoted in a publicity handout on Michael Reeves issued for the release of *Witchfinder General* (available in BFI library).

12 It is significant in this respect that one of the first people approached by Reeves when he went to America looking for work was director Don Siegel. As Pirie notes, the genre films of Siegel had provided a particular focus of interest for British cineastes of the late 1960s and in this can be seen as one part of the counter-cultural 'scene': Pirie, *A Heritage of Horror*, pp. 146–7.

13 *The Listener*, 23 May 1968, pp. 657–8.

14 *The Listener*, 30 May 1968, p. 704.

15 Hall and Jefferson (eds), *Resistance through Rituals*, pp. 64–5.

16 Pam Cook (ed.), *The Cinema Book*, London, 1985, p. 117.

17 Historically, of course, artists of the Romantic period had a number of complicated political allegiances: see Marilyn Butler, *Romantics, Rebels and Reactionaries: English Literature and Its Background 1760–1830*, Oxford, 1981.

18 Hall and Jefferson (eds), *Resistance through Rituals*, p. 61.

19 Jeffrey Weeks, *Sex, Politics & Society*, London, 1981, p. 260.

20 Jeffrey Weeks, *Coming Out*, London, 1977, p. 187.

21 Reeves's film was based loosely on Ronald Bassett's novel *Witchfinder General* (London, 1966), itself a part-fictionalised account of Hopkins's activities.

22 One striking example of this occurs later in the film when a wounded Stearne – the Witchfinder's assistant – removes a bullet from his arm with a torturing spike. As he screams in agony, the camera moves slowly away to a group of trees nearby.

    In his account of *Witchfinder General*, Pirie suggests that nature functions as a positive force. It seems to me, however, that nothing in the film offers itself as unequivocally positive, and that this is both the film's strength and its principal limitation. Pirie, *A Heritage of Horror*, p. 153.

23 The similarity between the two sequences is underlined by the presence in each of slow fades and tracks – rhetorical devices usually associated with a more leisurely content, their use here accentuating the violence of the drama.

24 Andy Medhurst, '1950s War Films' in Geoff Hurd (ed.), *National Fictions: World War Two in British Films and Television*, London, 1984, p. 37.

25 See Anna Coote and Beatrix Campbell, *Sweet Freedom: the Struggle for Women's Liberation*, London, 1982, pp. 9–47 for a tracing of the emergence of the Women's Movement in the late 1960s and early 1970s.

26 Terence Fisher on the handheld camera: 'It leaves me cold. The camera moves all the time, and one quite rightly wonders why'; on the zoom, 'a gadget'. Quoted in Harry Ringel, 'Hammer Horror – the World of Terence Fisher' in Thomas R. Atkins (ed.), *Graphic Violence on Screen*, New York, 1976, p. 37. However, Fisher has elsewhere expressed an admiration for *Witchfinder General*: see Harry Ringel, 'Terence Fisher Underlining', *Cinefantastique*, 4, no. 3, 1975, pp. 19–26.

27 One of the posters for the film showed a photograph of Lee balanced in the composition against a photograph of Charles Gray, with 'The Devil's Adversary' printed under the former and 'The Devil's Advocate' under the latter. Even here an awareness of a connection and similarity between these two figures is being signalled.

28 Dennis Wheatley, *The Devil Rides Out*, contained in four–novel compendium (*The Devil Rides Out, The Haunting of Toby Jugg, Gateway to Hell, To the Devil a Daughter*), London, 1980, p. 15.

29 Pirie, *A Heritage of Horror*, p. 63.

30 Two films made in this period – *Corruption* (1967, d. Robert Hartford-Davis) and *Scream and Scream Again* (1968, d. Gordon Hessler) – both depict the surgical destruction of young bodies by monstrous father figures (Peter Cushing in the first-named film, Vincent Price in the second). However – and this is the crucial difference between these films and *The Devil Rides Out* – here this is unquestioningly conflated with the destruction of the independent woman – most notably the policewoman murdered by Michael Gothard's android in *Scream and Scream Again* – resulting generally in a reactionary tone.

Horror and the family   6

The marginalisation of both Count Dracula and Baron Frankenstein in British horror cinema of the 1970s was only one part of a much wider rejection and casting out of those male authority figures who had been so important in earlier Hammer horrors. At the same time the question of the woman's desire – a troubling element in *The Sorcerers* and *The Devil Rides Out* – became a more pressing and unavoidable issue in 1970s horror, with this sometimes having surprising consequences for the sorts of films actually produced.

Clearly an important factor in this disruption of male authority, one that impinged on horror from outside, was the historical challenge delivered by the feminist movement of the early 1970s. But this needs to be linked with other influential factors, both those within and those outside the film industry. For instance, one can point to the increasingly politicised and rebellious youth culture of this period (youth, of course, being the principal target audience of British horror), with its vociferous dissatisfaction with and alienation from many of society's traditions and institutions and the often paternal authority embodied by these.

As far as the film industry itself was concerned, there was a general withdrawal of American finance in the early 1970s, coupled with steadily decreasing admission figures. This precipitated a series of crises in the industry. Because of both this and the decreasing popularity of its films in the States, Hammer, still the leading British horror company although now much less of a force in world horror, made fewer films with US money, turning instead to British companies like EMI for finance. (Indeed, some of its later films – *The Satanic Rites of Dracula* and *Legend of the Seven Golden Vampires*, for example – did not receive a wide US release.)[1] In the context of a decreasing home market and uncertain US sales more exploitable trends came to the fore. To a certain extent, this explains the proliferation of nudity and violence found within the genre in the 1970s.[2] It also explains why there was a general lowering of budgets, which had never been generous, as the decade progressed.

One result of these financial pressures upon the genre was the blandness of style which permeates many 1970s horror films. Nevertheless, significant work was still being done. This chapter will explore in particular the often ambivalent response of British horror filmmakers to the diminution or 'death' of the genre's fictional fathers. Of course, this sort of ambivalence had been seen before in the genre – in some of the later Frankenstein films, for example – but by this stage the possibilities for recuperation, for a covering over or an evasion of problems associated with male identity and authority, appear to have become extremely limited.

A figure that appears in British horror for the first time in the 1970s and expresses in a very concise way many of the ambiguities and contradictions of this period merits some discussion here. She is Carmilla, the lesbian vampire.

Carmilla

> 'I have never had a friend – shall I find one now?' She sighed, and her fine dark eyes gazed passionately on me. Now the truth is, I felt rather unaccountably towards the beautiful stranger. I did feel, as she said, 'drawn towards her', but there was also something of repulsion. In this ambiguous feeling, however, the sense of attraction immensely prevailed. She interested and won me; she was so beautiful and so indescribably engaging. (*Carmilla*)[3]

> By showing the lesbian as a vampire–rapist who violates and destroys her victim, men alleviate their fears that lesbian love could create an alternate model, that two women without coercion or morbidity might prefer one another to a man.[4]

The 'ambiguous feeling' of the female narrator of J. Sheridan LeFanu's *Carmilla* (1872), the novel upon which Hammer's *The Vampire Lovers* (1970, d. Roy Ward Baker), was based, betrays an ambivalence towards the figure of the lesbian vampire. On the one hand, indeed a 'vampire–rapist', a destroyer of young, innocent women; on the other, a sexual liberator of females trapped within patriarchal households and definitions of the feminine.[5] The novel acknowledges the strictly limited social confines of the woman's existence, with father and daughter leading a near solitary existence in a lonely castle. It is precisely these limits that Carmilla challenges.

Throughout she is characterised both by movement – she enters the tale in a careering carriage, the heroine Laura deduces that she has travelled great distances – and an ability to transcend boundaries; for example, the scenes in which she mysteriously disappears from a locked bedroom. The conclusion of the tale, in which she is trapped within her own coffin by various father figures, staked, decapitated and her body burned marks the cessation of that threatening mobility (threatening that is to patriarchal definitions of the place of the woman). However, it is a conclusion which does not fully contain that threat. Disturbing elements escape: for example, the fact that Laura is related on her mother's side to the vampiric Karnstein family; and stylistically, in the haunting qualities of the final lines: 'and often from a reverie I have started, fancying I heard the light step of Carmilla at the drawing-room door.'

One significant change made in the adaptation from novel to film was the characterisation of Carmilla. In LeFanu's tale she gives the appearance of being eighteen years old, 'slender and wonderfully graceful' while in the film, as played by Ingrid Pitt, she is obviously older and with a much more aggressive physical presence (a 'sexual juggernaut' according to one critic). This connects with a greater stress in the film on the inadequacy of male authority and power in the face of the threat she presents. Significantly, as was the case with the earlier *Dead of Night* and Hammer's own *The Gorgon*, this male inadequacy often takes the form of a diminution of the power of a man's vision.

The film's opening sequence, in which Baron Hartog attempts to destroy the vampiric Karnsteins, is instructive in this respect. That Hartog is doing this to avenge his beloved sister rather than a lover hints perhaps at a degree of sexual immaturity, the nature of which becomes clearer as the sequence progresses. Hartog steals the vampire's shroud and retires to a nearby tower where he awaits the undead's return. Eventually it appears, covered from head to foot in a voluminous white garment, moving through the mist in slow motion, one of the moments of 'intense dream-like beauty' discerned by Pirie throughout the Karnstein trilogy.[6] Hartog leans out of a window and waves the shroud in the air – a curiously childish gesture, which is followed by a close-up of the vampire's bloody mouth. He waits, sword in hand, as the vampire approaches. It turns out to be a beautiful woman. Hartog is transfixed as she advances, smiling, upon him. Suddenly his crucifix brushes against her breast, she bares her fangs and is promptly decapitated by the Baron.

This sequence clearly deploys sexually charged imagery. The bloody mouth, and the fanged, phallic power it represents, can be

8 Ingrid Pitt as Carmilla in *The Vampire Lovers*

read in this respect as a vagina dentata, with the decapitation which comprises the male response to this functioning as a kind of symbolic castration. Significantly, as far as some of our later remarks are concerned, the abrupt transition of the female vampire from beauty to destructiveness, especially when combined with Hartog's childish attributes, also suggests an alternation between a good, loving mother figure and a bad devouring mother figure. The power of this 'phallic' woman, it is implied, is in part the power of the mother over the child before the intervention of the Law of the Father – symbolised in this instance by the crucifix. (This approach can be associated with the work of psychoanalyst Melanie Klein, some of whose ideas feature later in this chapter.)

This configuration – man looking at woman followed by images of powerlessness – recurs throughout the film. For example, on the death of his niece, General Spielsdorf, who has been looking at Carmilla, drops his gaze. When he raises it, Carmilla, impossibly, has vanished. As Spielsdorf shouts her name, a succession of shots show empty rooms and corridors, the absence of Carmilla from all these reiterating her absence from the place of Spielsdorf's gaze. Here the patriarch is 'de-throned' through a revelation of the inadequacy of his gaze. Later, towards the end of the film, Carl, the film's notional hero, confronts Carmilla – whose mouth is bloody – with a sword which she promptly knocks out of his hand. In this revision of the opening sequence, the significance of this act could hardly be clearer. The conclusion to the film, in which Spielsdorf, Roger Morton and Baron Hartog together destroy a sleeping, unresisting Carmilla is, when seen in this context, hardly the climactic heroic victory of good over evil that one found in the earlier *Dracula*. Here instead the patriarchal order attains victory only through the total passivity of the threatening woman, a further sign of the inadequacy of that order as revealed in the film.

Placed alongside this vivid depiction of male inadequacy are scenes – usually taking place in domestic settings like bedrooms and corridors – in which male characters are either marginal or absent and where female characters look at each other in an erotically charged way. The central scene here is that in which Carmilla and Emma, the latter the daughter of Roger Morton, romp, semi-nude, through Carmilla's bedroom in the Morton household. On one level, these scenes service the commercial requirement for an exploitable female nudity.[7] But at the same time they signal a split in the film regarding the way in which the female body is represented. In some sequences (most notably the opening), it is, traditionally for British horror, the focus for childlike male fears and anxieties. In other sequences, it is the site for an essentially narcissistic female desire which the film insistently equates with lesbianism (this narcissism underlined by the fact that the female characters are often dressed alike, in long white nightgowns).

In its representation of female desire, *The Vampire Lovers* can be aligned with *The Devil Rides Out*: both acknowledge a female desire that is, to a certain extent, independent of male control while at the same time banishing this desire to a separate 'manless' space. But unlike *The Devil Rides Out*, *The Vampire Lovers* lacks an authoritative figure like Christopher Lee's Duc de Richleau (or even Mocata) to guarantee a patriarchal order. Hence the relative paucity of action in *The Vampire Lovers*: until near the end of the film no male character seems capable of doing anything to defeat Carmilla. However, despite this, *The Vampire Lovers* does place distinct limits on Carmilla's mobility and the female desire that she both represents and provokes. One can point here to the relentlessly voyeuristic way in which she and other women are portrayed in the film (with all this presumably presented for the gaze of a male audience). Also significant are the repeated cutaways to a mysterious male figure whom we presume is Count Karnstein, although we are given no firm information to support that supposition. These shots, which are only faintly motivated by that character's brief appearance at the ball near the beginning of the film, mark him as a final, somewhat arbitrary guarantor of the male look – he seems to have some sort of power over Carmilla – which, implicitly, underlines its weakness elsewhere in the film.

A sequel to *The Vampire Lovers* followed quickly. Compared to its predecessor, *Lust for a Vampire* (1971, d. Jimmy Sangster) proved to be a distinctly reactionary project, concerned as it seemed to be to undermine the power of Carmilla. One consequence of this is that Carmilla (now played by Yutte Stensgaard) in *Lust for a Vampire* is a much more passive figure than she was before, submitting herself as she does not only to an evil lord (presumably Count Karnstein) but also to what can only be described as her boyfriend, the film's hero Richard Lestrange. (It is significant that Lestrange turns out to be a horror novelist, an authoritative master of the very same discourse within which he himself appears.) At the same time, however, the film shows little interest in portraying a dynamic male authority in action. Instead it offers an increasingly complicated plot combined with elements of jokiness which together render *Lust for a Vampire* more an example of early 1970s camp, a curious hybrid of romance, comedy and thriller, than a horror film.[8]

The final Karnstein film, *Twins of Evil*, was released in 1971. It marked a further move to an unqualified objectification of the woman. This is most obviously signalled by the positioning of the twins in relation to the male characters. The fact that the rebellious, independent twin is presented as unequivocally evil while the obedient twin, the one who in effect knows her place, is virtue personified immediately lends a misogynist tone to the proceedings. The action of the film arises out of a conflict between the all-male Puritan group, led by Peter Cushing's Gustav Weil, and the decadent, vampiric Baron Karnstein. Both of these seek to dominate women in various ways. At the film's conclusion, the evil twin is beheaded and both Weil and the Baron are killed. Weil is replaced by Anton, the local schoolmaster, who had initially opposed the Puritan witchhunts but by this stage is leading the Puritans into battle against the vampires. The model of arrogant, domineering masculinity represented by Weil and the Baron is replaced by his more understanding and sensitive leadership, which in the end, it can be argued, functions as merely another form of domination. It is significant in this respect that Carmilla herself makes only a fleeting appearance and that the lesbianism which previously had signalled, albeit in a compromised fashion, a female desire separate from male definitions has been almost entirely removed.

Carmilla's reign as a powerful and independent female character in British horror was, perhaps not surprisingly, a relatively short one. But the very fact of her existence signalled that a change had occurred in the genre; quite simply, Carmilla would have been an unthinkable development a mere decade before. Importantly, the Karnstein films were not alone in addressing some of the problems and anxieties thrown up by what was by any standard a troubled moment in British social history. Neither were they unique in identifying the woman as a figure of instability in British horror. Recurrent preoccupations in horror at this time included a perceived weakness in paternal authority, a sense of fathers as both brutal and petty, and a conception of female power as a quality bound up with the maternal. The most striking thing about these films, that which binds them together into a group, is that they take quite explicitly as their focus something that, to a lesser extent, also concerned the Karnstein films – namely, the nuclear family.

Family horrors

Throughout the late 1960s and early 1970s, 'family' became an increasingly contested term. For the Women's Movement, it was the prime institution of patriarchal repression of women: 'Patriarchy's chief institution is the family. It is both a mirror of and a connection with the larger society; a patriarchal unit within a patriarchal whole.'[9]

For psychiatrists R. D. Laing and David Cooper, it enforced a more general repressiveness:

> The bourgeois nuclear family unit (to use something like the language of its agents – academic sociologists and political scientists) has become, in this century, the ultimately perfected form of non-meeting and therefore the ultimate denial of mourning, death, birth and the experiential realm that precedes birth and conception.[10]

For the various conservative moral movements of the time, however, it was the beleaguered repository of religious and moral value, that which bound modern society together and which had to be protected:

> In the Christian view of society the family is one of the vital parts of the structure. Church, state and family are the three institutions divinely ordained for the preservation of society . . . There must, at the centre of society, be a social unit where everyone can feel safe. Men and women are not given the emotional strength to live without the security which comes from love and trust.[11]

Horror films have often explored familial tensions. For example, there are some rather obvious parallels to be drawn between American and British horror productions in the 1970s. Both use family dramas to address in a variety of ways and from a number of different positions a widespread sense of social fragmentation. But while American horror films of the 1970s – which included, to name but a few, *The Exorcist*, *The Hills Have Eyes*, *It's Alive* and *The Texas Chainsaw Massacre* – with their present-day settings and their relatively realistic depiction of violence, tended to explore the social dimensions of this situation (with in particular the monstrous family used to symbolise a wider social corruption and bankruptcy), British horror, usually set in the past, away from everyday reality, dealt more with the psychological effects of the family structure.[12] For example, all the films to be discussed here take as their subject matter the ways in which individual characters enter into identification with familial roles – mother, father, daughter, son. This process is usually conceived of as repressive, often involving a violence which emanates from the older generation and is directed against the young. What emerges from this series of 'family' films are two different treatments of these issues: on the one hand, some films which contemplate a mother figure and her power, and, on the other hand, another set of films which take as their shared subject the rule of the father.

The power of the mother

'Mother is ancient history.'[13]

The drama in these films turns on the threatened or actual collapse of an already weakened patriarchal order provoked by the emergence of a very powerful and threatening mother figure (with fathers either ineffectual or absent). The principal conditions of this figure's existence are, firstly, that the characters around her are rendered childlike in some way or other, and, secondly, that the realm of maternal power is associated with the past, both the past (i.e. infancy) of the individual and of society in general. A knowledge or memory of this past has been repressed via the establishment of a patriarchal order. But now the mother returns with a destructive vengeance and in representing this return the films in question, consciously or otherwise, tap into what are essentially pre-oedipal fantasies about maternal power.

The pre-oedipal mother – as variously theorised by Freud, Jacques Lacan, Melanie Klein and Susan Lurie - is primarily an object, is the mother of the infant seen through that infant's eyes as a very powerful being. Although there is disagreement as to the relation this mother bears to the father, she is generally seen as embodying phallic attributes and, connected with this, bestowing a sense of completeness and plenitude. Significantly for the purposes of our argument, Klein further argues for her as a part-threatening, devouring object as the child projects upon her its own innate aggression.[14]

The trajectory of the British horror genre as described in previous chapters, with the woman as object beginning to speak in films such as *The Gorgon* and *The Devil Rides Out*, takes in these 'mother' films a new direction. Each film in its own way depicts one of these archaic mother figures – who by definition is an object for others, that which exists in the inaccessible past of each adult – as someone who is struggling towards an autonomous female identity. As one might expect, this project turns out to be an impossible one: the distance between an archaic past and the present day is simply too great to traverse and, in the end, this version of the pre-oedipal mother is altogether too destructive, too anti-social, to be accepted. It is as if when detached from her traditional role in British horror, the figure of the woman has here become unstable and liable to disintegration.

The three maternal dramas to be discussed here were all produced by Hammer. The first of these, *Blood from the Mummy's Tomb* (1971, d. Seth Holt) was adapted from Bram Stoker's *Jewel of the Seven Stars*. It opens with Margaret Fuchs, its contemporary heroine, asleep and speaking an unintelligible language. There follows a sequence in ancient Egypt in which Tera, Margaret's double (both are played by the same actress) is ritually poisoned and has her hand cut off. As the film progresses, it becomes clear that this destruction of a female physical integrity marks the founding of a patriarchal order. That this order is weak and subject to regression is immediately made apparent, however, by the fatal attack launched against the male priests responsible for Tera's execution.

Margaret's own mother is absent from the film (she dies giving birth to Margaret). Margaret's family is presented to us as a male-dominated institution with the woman therein an object to be transferred from father to her boyfriend. In the face of this situation, Tera embodies an awesome power from the past. As she herself puts it, 'I, Tera, Queen of Darkness, priestess of Ancient Egypt, have lived before. My spirit has never rested through all these weary centuries. My soul has wandered among the boundless stars while my mortal body waited.' She is separated, divided and seeking to regain that lost unity. One can note in this respect the stress laid in the film on restoring the physical integrity of Tera's body, which is reenacted on another level in the gathering of objects plundered from her tomb – the jaw of the ass, the cat, the serpent – so that the resurrection ritual can be carried through. What her prospective return threatens is the Law of the Father: 'no scheming and malignant priesthood, no repressive archaic laws or endless rituals of death. A land where love is the divine possession of the soul'.

Moreover, the present-day manifestation of male authority is shown as already weakened: paralysis afflicts Margaret's father shortly after the film begins and the doctor attempting to treat Margaret is ineffectual and eventually killed by her. Of her father's male archaeologist colleagues, one is confined to a lunatic asylum and another collapses at the mere sight of Margaret/Tera.

Insofar as *Blood from the Mummy's Tomb* identifies the nuclear family as an institution which favours male authority (albeit an ineffective one), then it aligns itself with much feminist thought of the day. However, at the same time, and arguably as a condition of the former, it offers no ideas about how this unjust situation might be rectified. Instead it exhibits a fascination with, and a subjection before the power of an ancient matriarchal figure. This fascination, and the move into the distant past that it involves, enables the film to avoid some of the pressing political issues, especially those to do with the family, that are implicit in its scenario. Inevitably perhaps, the only solution it can envisage is the total collapse of Margaret's family. *Blood from the Mummy's Tomb* ends with Margaret/Tera, badly burned in a fire, completely swathed in bandages and mumbling incoherently. This decidedly ambiguous image – is this Margaret or Tera and will the threat posed by Tera be renewed? – is symptomatic of a wider inability in the film to develop a coherent attitude to those feminist ideas which elsewhere it has either sought to incorporate or at the very least acknowledged.

Countess Dracula (1970, d. Peter Sasdy) arguably displays a more critical awareness than does *Blood from the Mummy's Tomb* of the relation between fantasies of maternal power and the familial and social roles assigned women in a patriarchal society.

Sasdy's film opens with the funeral of the Count, Countess Elizabeth Bathory's husband, the feudal patriarch of the region. As the priest intones the burial service, the Countess, an aged woman, looks out from behind her veil at Imre, a young, handsome soldier. This initial catching of the male body by the female gaze signals the prospect of the desiring female, which earlier horror films (particularly *The Sorcerers*, in which desire is also 'misplaced' in an old woman) had found threatening in the extreme. However, the centring of *Countess Dracula* on the female character sets it apart from these and thereby initiates a different approach.

As the film progresses, Elizabeth's look, and the desire it signals, is increasingly identified as a transgression against patriarchal definitions of the feminine which are seen to be founded on a double-standard opposition between virgin and whore. As Captain Dobi, the Countess's major-domo, puts it, 'Why should a man be slave to one woman when he can have the pick of any?' 'But if that woman embodies all the virtues?' Imre asks in return. Dobi again, asserting an inalienable patriarchal splitting of the woman; 'Mistress, friend and mother in one. Does such a woman exist?' 'You know she does!' replies Imre, thereby, and quite inadvertently, identifying the precise nature of Elizabeth's transgression. She wishes to cut across these definitions and identities, filling them all (mother, daughter, lover etc.) and contained by none, acquiring a unity which is conceived of as, yet again, essentially maternal. Restored to a youthful beauty by bathing in the blood of female virgins, Elizabeth takes on aspects of the pre-oedipal mother, in this case a Kleinian devouring figure – most explicitly at the film's conclusion when she attempts to consume her own daughter. She constantly seeks to acquire a plenitude which is only occasionally and temporarily realised; for example, in the scene in which she, newly restored to youth after having murdered a gypsy, rides to meet Imre by the lake, a brief use of slow motion suggests both the fullness and the transience of her satisfaction.

The pain of her necessary and inevitable return to her previous state works to underline the imaginary and unrealisable qualities of her escape. Elizabeth, whether young or old, is often placed behind bars and trapped within claustrophobic compositions. Her beauty is always temporary – dependent as it is on a constant replenishment of virgin's blood – and her satisfaction is consequently also temporary. The instability of her position is perhaps most cruelly expressed in the scene in which the local prostitute asks Imre whether he is thinking of his 'lady love'. This is followed by a sudden cut to an aged Elizabeth staggering through her bedroom. The moment suggests the impossibility of abolishing these divisive and defining roles through what is essentially a regression, an attempted escape, rather than an engagement with the conditions which have brought these roles about in the first place.

The doomed quality of Elizabeth's plan is further stressed by the film's intertwining of her crimes with her position of authority within a feudal society. Like her vampiric namesake, Countess Dracula terrorises the helpless peasants of the surrounding countryside, with her blood-letting activities depending on the absolute power that derives from her occupation of the castle. In a very important sense, Elizabeth's desire is a function of and stems from her class position. Connected with this is the fact that the majority of her victims, while certainly not of her own class, are of her own gender (her climactic killing of Imre is clearly accidental); appropriately enough, at the film's conclusion a line of peasant women line up to condemn her. In attempting to elude patriarchal definitions of femininity and constrictions of desire, Elizabeth is, like Tera, shown to be guilty of an egotistical selfishness. She ends in the film as she begun – confined.

Dr Jekyll and Sister Hyde (1971, d. Roy Ward Baker) is a curious concoction of a number of horror themes and motifs: Jack the Ripper, Burke and Hare and elements of Frankenstein as well as Robert Louis Stevenson's original literary source mingle in its convoluted plot. The film exhibits a camp humour which was becoming increasingly visible within the genre in the early 1970s, possibly as a response to the outdatedness of some of its conventions; and this, along with the plot, often distracts the film from the implicit logic of its own narrative proposition as announced in the film's title. However, inasmuch as *Dr Jekyll and Sister Hyde* does hold to that transexual proposition, it can be recognised as another maternal drama.

Perhaps the most surprising absence in a film about a man turning into a woman are anxieties around castration. Instead one finds the transformation signalled here as pleasurable, with Sister Hyde languorously admiring herself in a mirror; a return to an imaginary maternal plenitude, one which, as with *Countess Dracula*, is only temporary and achieved at the expense of murder. (Possibly the dagger that Sister Hyde carries is a distinctly phallic compensation for what is lost in Jekyll's transformation into a woman.) Jekyll/Hyde lives in a house conspicuously lacking in father figures; the Spencer family who live upstairs comprise only mother, son and daughter, while Jekyll's surrogate father, Prof. Robertson, is often absent and generally ineffective throughout. Like Countess Elizabeth, Hyde exists within and challenges standing definitions of femininity con- structed around a double standard, in this case the absolute Victorian division between virgin, represented here by the genteel Susan Spencer, and the working-class whores who become Jekyll/Hyde's victims. This is most evident in Hyde's mobility, as she moves freely between domestic interior – into which she brings a bright red dress, the colour signifying her dangerous sexuality – and fog-laden streets. She can be contrasted with Susan who after having moved into the house at the beginning of the film only ventures forth alone into the streets once and then narrowly escapes death at the hands of Hyde herself.

However, the potential posed by Hyde for a challenge to the social values (both those of the Victorian era and the 1970s) which have produced her is circumscribed by the fact that she is constantly seen as enacting a regression on the part of Jekyll: in an important sense, she belongs to him. It is significant in this respect that throughout the film Jekyll is constantly verbalising while Hyde remains comparatively silent. This is underlined by the child-like qualities of Jekyll, Susan and Susan's brother, Howard, and the way in which these further position Hyde as mother-object in their eyes; indeed she is often seen from either Howard's or Susan's point of view.

While it is true to say that there are moments which resist this, which work to suggest the possibility of a female subjectivity speaking from within this objectification – Hyde before the mirror, Martine Beswick's noteworthy performance in that part – these exist only in isolation. The climactic intervention of the police at the end of the film, and Jekyll/Hyde's subsequent fall from a building, stands as the final point of a narrative of objectification, from which Sister Hyde, never as formed as Elizabeth in *Countess Dracula*, always something less than a subject, cannot escape.

In all three of these films, a disorder within the family arises from a weakening of paternal authority. This in turn entails a recognition on the part of the filmmakers of a wider social shift in understandings of the family and in particular the position of the woman within this, which can be aligned with but is not reducible to the Women's Movement. In centring on a mother figure the films acknowledge the possibility of a new female subjectivity, but as a condition of this acknowledgement turn this gender-transformation, this coming-into-being, into, paradoxically, a regression. The consequent sliding between woman as object – held in the gaze of children and ineffectual men – and as matriarchal subject structures the progression of the films. It also explains the inconclusiveness of their

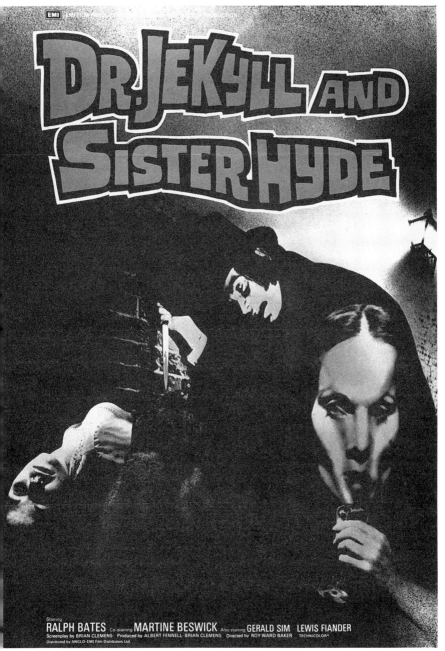

Director: Roy Ward Baker (British poster, 1971)

Director: John Gilling (British poster, 1967)

respective conclusions: a bandaged Margaret/Tera in *Blood from the Mummy's Tomb*; Countess Elizabeth awaiting execution in *Countess Dracula*; Jekyll/Hyde irrevocably split, with half of the face that of Jekyll, the other half that of Hyde, at the end of his/her film. Immobility, waiting and splitting: each of these marks an inability to decide, to chose between a fantasy of maternal power and a more questioning and overtly political engagement with those social shifts which, to a large extent, have moulded these films. It is in the articulation of these apparently incompatible elements – of present-day social reality and archaic mothers – that these maternal dramas acquire their peculiar contradictory character.

The law of the father

Operating alongside these depictions of the maternal are a group of films which find their way into problems associated with the family via the figure of the father, with this time the mother either marginalised or absent. In particular, these films concentrate on the difficult relations between fathers and their children, with the father often seen as preventing his children from becoming adults. The images of passivity with which they often conclude signal in this respect an inability to progress and develop within such a situation, where the only outcome possible is a violence that is often turned against the father himself, who in refusing to pass on his power, investing it totally in himself, isolates himself from the framework of relationships and identifications through which such power can be transmitted down through the generations. Seen in this way, these father-fixated films can be related to classic Hammer horror (even though of the four films discussed here only *Demons of the Mind* and *Hands of the Ripper* were actually produced by that company) insofar as the latter too often dealt with a problematised transmission of patriarchal power from one generation to the next. However, in 1970s horror the antagonism between generations has become much more intense and violent; moreover, as already indicated, these – and other British horror films of this period – lack those decisive problem-solving professionals who in earlier horror films had worked to manage this troubled situation.

What this means in effect is that historically specific problems in defining the family as a site for the transmission of patriarchal authority and values are here being dealt with in quite a different way from the way in which they are handled in those films which centre on the mother. In the latter, one finds recurrent images of regression to an archaic past, whereas in the present instance the notion of the father as absolute tyrant serves to freeze the family's development, permitting no interaction between generations: the generation gap with a vengeance, so to speak.

If a text was required that could sum up many of the attributes displayed by these 'father' films, one need look no further than the conclusion of *And Now the Screaming Starts* (1973, d. Roy Ward Baker) when the camera closes in on a passage in an open Bible: 'For I, the Lord thy God am a jealous God, visiting the iniquity of the fathers upon the children unto the third and fourth generation of them that hate me.' In the case of the film within which it is located, the iniquity derives from the actions of the feudal lord Sir Henry Fengriffen (Herbert Lom) and falls upon his grandson Charles (Ian Ogilvy). A flashback informs us how Sir Henry raped the bride of a servant and then cut off the servant's hand. The servant curses him; and this curse is finally realised many years after Henry's death when Catherine (Stephanie Beacham), Charles's new wife, is raped by the servant's ghost and eventually gives birth to a one-handed son.

The grandfather is the lord of the manor, a tyrant answerable to no one. The house into which the newly wed Charles and Catherine move is dominated by his forbidding portrait. This portrait in turn is associated with images of bodily (male) mutilation – a face without eyes, a severed hand. In earlier Hammer films, with their distinctive oedipal qualities, such wounds functioned as symbolic castrations dealt by a father figure as a punishment for the desire for a mother figure. Here, however, these wounds symbolise instead a more general and undirected interdiction, a refusal of adulthood. The outcome of this is that there is no way forward for the young people in the film; their desires, their emotions, are rendered ineffectual. This, it appears, is especially the case for the young male. At the end of the film Charles, who has been insistently denying the efficacy of the curse, sees the one-handed baby. Immediately, he rushes to his grandfather's tomb and disinters his skeleton. Unable to father a child, to become a father himself, he rants against the figure who selfishly held that power to himself. Male potency is no longer available – is realisable only in flashback form – and Charles has no option but insanity.

Catherine's function within this is to serve as the vessel for the execution of the curse. Although it is her voice that initiates the narrative – with the Rebecca-like 'In my dreams I go back to the year 1795 . . .' – and her actions, the search for the truth about the family into which she has married, constantly further the narrative, in the end she actually discovers very little. In this, *And Now the Screaming Starts* differs from other 'father' films which deal more with the troubled relations between fathers and daughters, with the family identified both as an arena for a male tyranny and as a prison for women, the latter doubly powerless insofar as they are both young and female.

One product of this way of seeing is that, unusually for period horror, two of these films, *The Creeping Flesh* (1972, d. Freddie Francis) and *Hands of the Ripper* (1971, d. Peter Sasdy) lack even a notional male romantic lead to which the heroine–daughter – Penelope in *The Creeping Flesh* and Anna in *Hands of the Ripper* – can be linked at their respective conclusions. To this can be added, in a qualified sense, *Demons of the Mind*: its heroine Elizabeth's romantic interlude with Carl near the beginning of the film is characterised, through an unnaturalistic absence of dialogue, as unreal and dreamlike.

This general absence of normative heterosexual relations can be seen to derive from the father's refusal in each film to share his power with any other male; insofar as these films conjure up a domestic world that is bounded by the authority of the father, the very possibility of a young male rival to challenge successfully this authority seems unthinkable. The conventional 'career trajectory' of the woman – from daughter to wife – is thereby made unavailable, and Penelope, Elizabeth and Anna are shown in the main as motherless daughters whose eventual insanity functions as a response to their fathers' refusal to accept them as separate and independent beings. Because there is no hero as such who can save the daughter and restore patriarchal authority in a more just (i.e. less visibly domineering) form, an incurably violent antagonism between father and daughter often ensues. As with other horror films of this period, the positioning of the woman within the family is identified as both repressive and troubled; but one of the conditions of this is that the films in question are unable to offer any credible solution to this problem.

The first half of *The Creeping Flesh* depicts with considerable economy and intelligence the Victorian archaeologist–explorer Emmanuel Hildern's loving oppression of his daughter, Penelope, whom he regards as solely his possession. As he puts it, 'Ever since your dear mother died, you've been everything to me.' Penelope has been kept in ignorance of her mother's confinement to a lunatic asylum, a confinement, it is hinted, motivated by Hildern's fear of an active female sexuality. This daughter's main domestic function, the management of household affairs on inadequate funds, clearly imposes a great strain upon her, one that is not recognised by a father more interested in scientific research. Her nascent rebellion against her father's domination is signalled through her rediscovery of her mother and the independence she represented. She reads a magazine called 'Romance' – a genre conventionally associated with female desire – that belonged to her mother and then, disobeying her father, ventures into her mother's room. There she finds the letter which earlier in the film had informed Hildern of his wife's death. Letting down her hair and putting on her mother's red dress, she begins to play the piano. On entering the room, Hildern initially mistakes her for his wife, but then he chastises her for her disobedience. She responds angrily, crying 'All the time she was a prisoner, like me!' It is at this point, in a shot which could be read as showing Hildern's subjective image of his daughter, he observes in her the first signs of insanity. This is promptly followed by a more obviously subjective flashback depicting Hildern's wife's descent into madness, identified here with both her sexual licentiousness and her career as a dancer. The problem for Penelope at this point is, quite simply, that she has nowhere to go. The film makes it clear that she knows nothing of the outside world, indeed is forbidden to stray far from the house, and there is no hero who can rescue her (unless one counts the escaped lunatic Lenny whom she eventually encounters and who can arguably be seen as a parody of such a figure).

Hildern's response to the threat to his authority posed by his daughter is intertwined with his experiments on the ancient skeleton he has brought back from his archaeological expedition. This object is described as being one of 'the Evil Ones' who walked the earth before mankind. Water is spilled accidentally onto one of the skeleton's fingers and, miraculously, flesh and blood appear there. Using this blood, Hildern manufactures a serum against what he believes to be the 'pure evil' bacillus alive in the Evil One and promptly injects this into his daughter in order, as he sees it, to protect her from her mother's insanity. The serum fails and she becomes 'evil', that is like her mother, wearing a red dress, letting down her hair, dancing. Needless to say, the equation made here – between female independence and archaic, absolute Evil – is hardly a progressive one. Importantly, however, it is an equation not supported by the film but rather located firmly within Hildern's somewhat questionable logic. It is significant in this respect that while in the throes of the madness induced by her father, Penelope attacks three men (a drunken sailor, a lecherous 'cad' and the lunatic Lenny), each of whom, in their greed and self-centredness, can be seen as stand-ins for her own father. Appropriately, at the end of the film it is she, now entirely an object, without speech, who lets the Evil One – by this stage resurrected as a vengeful monster – into the house in which a terrified Hildern is hiding.

Hildern's attempted objectification of his daughter within both the home and a scientific experiment backfires when he loses one of his own fingers to the monster. This punishment is offered to us as having a certain amount of justice to it, not only because earlier Hildern had severed one of the monster's fingers but also because we have seen what Hildern has done to his own daughter. Here, with the monster's incursion into the house that was previously Hildern's domain, he is, in a sense, made to suffer for his selfishness. In the film's remarkably bleak conclusion, which takes place in an asylum earlier identified as repressive and inhumane, Penelope is pronounced incurably insane and locked up with her father; this family has failed. In what can be seen as both a patriarchal damage-limitation exercise and an inability to produce a more positive ending, a brutal form of patriarchal authority is reinstated in the form of Christopher Lee's asylum director.

Similar tensions and ambiguities gather around the father in *Demons of the Mind* (1971, d. Peter Sykes). In the credit sequence, for example, photographs of a cruel-looking Baron Zorn and his two children, Elizabeth and Emil, are joined together in the frame. This juxtaposition is repeated at the film's conclusion when in rapid succession one finds images of Zorn impaled by a giant, flaming cross, the son he has just shot dead and the daughter screaming insanely.

In this and other ways, *Demons of the Mind* displays a self-consciousness in its representation of the family as a repressive institution, in so doing drawing on a Laingian critique that turns on the idea of familial repressiveness causing youthful insanity: at one point Carl, a student, remarks to Zorn, 'Elizabeth's not mad now, but you and this house will drive her mad.' However, while Laing often identified the mother as the main agent of this repression inasmuch as she refuses to let her children go, here the mother is absent, accessible only via the Baron's subjective and lascivious memories of her.[15] These in turn can be linked with Hildern's memories of his 'insane' wife in *The Creeping Flesh*: in both, insanity is equated with a threateningly independent female sexuality. Like *And Now the Screaming Starts* and *The Creeping Flesh*, *Demons of the Mind* locates the problem with the family in the figure of the selfish, tyrannical father. Here, as is the case in a slightly different way with *Countess Dracula*, this function is doubled by his position as the head of a feudal social hierarchy. Hence the peasant revolt at the end of the film can be seen as a re-enactment on another level of the children's attempted, and thwarted, rebellion against the father.

The precise nature of this tyranny is made clear in the Baron's first appearance after the credit sequence. When Elizabeth arrives home, he is found praying at his wife's tomb. Associated from the beginning with death, and a concomitant objectification of the mother, he greets his daughter thus: 'Child of my flesh, my blood.' As is confirmed later by an incredulous doctor who remarks of the children, 'They're extensions of your being in some grotesque way,' Zorn is unable to see either her or Emil as individuals separate from himself. Referring at one point to his ambitions for his family, he says 'I want it to be as it was.' Like Hildern in *The Creeping Flesh*, he selfishly stands in the way of his children's maturation.

The film as a whole moves away from the bourgeois domesticity that characterised the settings of *The Creeping Flesh* and *And Now the Screaming Starts*. It opens instead with Elizabeth reaching up to the sky through the bars of a coach window: a poetic representation of her entrapment as opposed to the domesticated realism found in *The Creeping Flesh*. More revealing comparisons can be made between Cushing's restrained performance as Hildern and the more melodramatic acting style evident in *Demons of the Mind*, Hildern's claustrophobic household and Zorn's spacious baronial hall. *Demons of the Mind*'s setting would seem then to enable a more overtly symbolised portrayal of the father's activities. This is perhaps most clear at the film's conclusion when, unlike Hildern in *The Creeping Flesh* who merely loses a finger, Zorn is staked with a giant cross, which also aligns him with that other aristocratic figure of absolute feudal authority, Count Dracula.

However, while the form of the father's punishment might be different, its function remains much the same. The tyrannical father is destroyed, but only at the cost of the destruction of his failed family: hence the insanity of its sole surviving member. A violently repressive patriarchal system, represented here by an itinerant priest who is at first weak and disorientated but gains authority as Zorn declines, is put in its place. The despair of the conclusion stems yet again from a simultaneous recognition of this reinstatement of repression and an inability or unwillingness to offer anything in its stead.

Henry Fengriffen, Emmanuel Hildern and Baron Zorn, in their selfishly holding on to the women in their power, all exhibit characteristics of the primal father as identified by Freud in *Totem and Taboo*, his account of the founding of a patriarchal order. In Freud's version, the selfish father keeps all the women in the tribe to himself. This situation is finally overcome when the sons – the primal horde – kill and eat the father: 'and in the act of devouring him they accomplished their identification with him, and each one of them acquired a portion of his strength'.[16] However, these films conclude differently: in both *The Creeping Flesh* and *Demons of the Mind* the bad father is punished by another father figure. (The mob in *Demons of the Mind* is less a primal horde – little time is spent elaborating on the relationship between the Baron and the peasants – than it is a generically conventional device which functions here as an extension of the priest's influence.) It is also the case that the agencies of this punishment are only partially motivated by the narratives in which they appear, or rather that motivation takes a more nakedly ideological form than had been seen before in the genre.

The monster in *The Creeping Flesh* can be related to a Lovecraftian horror tradition that was generally alien to British horror and is filmed in an accordingly strange way, with the camera positioned in one instance behind its eyes (a repetition of an effect in the 1965 film *The Skull*: both this film and *The Creeping Flesh* were directed by Freddie Francis); it is also not destroyed at the end of the film. In *Demons of the Mind* the priest's appearance – he is first seen wandering through the forest – is never fully explained although his thematic function – the punishment of Zorn – is clear. This partial arbitrariness, which is arguably the only means by which these films can produce an ending, functions as a final abrupt closing down of

some of the possibilities for a more intensive interrogation of the
family and male authority within it that have been raised earlier in
each film. The closure thereby attained is an ambivalent one, usually
seen as the inevitable return of a social and psychological repressiveness: hence the far from happy endings of *And Now the Screaming
Starts*, *The Creeping Flesh* and *Demons of the Mind*.

Perhaps more than any other film in the group, *Hands of the
Ripper*, which tells of the exploits of Jack the Ripper's daughter,
reveals and to a certain extent dwells upon this inability to see
beyond a certain point. The bad, selfish father is present in *Hands
of the Ripper* in the forms of both Jack the Ripper and the
psychoanalyst Dr John Pritchard. (The similarity in names is, I
think, significant.) Like Hildern, Pritchard is the authoritative head
of a Victorian household. Also like Hildern, he balks at the prospect
of his offspring's independence: hence his lack of enthusiasm over
his son Michael's forthcoming wedding and his coolness towards
Michael's blind fiancée, Laura.

This quality of Pritchard's character also manifests itself in his
attempts to cure Anna, Jack the Ripper's daughter, of her apparent
insanity. This in itself seems a perfectly laudable aim, particularly
when compared with the hypocrisy of Dysart, an MP and as such a
spokesperson for the Victorian establishment. However, as the film
progresses, Pritchard's actions become increasingly questionable.
For one thing, he covers up several of the murders that have been
committed by Anna. For another, his professional relationship with
Anna is clearly informed and undermined by his desire for her.
This is apparent from the beginning when he moves Anna into his
dead wife's room and has her dressed in his dead wife's clothes.
(Importantly, this room was reserved for Laura, his prospective
daughter-in-law; Pritchard's installing Anna there is another way of
forestalling a youthful encroachment on his space.) It culminates in
the scene near the end of the film in which Pritchard finally kisses
Anna and in so doing inadvertently triggers her murderous attack
on him.

If Pritchard's motivations are not what they initially seem, neither
is the cure he seeks for Anna's illness necessarily a good thing. *Hands
of the Ripper*'s pre-credits sequence, in which Anna's real father, Jack
the Ripper, stabs her mother to death while she, a child, looks on,
suggests that this illness arises from Anna's misidentification before
what is signalled – through non-conventional lighting and music, its

organisation around a child's gaze – as a primal scene, the moment, it has been argued by Freud, when a child either witnesses or fantasises witnessing its parents making love. Freud also indicates that the child views the sexual act as one involving violence. In *Hands of the Ripper*'s primal scene, this violence has become literal; the gender roles offered therein assigning the male the active part and the female the passive, and ensuring that Anna has only two identificatory options, two ways into the scene: mother–victim or father–aggressor.[17] She choses the latter, and the film subsequently interweaves this with Pritchard's activities. In a very important sense, what Pritchard is trying to do is put Anna back in her proper, gendered place, 'emasculating' her in order that she can become 'a lady'. This is made clear when on their first meeting, in an action replete with symbolically castrating overtones, he treads cruelly on her foot.[18]

Throughout *Hands of the Ripper* Anna resists being precisely what Pritchard wants her to be, that is a mother–wife, the object of his own desire: as the doctor says 'All you have to do is learn to become one of the family.' Later, when Dolly, Pritchard's housemaid, calls her a lady, Anna uneasily replies 'But I'm not a real lady yet.' In fact, much of her violence is directed against women who refer to her femininity or beauty or attempt to put her before a mirror: she actually kills Dolly the housemaid with a broken mirror. These killings enact a symbolic rape, with sharp objects – a poker, hat pins – piercing the female body, and are accompanied by the voice of the Ripper calling Anna's name in what can be read here as a psychological interpellation, a calling of her to a particular male identity. In this respect, Anna is contrasted within the film to Laura, the 'good' woman, who is blind, dependent on men for her vision. The latter knows her place, having already entered into a socially correct identification of femininity.

In the Victorian world of the film, where femininity is arranged and defined through the double standard, Anna's actions could be seen as a transgression of and challenge to patriarchal structures of oppression that has distinct feminist possibilities. Like the mother figures discussed above, she has a mobility that is not available to the constantly chaperoned Laura, moving as she does from domestic middle-class household to working-class street, from virgin to prostitute; she can see the undesirability of woman's place, unlike Laura who literally cannot see anything.

However, these possibilities, and the critique of patriarchy they necessarily entail, are not realised within *Hands of the Ripper* because, quite simply, Anna, the reluctant woman, in resisting a patriarchal defining of her identity, acts as a male would. The symbolic rapes of other women have already been noted. In support of this, one can add the scene in which Anna punishes Pritchard by running him through with a sword, an act which aligns her with the monster in *The Creeping Flesh* and the priest in *Demons of the Mind*. The only possibility of action within a world-view that assigns the woman to passivity – and here, on one level, *Hands of the Ripper*'s ideological position, or rather the horizon beyond which it is unable to see, seems to be bound to the Victorian patriarchal society which elsewhere it criticises – is conceived as masculine, and because Anna cannot in the end actually be a man, her resistance is rendered impossible, with no hope of a successful resolution. The form of such a resolution cannot be envisaged within the film's terms of reference; it is literally unthinkable. Instead Anna vacillates between male and female positions in an increasingly violent series of events that culminates in her own death. The conclusion of the film, in which Anna and Pritchard die in each other's arms to the strains of Verdi's Requiem Mass, finally transforms this impossibility into a despairing acquiescence in the face of a deeply felt social injustice.

But at the same time *Hands of the Ripper* does exhibit an awareness of its own inability to portray activity within this society in anything other than masculine terms. The most visible example of this is the 'Votes for Women' slogan that appears on an East End wall past which Anna and Pritchard walk shortly after Anna's murder of a prostitute. A sign of political organisation, it is juxtaposed with Anna's individualist 'masculine' solution; however, the juxtaposition is arbitrary, a directorial comment made behind the backs of the characters, which underlines the separateness of Anna's approach from a more overtly politicised strategy.

In addition, Pritchard's single-minded pursuit of the truth about Anna – a pursuit which takes him through all levels of Victorian society, from the royal medium to the East End of London, and which finally leads him to Jack the Ripper, one of the guarantors, as it were, of the Victorian double standard – always has the possibility within it of revealing and interrogating social structures of power and subjection. (Indeed the film does dwell in some detail on Victorian sexual hypocrisy and repressiveness.) But in the end, both Pritchard and the film itself retreat from this possibility: a dying Pritchard renounces his scientific quest and states that Anna is possessed, a view which puts him alongside the reactionary Dysart whose suggested solution to Anna's problem is to have her hanged. Finally and inevitably, Anna and Pritchard, each in his or her own way socially transgressive figures, perish while Laura and Michael, the morally and sexually conventional couple, survive; meanwhile the identity of the Ripper and the truth about patriarchal attitudes that he embodies remains concealed.[19]

Like their maternal counterparts, *Hands of the Ripper*, *Demons of the Mind*, *The Creeping Flesh* and to a lesser extent *And Now the Screaming Starts* explore a crisis of authority within the family. That these films' treatment of this is ambivalent and often downright contradictory can be assigned to a general unwillingness or inability to jettison completely those fathers/patriarchs (while at the same time representing them as monstrous) who in the past had been so important in defining the identity of British horror. To do such a thing would involve a radical rewriting of the genre which no film appears capable of initiating.

   Seen from this perspective, the Karnstein and 'mother' films from the 1970s, which do tend to push aside such figures of patriarchal authority, are far more challenging to pre-existing generic structures and conventions in their positing of a desiring, active female subject. As has already been demonstrated, it is a challenge which is quickly contained and neutralised. Female desire in *The Vampire Lovers* is made increasingly subject to a male authority as that mini-cycle progresses, while the power of the mother is even more tentatively presented. What these films offer then is a definite rupture within British horror, a moment of potential change, a partial moving away from an objectification of the female, which is quickly closed down. Conversely, in the 'father' films one finds a constant objectification of the woman accompanied by an often revealing presentation of patriarchal institutions of repression. The categorisation of 'mother' films as radical and 'father' films as reactionary or conservative is clearly reductive, taking no account of the structuring contradictions of each group. In effect, these films offer a variety of responses to the same problem, namely the threat posed by the possibility of a desiring female subject, of female identity separate from male definitions of it, in the broadest sense to patriarchal definitions of gender, but more particularly to an unquestioning objectification of the female upon which the genre in the past had profitably constructed itself.

Notes

1 Hammer also underwent a change of ownership at this time.
2 The increasing permissiveness of British film censorship was another factor in this.
3 J. Sheridan LeFanu, *Best Ghost Stories*, New York, 1964, p. 289.
4 Bonnie Zimmerman, 'Daughters of Darkness: the Lesbian Vampire on Film' in Barry K. Grant (ed.), *Planks of Reason: Essays on the Horror Film*, Metuchen NJ and London, 1984, p. 156.
5 An undoubted influence on the composition of Bram Stoker's *Dracula* (1897), *Carmilla* shares with that work the notion of the vampire as sexual liberator coupled with an inability to conceive of that liberation as anything other than death.
6 David Pirie, *The Vampire Cinema*, London, 1977, pp. 98–123.
7 This exploitative intent on the part of the filmmakers is revealed by the following remarks made by Tudor Gates, the writer of all three Karnstein films: 'I went to see a number of Hammer films. While I enjoyed them, the one thing that struck me was that they were terribly outdated, at least for the modern cinema-going public. That was the time over here when the floodgates of censorship opened. I felt that the thing to do was to bring Hammer Films up to the seventies. So I deliberately threw in the nudes and the lesbians and all the rest of it.' *Little Shoppe of Horrors*, 8, May 1984, p. 43. This whole issue of this valuable fanzine is dedicated to the Karnstein trilogy and provides useful background information.
8 For discussions of camp, see 'Notes on Camp' in Susan Sontag, *Against Interpretation and Other Essays*, New York, 1966, pp. 275–92; George Melly, *Revolt into Style*, London, 1970.
9 Kate Millett, *Sexual Politics*, London, 1971, p. 33; see also Eva Figes, *Patriarchal Attitudes: Women in Society*, London, 1970 ('Habits are perpetuated in that bastion of social conservatism, the family', p. 169), Shulamith Firestone, *The Dialectic of Sex: the Case for Feminist Revolution*, London, 1971 ('unless revolution disturbs the basic social organization, the biological family – the vinculum through which the psychology of power can always be smuggled – the tapeworm of exploitation will never be annihilated', p. 12) and Germaine Greer, *The Female Eunuch*, London, 1971, especially pp. 219–38.
10 David Cooper, *The Death of the Family*, Harmondsworth, 1971, pp. 5–6; see also R. D. Laing, *The Politics of the Family*, London, 1971.
11 Sir Frederick Catherwood, 'A Christian View' in *Pornography: the Longford Report*, London, 1972, p. 140.
12 See Robin Wood, 'An Introduction to the American Horror Film', in Bill Nichols (ed.), *Movies and Methods – Volume 2*, Berkeley, 1985, pp. 195–220 and Tony Williams, 'Family Horror', *Movie*, 27–8, winter 1980/spring 1981, pp. 117–26.
13 Susan Lurie, 'The Construction of the "Castrated Woman" in Psychoanalysis and Cinema', *Discourse*, 4, 1981–2, p. 59.
14 See J. LaPlanche and J.-B. Pontalis, *The Language of Psychoanalysis*, London, 1985, section on 'preoedipal'. For a formulation of the notion of the devouring mother, see Melanie Klein, *Contributions to Psycho-Analysis 1921–1945: Developments in Child and Adolescent Psychology*, London, 1964.

15 Juliet Mitchell, *Psychoanalysis and Feminism*, Harmondsworth, 1975, pp. 277–92 for a critique of Laing which argues that his work takes insufficient account of the role of the father within the family.

16 Sigmund Freud, *Totem and Taboo*, London, 1950, p. 142

17 See John Fletcher, 'Poetry, Gender and Primal Fantasy', in V. Burgin, J. Donald and C. Kaplan (eds), *Formations of Fantasy*, London, 1986, pp. 109–41 for a discussion of the multiple identifications offered by and available within the fantasy of the 'primal scene'. It appears that *Hands of the Ripper*'s primal scene is much more rigid and constrained in this respect, permitting only an either/or (male/female, active/passive, murderer/victim) identification for Anna; to a certain extent, this is one of the limitations that the film is unable to transcend.

18 In Emily Bronte's *Wuthering Heights* the rebellious Cathy suffers a similar 'wound'. See Sandra M. Gilbert and Susan Gubar, *The Madwoman in the Attic* (New Haven and London, 1979) for a discussion of this novel which bears some relevance to *Hands of the Ripper*.

19 For a historical reading of the Ripper in these terms, see Judith R. Walkowitz, 'Jack the Ripper and the Myth of Male Violence', *Feminist Studies*, 8, no. 3, autumn 1982, pp. 543–74.

Conclusion

David Pirie concluded his 1973 study of British horror cinema with an optimistic call for a regeneration of the genre: 'On present reckoning at least (although it is much too early to say with any certainty), the gothic cinematic revival in England looks like having a more lasting popular success than the original literary movement from which it derives.'[1] Unfortunately, Pirie's optimism was premature. British horror as a distinct category of a national cinema was not to survive the widespread collapse in British film production that occurred in the mid 1970s.

This 'demise' of British horror was all the more unfortunate in that around the time of Pirie's writing there were isolated signs of new approaches appearing within the genre. Films from this period which exhibit decidedly innovatory qualities include *The Wicker Man* (1973, d. Robin Hardy), *Frightmare* (1974, d. Peter Walker) and *Death Line* (1972, d. Gary Sherman). The latter two are particularly notable for taking as their principal subject matter cannibalism – a theme usually associated with American and Italian horror of the 1970s – and working to locate this within a recognisably class-ridden British social reality, often with extremely disturbing results.

More recently, two films in the genre have achieved a degree of critical and commercial success. *Company of Wolves* (1984, d. Neil Jordan) draws on a variety of sources (fairy tales, Breughel, Arthur Rackham, surrealism etc.) in its stylised depiction of a young woman's awakening sexuality. *Hellraiser* (1987, d. Clive Barker) is part of what has been termed by some critics 'body horror'. Characteristically for this type of horror, the film utilises sophisticated cosmetic effects to construct extremely realistic images of the human body torn apart and rearranged. It has been argued that this fascination with bodily destruction is an expression of a broader inability to find an Other upon which inner fears can be projected and materialised.[2] While both *Company of Wolves* and *Hellraiser* are in many ways impressive, it is significant, however, that neither attempts to engage in any meaningful sense with a specifically British reality. Unlike, say, Hammer horror which did very much locate itself in relation to nationally specific issues and anxieties, these recent British horrors look elsewhere for their effects and meanings.

This book has sought to demonstrate that the horror films produced up until and through the 1970s, and most notably those associated with Hammer, comprised an important – albeit controversial – intervention into British cinema and British film culture. From the perspective of today, they remain fascinating documents of a particular period in British cultural history. If there is to be a regeneration of British horror understood in a nationalistic sense – and with the current state of the British film industry this seems most unlikely – the individuals involved would do well to think carefully about these earlier horrors, both their characteristic strengths (for example, their liberating iconoclasm) and their limitations (especially their fatal fascination with the law of the father).

In the meantime we have the films themselves to view, enjoy (possibly), discuss. However, I do think there should be limits to this process of reviewing and remembering, limits which I have tried to respect throughout this book. In particular, we must constantly be aware of British horror's disreputability, for this quality comprises an integral part of the genre's working. It is a fundamental condition of British horror's existence that no one 'really' takes it seriously; therein lies dispensation for its transgressions, its often very lucid uncoverings and explorations of structures and assumptions that otherwise would have remained hidden.

'I read many reviews of our films with total amazement. I really do. For instance, when the National Film Theatre gave us a two-week season I was horrified. I thought if they made us respectable it would ruin our whole image.' Michael Carreras is quite right to be worried. Rendering these films worthy and respectable would be doing them a disservice. More, it would be like forcing them into the light and then watching helplessly as they crumble into dust.

Notes

1 David Pirie, *A Heritage of Horror: the English Gothic Cinema 1946–1972*, London, 1973, p. 165.
2 On 'Body Horror', see two articles in *Screen*, 27, no. 1, January–February 1986: Philip Brophy, 'Horrality – the Textuality of Contemporary Horror Films', pp. 2–13 and Pete Boss 'Vile Bodies and Bad Medicine', pp. 14–24.

Index